THE STRUGGLE FOR RECOGNITION:

Canadian Justice and the Métis Nation

Edited by
Samuel W. Corrigan and Lawrence J. Barkwell

Cover Design by Rod Carleton.

Pemmican Publications Inc. gratefully acknowledges the assistance to its publishing program by the Manitoba Arts Council and Canada Council.

Printed and bound in Canada by Hignell Printers Ltd., Winnipeg

Canadian Cataloguing in Publication Data

Manitoba Métis Federation Inc.
The struggle for recognition:
Canadian justice and the Métis nation

Contains the evidence presented to the Manitoba Aboriginal Justice Inquiry.

Includes bibliographical references.

ISBN 0-921827-20-2 (cloth); 0-921827-18-0 (pbk)

1. Métis - Manitoba - Criminal justice system.
2. Criminal justice, Administration of - Manitoba.
I. Corrigan, Samuel W., 1939-. II. Barkwell, Lawrence J., 1943-.
III. Manitoba. Aboriginal Justice Inquiry. IV. Title.

KF8228.M693M265 1991   345.7127/05/08997
KEM529.M3 1991   C91-097003-3

 PEMMICAN
PUBLICATIONS INC.

412 McGregor Street / Winnipeg, Manitoba / Canada R2W 4X5

Dedicated to

All the people of the Métis Nation

TABLE OF CONTENTS

ACKNOWLEDGEMENTS

The Manitoba Métis Federation Inc., on behalf of all Métis, gratefully acknowledges the dedication, commitment and countless hours of work that were contributed to ensure a successful publication of this important book.

The original suggestion for this volume came from the Manitoba Métis Federation Inc. Justice Committee: Ron Richard, David Chartrand and Denise Thomas. The initial intention was to publish the Manitoba Métis Federation Inc. submission to the Manitoba Aboriginal Inquiry of November 1989. The idea quickly grew to publish a volume that would incorporate both historical and contemporary Métis issues and that would reflect both the contributions of the Métis and the injustices suffered by the Métis in the Canadian governmental system.

Under the leadership and vision of the Manitoba Métis Federation Inc. Board of Directors, the team of researchers and writers began the arduous task of bringing the book to completion.

Contributions were made by writers (Lawrie Barkwell, Mike Brogden, Sam Corrigan, David Gray, Audreen Hourie and Lyle Longclaws) and by staff member Ed Swain. Professor Brogden participated with the assistance of a travel grant from the British Academy.

Acknowledgement is also given to the staff of the Public Archives of Canada, Glenbow Institute, the Public Archives of Manitoba, and the many other people, both Aboriginal and non-Aboriginal, who assisted with data collection and analysis and who provided a critical review.

W. Yvon Dumont
President, Manitoba Métis Federation Inc.
July, 1991

METIS PEOPLE AND THE 'JUSTICE' SYSTEM

Preface:

W. Yvon Dumont
President, Manitoba Métis Federation Inc.

We hear much about the involvement of Aboriginal peoples in the 'criminal justice system'. There are statistics in this book concerning the involvement of our own people, the Métis people in the criminal justice system. We are, of course, generally represented and in fact, over-represented, in the wrong end of that system. We are the clients and the victims of the 'criminal justice system'. That is not an opinion. It is a fact revealed by the statistics to anyone who cares to examine the record. What is immediately striking to the observer is the misnomer that is the label 'criminal justice system'. I am not able, and in fact I have not heard or read of anyone who is able to describe the theory of justice that would support the kind of involvement that the Métis people have in this condemnable system. It is the object of this book to present some statistics and some views to cause the reader to pay attention to the issues which demand attention if any notion of justice is in fact to be associated with the system that polices, puts on trial, assesses, sentences, jails and otherwise deals with our people. Justice has certainly eluded us in this country since it was taken over by the new immigrants in the past century. The search for justice by our people has been a constant and fruitless quest. It is certainly not a new demand that has been caused by any recent changes in particular. Let me illustrate by referring to the following quotations. They are extracts from a petition drafted by our forefathers, in my home community of Saint-Laurent in Manitoba. They were addressed to the federal government and they were drafted March 16, 1908:

All those millions are the proceeds of the land, which is our inheritance. Our forefathers have fought and shed their blood to defend and preserve that inheritance. Now today we are robbed of it, and our children are driven out like the buffalo, which has now disappeared from the prairies. That inheritance was deeded to us by our forefathers, and sealed with their blood. It is our [inalienable] right, which no civilized nation can deny. Misery, discontent, sorry, and wars are the result of injustice... We appeal to you in the name of justice, which is the greatest peace factor of the civilized nations of the world.

(Napoleon Chartrand's diary)

Today we are still seeking to redress that injustice. We are fighting the governments, of both the province and Canada, in the courts. In the courts we are seeking our inheritance, which is the lands promised to us in the Manitoba Act. We know how important is the security that is provided by our inheritance, by our land, in assuring a proper foundation upon which our people can be allowed to prosper peacefully and away from the misery and sorrow that is documented the system now visits upon us. But we are not awaiting quietly for the outcome of the judicial process. We are actively discussing with the same two governments ways in which we can, within the existing system that has so falsely been imposed upon us, increase the decision-making power of our people over all the public matters that affect them. We must change the way things are. Justice can not tolerate us continuing to be dealt with by government bureaucracies peopled by strangers to us. Justice can not tolerate decision-making by people who prefer to 'put us in our place' than to establish a proper place for the Métis people in a country whose wealth and power have been developed out of our inheritance.

We know that all reasonable minded Canadians and Manitobans will agree to join us and to work constructively towards the creation of a new system in which justice is much more than a easy label. We owe this continuing struggle to our forefathers. We owe this continuing struggle to our children and to their children. Let us work to wipe away the injustices of yesterday and to create true justice for all of us.

INTRODUCTION

Samuel W. Corrigan

This is a book about justice, Canada and the Métis Nation. It attempts to weave together the twin themes of equitable justice and self-determination with the development of Canada and the persistence of organized Métis society. It does so by reviewing three time periods, the era prior to the development of the Province of Manitoba in 1870, the 1980s, and the era beginning with 1990, the coming future of the Métis in Manitoba. Each of these themes and time periods merits some explanation in terms of the content of this book.

By equitable justice I refer to the systems and processes by which a people maintain social control and encourage social development. In all agglomerations of humans there are some individuals who behave in ways which offend others, and there are forms of behaviour which are considered anathema to a majority of the people. Every society develops means of dealing with these behaviours, either by forms of punishment or correction, and often with both together. We have developed words to convey the sense of these patterns of thought and behaviour, words such as *justice* which presumes the rightness of state reaction to individual anti-social behaviour, *courts*, connoting the all-powerful, semi-independent mediating arm of the state, and *police*, the branch of government designed to root out undesirable behaviour and bring offenders to the attention of the courts.

The philosophy of the justice system in Canada is exemplified by the theory that police in our country are not subject to specific direction by political bodies; they serve not the political masters, whether they be town councils, police commissioners or attorneys-general, but rather the interest of the state itself, that is the maintenance of orderly social relations within the collective of individuals of which the state is composed. In practice, of course, this philosophy often leads police forces to walk a tightrope between responsibility and accountability to the individuals chosen by the electorate on the one hand, and their own perception of the need for social control on the other. Few jurisdictions in Canada have been able to work out, without a great deal of pain, a satisfactory means of developing and maintaining a balance between the need for independence of social control and the need to ensure that social control serves the whole state rather than only some parts of the state.

Justice in Canada means simply the maintenance of orderly social relations within the multitude of societies which make up the country. To that end, Canada has developed one set of criminal laws (and two sets of civil laws!) given expression through hundreds of policing mechanisms and a myriad of court systems, and conducted through a multitude of penal systems and a tiny number of largely-ignored rehabilitative systems. It is no secret that the Canadian system of justice imprisons proportionately far more people, at vast cost, than do systems in most other western countries, and with dramatically less emphasis upon either rehabilitation or correction than in most western societies. The problems with the justice system in that sense have long been understood and ignored and will, I suggest, be understood and ignored long into the future. It is possible, however, that one segment of Canada, the Aboriginal societies of our country, may be allowed(!) to develop new systems of equitable justice which ensure the maintenance of orderly social relations and permit social development through an emphasis upon rehabilitation rather than punishment.

The papers by Brogden and Barkwell in the first part of this book detail the existence of Métis systems of equitable justice in the 19th century, systems developed by groups of people to ensure the continuance of their societies with no more than an absolute minimum of disruptive behaviour. These were systems, as in St. Laurent on the Saskatchewan River, which grew out of the recognition by the people themselves of a need for justice for all. They were developed by the people, were operated by the people, and were by all accounts successful in maintaining social order and essentially harmonious social relations. They developed out of the recognition by the Métis of patterns and standards of desirable behaviour in other Aboriginal societies, of the knowledge of particular needs in Métis society, and of an awareness of British and Canadian systems of justice. It was, perhaps, the very success of these systems of equitable justice, and the fact that they arose as a form of self-determination—that is, were developed by the Métis themselves—that led Canadian governments and Canadian institutions to decimate them, to destroy both the systems and the fabric of the societies which developed them. As Brogden and Barkwell describe, the Canadian government, determined to impose a single set of criminal laws upon the country—no matter how cruel or irrelevant such an idea might be—effectively abolished the workable and democratic systems of the Métis and criminalized the people with labels and rationales. Then, perplexed that so many individuals fell into their undesirable categories, they expanded the justice system into a massive body of police, courts and penal institutions to contain and service this artificial but now self-sustaining world. Today it is a service industry providing uncountable jobs and rewards for non-Aboriginal people, and degradation and punishment for Métis. There are strong indications in these papers that the instruments used by the state in the 19th century, the police, the courts and the prisons, simply failed to comprehend the clearly workable and efficient nature of Métis society and Métis justice systems. But in their ignorance they served the state well by destroying, painfully and over a long period of time, much of that pride which was exmplified in the fact of Métis self-determination. One is tempted to speculate: was it not really the fact that the Métis developed their own workable democratic systems of justice and government which led Canadian governments to spearhead such an orgy of local destruction and mass devaluation? Was the pride in being Métis and maintaining one's own system of peace and order a threat to central governments elsewhere? It would seem to have been so.

The second section of this book is concerned with the present, essentially with the results of those processes of eliminating self-determination and of imposing external and inappropriate control measures with the net effect of criminalizing the Métis people.

Three of these papers outline the present situation of Métis people in the youth justice system of Manitoba, the child welfare system of Manitoba, and the correctional (penal) system of Canada. The statistics alone are appalling. The stories behind those statistics are even worse, reminiscent in many ways of 1930s Germany or 1980s South Africa (both regimes where gross human abuse was legitimated by courts upholding laws). Many people will bridle at the above statement, and point out, as was noted before the Aboriginal Justice Inquiry in Manitoba in 1989, that people who do the crime also deserve to do the time. It will certainly be said that the system allows free legal representation, free counselling via court communicators, a multitude of court appeals, and a correctional system with numerous early release possibilities for those who are "well-behaved"! What absolute impertinence! The simple fact, patiently described in the chapter on devaluation, is that Métis people across the west have been so put down for over more than a century, have suffered such degradation and loss of opportunity, that many have in fact broken the recognized laws or behaved in ways which are fully seen by the Métis to be undesirable in society. But the measures used to deal with the law-breaking and antisocial behaviour within the community have served only to stimulate further crime and family breakdown, not to correct undesirable behaviour or to improve social relations. The solutions developed by non-Aboriginal people in a society which destroyed a coherent and workable Métis justice system have themselves become much of the problem.

The statistics in those three papers alone bespeak untold misery. The greater tragedy, however, has been Canada's (and Manitoba's) response to the numbers indicating increasing family and community breakdowns: it has been largely one of expanding the penal system, of developing new means which effectively separate Aboriginal children from Aboriginal families, and of blaming equally the offenders and the messengers who seek to rehabilitate and reform rather than punish. Many offices of the bureaucracy and many planners and researchers worry about the statistics, but their answer of expanding their systems is rooted in a fallacy. The fallacy is that of wringing non-Aboriginal hands and asking "What can we do to help these people?" rather than listening to the simple message expressed by the Métis so clearly for over 175 years now: "Allow us to look after ourselves!" As is clear from the first section of this book, Métis self-determination led to a workable system of justice. There is absolutely no reason whatsoever to suggest that the Métis (and other Aboriginal peoples as well, of course) are either incapable or unwilling to develop and administer a system of equitable justice in their own communities. To suggest otherwise, in the face of this history and these statistics, connotes racism.

The paper on the Longbody Creek Métis is an example of what the Métis can do in a short period of time and while under considerable stress. It says something else, too, for it speaks eloquently of the ability of the Métis to determine their own life ways, to develop a community of their own, form a local government and get on with their lives. Like the Métis of St. Laurent the Métis of Longbody Creek practised self-determination in the face of adversity. And the fact that they received some assistance from the Manitoba government demonstrates that at least some individuals in the bureaucracy recognize both the desirability and the advantages of Métis self-determination. Further, as the authors of that paper note, even the misguided and selfish efforts of the immigrants to force the Métis to give up their language in favour of French have failed to eliminate the community consciousness of the Métis as Métis.

The third section of this book addresses the future. Although it deals with matters of 1990 and 1991, the real concern is the twenty-first century. The submission and recommendations of the Manitoba Métis Federation to Manitoba's Aboriginal Justice Inquiry are presented, again with horrifying statistics, but with easily realizable suggestions for improvement. The recommendations take a major step in planning for something the Métis once had, a system which was stripped from them in the course of the legal repression noted in the first section of this book. This is no less than a workable, efficient, well understood, recognized and fair system of justice, a function of the self-determination of the Métis of the community of St. Laurent.

Many Canadians fear self-determination—or self-government, to use another popular phrase connoting the same thing—without realizing that it is the cornerstone of the Canadian system. It was the right of self-determination which the Métis sought in 1870, and achieved with the creation of the Province of Manitoba. As the composition of the population shifted, as the governments of the day—non-Aboriginal governments, that is—fumbled the land question, Métis emigrated in large numbers to the territories to the west. The continuation of a Métis presence in Manitoba was gravely endangered. Nonetheless many Métis communities survived, small groups of people who continued to speak Michif, who solved community problems internally, who worked hard to maintain themselves, their families, their society. This was done against great odds. As a minority the Métis were subject not only to those same national criminal laws which supplanted local justice endeavours, but also the devaluation by the majority which contributed to such poverty and to so many social problems.

I noted that Canada is founded upon self-determination. Each of the provinces is a model for self-determination and each has the power to create internal units—cities, towns, villages, hamlets, districts, municipalities and so on—with a significant measure of self-determination. That means simply the right of people to organize and govern themselves in certain areas of endeavour, including the right to raise and spend revenue. It means also, partly because of national legal standards, but largely because of bureaucratic and planning intransigence, that the areas of activity in which a community can make its own decisions are very limited and the powers which it might exercise are jealously guarded by senior governments. As well, of course, non-Aboriginal Canadians are generally unable to perceive of fields of action or authority in cultural or social terms; rather, everything must be circumscribed by territorial boundaries. Thus, without a formal land base, self-determination for a culture or society is inevitably denied. It was this problem which led the Provisional Government of 1870 to insist upon a Métis bloc of land in the new Manitoba, although the plan came to naught in the ensuing years of the 19th century. It is still this problem which bedevils the Métis now, as it seems that the twin ideas of land and self-determination in the criminal justice and family welfare spheres constitute blinkers for provincial and federal governments.

What is missing from government planning is the ingredient referred to in several papers in this volume and dealt with in the review of the Manitoba Métis Federation suits against the governments of Canada and Manitoba: simplicity and efficiency. Quite apart from any aesthetics of political philosophy, democracy—read self-determination—is a preferred form of government because it generally works: efficiently, effectively and with obvious widespread support from its practitioners. There is every reason to believe, moreover, that self-determination for an Aboriginal community such as the Métis of Manitoba would not only be more practical, in terms of lessening the damage inflicted by the contemporary non-Aboriginal justice, family welfare, and economic systems, but would also be financially far more efficient and cost effective. While many would wish to maintain the extremely expensive penal systems and rigidly structured family abuse systems now in place for non-Aboriignal people, all indications are that Aboriginal-designed systems for Aboriginal communities would be less expensive and far more practical than those imposed institutions which currently seem to have lives of their own.

To return to my initial statement, this is a book about justice, Canada and the Métis Nation. No single society can have a corner on justice, for, by its very nature, it is a function of self-determination. Both Canada, in its early political form before 1870, and the Métis had systems of justice developed by people for people, both workable in their context. As Canada developed, a single system of criminal law, and its extensions into areas as diverse as language, religion and family life, was extended to overwhelm successful, viable Métis communities. The results were and are disastrous. But as this book points out, there is every reason to recognize self-determination within Canada for the Métis Nation, allowing the development once again of Métis justice and family systems created by the Métis for the Métis. The renaissance of the Métis Nation will be complete only when Métis themselves can once again tackle Métis problems successfully, as they did so well prior to 1870. When that happens, and only when that happens, will we see any significant improvement in the statistics presented here.

Part One

Legal Systems of the

Nineteenth Century

INTRODUCTION: CRIMINAL JUSTICE AND COLONIZATION

M. Brogden, Liverpool Polytechnic [1]

Between the 1820s and the 1890s, Métis peoples in the West experienced dramatic changes in their social and legal status. At the high point, they enjoyed a substantial degree of legal autonomy in which their democratic traditions produced progressive and solidary forms of criminal justice. By the end of that period, many western Métis had been transformed into legal rejects. After Batoche, they were embedded in a different, alien, legal culture, which offered—superficially—citizenship and social equality, but which in reality degraded them as unequals. Understanding the present experience of Aboriginal people in western Canada in the criminal justice process entails appreciating their nineteenth century legal history of combating partisan law under the Hudson's Bay Company, and of evolving their own traditions of informal justice at Red River and later in the prairie townships, before being subjected to the marginalization strategies of English common law, and of its enforcers, the North West Mounted Police (NWMP). In preparation for their twentieth century status, they were subject to the legal degradation that the English common law reserves for those at the bottom of the social pile.

Part I of this volume explores both the summit and the valleys of the Métis experience with the criminal justice process. In the second quarter of the nineteenth century, they strove on the legal plane to obtain the right to economic self-reliance, for the legal authority to compete as traders with the Hudson's Bay monopoly. In the late 1860s on Red River, and in all the small townships of the South Saskatchewan in the early 1870s, Métis communities practised a democratic legal tradition as legal cultures which emphasized representation, humanity and the principles of reparation and mediation. By the time of the Batoche rising in 1885 and more evidently in the aftermath of that disaster, they were the target of a legal institution, the

1

NWMP, that had created its own *raison d'être* through the marginalization and segregation of the Aboriginal people of the Canadian prairies.

PATHOLOGICAL PERCEPTIONS OF THE METIS PEOPLES

Central to the denial of the Métis legal traditions as Sprague (1988) has shown more generally, in the tradition of white colonizing societies encountering Aboriginal people of mixed race, Métis people were perceived through the lens of a social Darwinism as a kind of lesser species, out of joint with the times. As Aboriginal peoples, they were caricatured as uncivilized, the remnant of a savage culture born out of the buffalo chase, the beaver hunt, and the sporadic labour required of early transportation. Secondly, as people of mixed race, they were not to be endowed with the romanticized values of the Indian: no European scribe penned sonnets in praise of the noble Métis. The Indian races could be given a certain standing in Victorian literature as the remnant of a unique, if outdated, culture. Nor could the Métis be ascribed the power to reason, the commitment to the honest toil and long-term planning of the white settlers.

When combined with the input of European Christianity, the mercantile exploitation of Aboriginal peoples, both Indian and Métis, was legitimized by differentiating between the civilized law-abiding (Christian) and heathen "natives", who were to be tutored like children unfamiliar with reason and law, relegated to a lower status in the social structure. Métis, within the traditions of English imperial language, were portrayed in a demeaning, condescending discourse. Racism combined with the language of gender to caricature their backward characteristics.

A contemporary Anglo-Saxon perception:

....the French metis are a very different race....almost all the national characteristics of the Scotch are reproduced in almost their native strength in their half-breed children....when a Scotch voyageur took to himself a wife from the Indian tribes, he let it be distinctly understood that he considered himself superior to his escort, who carried out his wishes to the letter....the children were brought up in the way he thought best. The French coureur de bois always regarded his Indian spouse as his equal and let her have her own way in bringing up of children and consequently, the Indian characteristics came to the front. In this way, there was formed a race, hospitable, careless, generous, having many of the noble qualities of the Indian and the French. But totally without mental ballast, fickle in their dispositions and easily influenced either in the right or wrong direction.[2]

European colonization embodied the thesis of the inexorable tide of civilization, advancing against the impedimenta of barbarism and unreason. In the conventional histories, even those (Sprague, 1988) that suggested some sympathy with the Métis case, they were regarded as primitive people irrationally obstructing the march of industry and of planned society. In Stanley's pioneering work (1960), they appear as both erratic and petulant, the assumed inconsistencies of a primitive people, failing to recognize their own best interests as embodied in the grander designs of the white dominion and rejecting the educational and moral instruction required by a more sophisticated society.

Their principal occupations—freighting and the production of plains provisions—were seen through European eyes as distractions rather than occupations, reflecting a pathological inability of the Métis to adapt to the requirements of social change. For example, the failure of the farming attempts by many Métis was interpreted and depicted as a consequence of an innate incapacity for sustained and organized husbandry. Such perceptions focused on, amongst other targets, the attitude to law and to legal institutions of the western Métis.

LAW, COLONIZATION AND THE METIS

Conventional accounts of the legal processes of nineteenth century western Canada—of Métis, of Indians, and of white settlers—rely entirely upon such pathological perspectives. The many histories that eulogise the frontier role of the then North West Mounted Police (for example, McLeod, 1976), largely ignore pre-existing forms of Aboriginal legal process and policing.

In orthodox histories, law enforcement on the plains only appeared with the formation of the NWMP and the long march across the future Saskatchewan and Alberta in 1874 in pursuit of (largely mythical) whiskey traders' forts. They wrongly assume that the formation of the legal institutions of western Canada was the culmination of an evolutionary rational-legal diffusion. Police history, in particular, has been stunted by the failure to recognize indigenous law enforcement processes (Brogden, 1987) as well as to appreciate the role of the legal institutions in social struggle.

Critically, understanding the legal experience of Aboriginal peoples in the formation of modern Canada involves acknowledging the way the colonial society, through institutions from medicine to criminal justice, sought to re-mould these cultures in its own image. Legal structures imposed by a colonial power—as in the case of the NWMP—are part of a seamless web of institutions by which a colonial state seeks to construct its own legitimacy while denying authority to existing Aboriginal practices.

3

The central problem for the British state and the Ottawa surrogate, especially in the later part of the nineteenth century, was how to maximize imperial control at minimal costs. Coercion was expensive as the Hudson's Bay Company had earlier found at Red River, and often counter-productive. Persuasion through education, through the incorporation of an Aboriginal elite (as happened to the Métis at Red River) and through the more general development of 'civilized' colonial institutions was more complex and longer term, but ultimately more effective.

In practice, the expansion and consolidation of the wider Empire was achieved primarily through extending the legitimation of institutions with a British lineage in the colonial territories. British models set the standard for normality and civilization. The NWMP, for example, was one of a hundred and forty colonial police forces that were derivatives of the British-sponsored Irish Constabulary. However, the police and law were only two components in a range of imperial apparatus through which European rule was accomplished at minimal costs.

Initial conquests might be through the mailed fists of the Canadian militia or the NWMP but long-term colonization required a degree of acceptance by the colonized. Education, medicine, and especially law, were important in this process. One NWMP report on the Métis manages to capture the spirit of all these types of institutional colonization, emphasizing Aboriginal pathology in exhorting evolutionary tutelage.

> Amongst the native peoples of the West, ideology of empire was to be conveyed through educational training! It appears that a manual training-school, with a model farm attached should be established among the half-breeds. In no other way can the young children be brought under a desirable healthy influence. The effects on the present generation, as well, would be most beneficial, enabling them to see what patience and industry can establish. It would be necessary for such a school to teach the very elements of social economy; to train the boys as farmers, blacksmiths, carpenters etc; the girls to perform household tasks.... [3]

Similarly, medical institutions were instrumental in the civilization of the Aboriginal people. Conceptions of illness, of diagnosis, of cure, and the approval of recognized medical practitioners (by London accreditation rather than by local tradition) were reconstructed within the normality of colonial civilization. "It might be interesting to note that they live entirely without medical advice. A case came to my notice last year in which an attempt had been made to cure flatulent dyspepsia by a series of gashes across the stomach, a proof that some rational education should be established amongst them."[4] Métis survival on the inhospitable plains of western Canada for a century or more without that advice is somehow ignored.

Law—the complex body of English legislative tradition and in particular, the institution of the NWMP with many of its local superintendents combining in one office, arresting, prosecuting and judicial functions—was a further device by which the "lesser-evolved" races could be persuaded and coerced into the mainstream of "civilized" Empire. Traditional law was denied existence. The prairies were virgin soil for legal implantation. Hence the first Inspector of the NWMP justifying the role of that force in the prairie provinces

> ....not long ago, these wild Indian tribes of the far West were accustomed to regard murder as honorable war, robbery and pillage as traits most ennobling to mankind....the most savage tribes...free from restraint and any sort of control, waged indiscriminate warfare with each other and with mankind....Law, order, and security of life and property were little observed, civil and legal institutions almost entirely absent. [5]

Common law and criminal code, adversarial due process, and an occasional separation of the powers of the legal personnel were fruits to be grown where only rocks had appeared before.

Social control through law, however, is not limited to utilizing the charges and powers within the criminal law. In the early days of state formation often the only important state institution was the police. That body was not solely concerned with law enforcement. It had the larger mandate of conduct in the initial administrative requirements of the colonizing state. Critically, the police institution in those early days was the major unit of local administration, supervising health campaigns including innoculation of both people and cattle against disease, and acting as a census agent of the inhabitants of the new territory. It was often, as in many British African colonies, the instrument of taxation. In the case of the Aboriginal peoples of western Canada, it was also an agency of relief. But in each of these activities, its primary function was that of social control, of control as informed by the mandate from the central state and through the filters of its own occupational prejudices and stereotypes. The NWMP in all its practices with regard to the Métis, chastizing them under the vagrancy law or feeding the destitute (in return for forced labour), acted in accord with its master's view of their own needs, not those of the Aboriginal peoples.

The western Métis in the late nineteenth century, like other Aboriginal peoples, were subject to several ordering strategies by the Ottawa government, mainly through education, medicine, but predominantly through criminal justice institutions. The history of the Canadian frontier in the nineteenth century includes the use of the criminal law and relief of destitution to segregate some Aboriginal peoples and to marginalize others. Criminalization of the Métis, the supplanting of Aboriginal law and legal institutions, and the eventual structuring of Aboriginal peoples as a dependency class, were central to the colonization of western Canada.

NOTES

1. Mike Brogden received a grant from the British Academy in support of his participation in the production of this section of the book.
2. Daily Intelligencer, 12th May, 1885. See also: Bourgeault, 1988:55
3. NWMP Prince Albert Report, 1888.
4. Ibid.
5. NWMP Annual Report, 27th December, 1875.

EARLY LAW AND SOCIAL CONTROL AMONG THE METIS[1]

Lawrence J. Barkwell

The Canadian state has never tolerated autonomy for indigenous people whether it was in terms of participation within the legal system, other spheres of social control, or political action. Stark illustrations of this are offered in the Canadian government's unwillingness to accommodate the Métis nation under Louis Riel in the nineteenth century or to grant any significant measure of sovereignty to Indian people in the second half of the twentieth.

To discover indigenous people with any type of formal legal autonomy in North America, the irony is that one has to look to the U.S.A. There, Indian Tribal Courts and codes of law exist while in Canada they do not. Indeed, little or no customary law has been incorporated into Canadian law, let alone has it survived in a coherent form, though a little customary usage has. In this respect the pacification of the Canadian Indian has been even more complete than that of the Australian Aboriginal people. The federal government in Australia has for some years referred to its Law Reform Commission the task of examining and retrieving Aboriginal customary law. Thus in Canada, unlike other colonized societies, the study of traditional law reveals little about the contemporary state of pacification; instead we must look at other aspects of the apparatus of social control (Havemann, 1983:3).

On May 2nd, 1670, King Charles II granted a Royal Charter to the Governor and Company of Adventurers of England Trading into Hudson's Bay, appointing them "true and absolute Lordes and Proprietors" over the basin whose waters flowed into Hudson Bay. In addition to its trading privileges, the Company had jurisdiction to "judge all persons belonging to the Governor and Company, or that shall live under them, in all cases, whether civil or criminal, according to the laws of this Kingdom and execute justice accordingly" (Stubbs, 1967:3).

The charter provided for the appointment of Governors and Councils in Rupert's Land empowered to enforce law and order, by penalties and punishments in accordance with the current laws of England. If an offence was committed in a part of Rupert's Land where there was no Governor and Council, the Chief Factor of the district had authority to send the offender to England for trial.

Hudson's Bay Company officials did not attempt to exercise jurisdiction over the Indians, except when they committed offences against the Company or its employees. Sir George Simpson, the Governor of Rupert's Land from 1821 to 1860, made this policy clear in his evidence before the Select Committee of the Imperial House of Commons on the Hudson's Bay Company.

> They are under our jurisdiction,...when crimes were committed upon whites, but not when committed upon each other; we do not meddle with their wars.[2]

Up until 1803, both alleged offenders and witnesses in cases involving serious offences were sent by the Company to England for trial. This procedure, which could take the better part of two years, was grossly unfair to all involved. In an effort to correct this burden of expense and delay, the Canada Jurisdiction Act was passed by the British Parliament in 1803. The Act provided in part:

> Offences committed within any of the Indian Territories, etc., shall be tried in the same manner as if committed within the provinces of Lower or Upper Canada. The Governor of Lower Canada may empower persons to act as justices for the Indian Territories, etc., for committing offenders until conveyed to Canada for trial, etc.[3]

Matters of law and order in the west gradually came to the attention of both Imperial and Canadian authorities more and more often. The developing conflict between the Hudson's Bay Company and the partners of the North West Company, and the significant fears of the Métis over the arrival of the Selkirk settlers in the Red River area, served to escalate tension and the possibility of violence. Although no group desired physical conflict, violence finally occurred with a fight between armed parties of settlers and Métis at Seven Oaks on the Red River in 1816.

SEVEN OAKS: CONFLICT AND TRIAL

By June of 1815, the Métis had escalated their demands that the settlers at the forks of the Red and Assiniboine Rivers leave the area. Peter Fiddler, acting as head of the settlers, negotiated with the Métis chiefs at their camp at Frog Plain. On June 20, Peter Pangman instructed Peter Fiddler that no colonists were to remain, but that a limited number of Hudson's Bay Company servants might stay, as it was to the advantage of the Métis to have competing trading companies in the area. Pangman also requested payment of an annual tribute to the Métis. Chief Peguis then tried to intervene on behalf of the colonists, but to no avail. On June 24, 1815, he was the bearer of the Métis order, signed by Cuthbert Grant, William Shaw, Peter Pangman and Bonhomme Montour, that Fiddler was to leave with the colonists.

On June 25, Peter Fiddler countered with the following terms (Macleod, 1963:29):

Proposals of Peace delivered by us to the Half Breeds, 25th June, 1815.

Peace

In the year of our Lord 1815 this 25th day June & His Majesty's Reign the Fifty Sixth. 1st. It is hereby promised that peace & amity shall hereafter ever exist between the people of this settlement and the Half Breeds & that all that has been done on both sides shall be forgiven.

2nd. It is furthermore agreed that the Half Breeds shall ever enjoy the full liberty of running the Buffalo and living according to the custom in which they have been brought up.

3rd. And it is also agreed that they shall not be subject to any Local Laws that may be hereafter established unless they finding the good effects of living a civilized life shall come forward and ask to be admitted into our society, then they shall be considered as one of us and shall enjoy all the Privileges we may possess.

4th. And it is further promised that whatever presents may be given annually to the Indians, that the Half Breeds shall have an equal share in them.

Red River Settlement, 25th June, 1815.

Cuthbert Grant and the other Captains of the Métis rejected this proposal and responded with one of their own which was then accepted by James Sutherland and James White on behalf of the colonists of the Red River Settlement (Ibid:29):

Métis Treaty Terms

1. All settlers to retire immediately from this river, and no appearance of a colony to remain.

2. Peace and amity to subsist between all parties, traders, Indians, and freemen, in future, throughout these two rivers, and on no account any person to be molested in his lawful pursuits.

3. The honorable Hudson's Bay Company will, as customary enter this river, if they think proper, from three to four of their former trading boats, and from four to five men per boat as usual.

4. Whatever former disturbance has taken place between both parties, that is to say, the honorable Hudson's Bay Company and the Half breeds of the Indian territory, to be totally forgot and not to be recalled by either party.

5. Every person retiring peaceable from this river immediately, shall not be molested in their passage out.

6. No person passing the summer for the Hudson's Bay Company, shall remain in the buildings of the Company but shall retire to some other spot, where they will establish for the purpose of trade.

Cuthbert Grant,
Bostonais Pangman,
Wm. Shaw,
Bonhomme Montour,
The Four chiefs of
the Half-Breeds,
James Sutherland,
James White.

Red River Indian Territory, Forks, Red River, 25 June, 1815.

Such were the terms of the first treaty which asserted the rights of the Métis as a free Aboriginal people.

The Seven Oaks incident was really a culmination of the ongoing trade war between the North West Company and the Hudson's Bay Company, with the Métis fighting in defense of North West Company rights and for the rights of the Métis as a free Aboriginal people.

COURT SYSTEMS OF EARLY MANITOBA

One of the first major trials involving accused Métis men held under the Canada Jurisdiction Act was the murder trial of two of Cuthbert Grant's men, Paul Brown and Francis Boucher, charged with killing Governor Robert Semple at Seven Oaks on June 19, 1816. The trial was held at York, Upper Canada, in October 1818, before a court of Upper and Lower Canada with Chief Justice Powell presiding. Both men were acquitted of the charges.

As a result of the Seven Oaks incident a Royal Commission was appointed to look into the governance of Rupert's Land. The Commission reported to Parliament in 1819, resulting two years later in "An Act for regulating the Fur Trade and establishing a Criminal and Civil Jurisdiction within certain parts of North America" which was passed two years later.

This Act provided for the extension of the provisions of the Canada Jurisdiction Act to all the territories previously granted to the Hudson's Bay Company. The Courts of Upper Canada were to have the same civil and criminal jurisdiction within the Indian territories as they had within the limits of the Province. Justices of the peace were appointed to determine cases in the Indian territories. They were empowered to hold Courts of Record for the trial of criminal offences (excepting felony charges subject to capital punishment) and civil trials in which the cause of action did not exceed two hundred pounds. All other cases were to be tried in the Courts of Upper Canada.

Non-Aboriginal Judicial and Correctional Systems

In 1821, the fur trading companies were amalgamated and Rupert's Land was reorganized into four Departments, each with its own Governor and Council. The District of Assiniboia in the Northern Department, which included the Red River Settlement, was divided into four judicial districts, each with a court presided over by a magistrate or a justice of the peace. These courts could only deal with minor cases. More serious matters were heard by the General Quarterly Court composed of the Governor and Council.

To improve this system, the Governor and Committee in London provided in 1839 for the office of a Recorder of Rupert's Land. This individual was to be a person trained in law whose duties were to direct the proceedings of the General Quarterly Court and to serve as a member of the Council of Assiniboia. For all criminal cases, and for civil claims over 10 pounds, a jury was to sit with the Recorder and the other members of the court to determine questions of fact.

In 1835, the first prison had opened in Upper Canada at Kingston. The rules at this prison were enforced by a particularly harsh regime of corporal punishment. In 1846, there were sixteen children under the age of sixteen at the Kingston Penitentiary. It is reported that a ten-year-old boy serving a seven year sentence was whipped on seventy-one separate occasions for offences as minor as making faces and misbehaving at the dinner table. In 1841, a fourteen-year-old girl was whipped four times in the space of three months (Gosselin, 1982:72). In 1847, over 6,000 punishments were imposed on 500 prisoners. It was estimated that each prisoner was flogged on average four or five times per year for what one could only characterize as administrative infractions.[4] Banishment was established as a punishment in Upper Canada in 1802 and was only abolished in 1902. At the same time transportation to New South Wales or Tasmania was used as an alternative to hanging for theft. Many did not survive the sea voyage and many more died in those penal colonies. In 1859, there was discussion of making the Hudson's Bay territory into a penal colony but this did not come about.

It is fair to say that the Métis, especially those living out on the plains, viewed these legal systems as oppressive, irrelevant and detrimental to their way of life. The Métis openly defied officers who tried to stop their free trading activities. In defiance of Hudson's Bay Company law, one Métis trader was quoted as saying, "Take me prisoner, this is my country, I shall have justice" (Giraud, 1986 [II]:361).

Métis Judicial and Correctional Systems

The reports of Alexander Ross (1856) and Father Alexis André (1873) establish conclusively that Métis communities in western Canada practised forms of criminal justice that were far in advance of anything that the Canadian state had to offer at the time. As Ross (1856:381) pointed out, "....we have...no tread-mills, no hulks, no pillory, no penitentiary, no white sheets, no Botany Bay. Fortunately, our only available punishment is generally speaking quite sufficient." Métis social organization was both communal and democratic. Leaders were elected and laws which had been passed on verbally over the years were usually ratified or changed at public assemblies.

Métis legislation in those days was highly progressive, containing reparative, restitutive measures with minimal reference to the corporal punishments of Upper Canada. This was in striking contrast to the regime in force at Kingston penitentiary as noted above. From the historical records of the day, it is clear that Métis methods of social control were inspired by concepts in force among the prairie Aboriginal population. The Métis structured their policing on a warrior society model although generally penalties applied to offenders were substantially less, and in no case led to death (Giraud, 1986[II]:361; Dusenberry, 1985:122-123). The structure was also democratic in terms of the annual election of all key officials (if one can overlook the exclusion of women from voting participation).

Others besides the Métis in the community took exception to the way in which the rule of law was being implemented in Assiniboia. Councillor Alexander Ross saw little need for a Recorder with legal qualifications. "In the place of the simple honesty, which marked our proceedings hitherto [bringing such a man into the colony] has a tendency to substitute the quibbles and technicalities of law, which few but lawyers themselves comprehend (Ross, 1856:376)." One can also note that the legal system was not fairly adversarial as there were no other lawyers in the district and accused persons were routinely tried without defence counsel.

The laws of the District of Assiniboia were consolidated and codified in 1841, 1852 and 1862 by Recorder Adam Thom. Ross was also critical of this process, commenting that: "It was the Recorder that penned them; it was the Recorder that argued them through the council in a masterly manner; it was the Recorder that interpreted them, so as to make their inevitable generalities fit particular cases....People said he possessed the gift of twisting and untwisting his interpretations, so as always to fit his own cause (Ross, 1856:383)." In actual fact, however, this largely Métis community was self-regulating, so little use was made of the General Quarterly Court of Assiniboia for want of cases.[5] In 1857, Sir George Simpson reported that in the previous thirty-seven years there had been only nineteen major crimes brought to court (Stubbs, 1967:11).

In 1849, in England, Alexander Isbister petitioned the Colonial Office regarding the inherent Aboriginal rights of Indians and Métis, independent of colonial law. The petition also requested representative government with control over lawmaking and the administration of justice. It was an effort to escape the oppression of the Hudson's Bay Company through recognized self-government (Isbister, cited in Cooper, 1988:129).

Objects Sought By The Petitioners

1. Protection in their rights of liberty to trade in furs as well as every other production of the country. The Natives of Rupert's Land, whether Indians or half-castes, consider that even had the charter of the Hudson's Bay Company been good and sufficient in point of law (which it is not), it could not deprive them of rights inherent and inalienable in their ancestors, and, of course, inherited by them as their descendants. The charter

13

being, however, illegal, and virtually admitted to be so by the Company themselves, by the fact of their having been under the necessity of petitioning Parliament for its confirmation, which they did in the year 1690, the claims of the Hudson's Bay Company—untenable even as against other traders from Britain—are of no force whatever against the Natives of the country, who irrespective of all such considerations, have the right, of which no King or Parliament can deprive them, of trading with whom they please.

2. That all lands sold to settlers should be legally secured to them.

3. That the Company be bound to make payments, if so desired, in the current coin of the realm.

4. That the settlers be invested with full corporate rights, have the power of choosing their own magistrates, and a voice in the passing of their own laws.

5. That some provision be made for the independent administration of justice, and the adequate supervision of the Company's own officers.

6. That the laws in force in the colony for the prevention of the sale of spiritous liquors to the Indians be binding equally on the Company and the Settlers.

7. That, in consideration of the Company's retaining in their own hands the entire commerce and shipping of the country, they provide in their vessels, at a reasonable charge, accommodation for the imports and exports of the colony.

Rules of the Buffalo Hunt, 1840

Nowhere was Métis social organization more evident than in the structure of the annual buffalo hunts. These hunts involved large numbers of people, huge amounts of equipment and travel over long distances into the United States. The Métis were usually accompanied by their relatives from among the Cree, Saulteaux and Assiniboine Indians. A number of different communities were also involved. The Métis party leaving White Horse Plains and travelling south-west, for example, would pick up members from the Souris River and Turtle Mountain areas in the United States. The party leaving the Red River settlement would travel south to Pembina where they would be joined by Métis and Indians from what is now northern Minnesota and north-east North Dakota. These groups preferred to travel with the large Canadian contingent, as it was considered dangerous to travel too far into Dakota (Sioux) territory in small groups. Over the years it became the custom of many Métis to winter on the southern and western plains rather than to travel all the way back with the main group.

In 1854, Father Belcourt reported that there were approximately 2,000 Métis living around Pembina. He noted hunting expeditions originating in the district of Assiniboia with as many as 5,000 Métis and Indians. These parties went up the Missouri River to just below Fort Mandan. He was concerned about the impact of these large numbers of "British half-breeds" hunting buffalo; to end these incursions he asked the American government to place a military post at Pembina Mountain where local Métis could be mobilized as militia "....with the idea of cowing the British and the Indians...." from Canada (Voegelin and Hickerson, 1974:137-138).

Ross (1856:248) reported in detail on an expedition which left the Red River Settlement on June 15th, 1840. When the roll was called at Pembina, 1,630 people were present with 1,210 Red River carts. Ross noted that the officials for the trip were named and installed into office without the aid of writing materials. The first step was a council meeting for the nomination of chiefs or officers. Ten captains were named; the senior officer at that particular assembly was Jean Baptiste Wilke, who also held the position of president (1856:248).

Each captain had ten soldiers under his orders. Ten guides were also appointed. The camp flag belonged to the guide of the day. Once this flag was raised in the morning, the guide was the chief of the expedition and the captains were subject to him. When the flag was lowered, the captains' and soldiers' duties began. These *dizaines* formed a police force—they looked after the execution of laws or judgements, protected the caravan from attack, guaranteed property against theft and mounted guard during the night (Giraud, 1986 [II]:143; McDougall, 1903: 72-79).

Before leaving Pembina the captains and other chief men held a council to set down the rules of the expedition. These provisional governments showed constant recourse to election according to Métis custom of the day, and showed respect for the freedom of the individual. It gave them leaders of their own choice and as a consequence, the leaders' authority was freely accepted (Giraud, 1986[II]:143). Those rules were documented by Ross (1856:249-250) as follows:

1. No Buffalo to be run on the Sabbath-day.

2. No party to fork off, lag behind or go before, without permission.

3. No person or party to run buffalo before the general order.

4. Every captain with his men, in turn, to patrol the camp, and keep guard.

5. For the first trespass against these laws, the offender to have his saddle and bridle cut up.

6. For the second offense, the coat to be taken off the offender's back, and be cut up.

7. For the third offense, the offender to be flogged.

8. Any person convicted of theft, even to the value of a sinew, to be brought to the middle of the camp, and the crier to call out his or her name three times adding the word "Thief", at each time.

Ross also made the following observation (1856:250):

....virtue is fostered among them by the mildest of means; for what do such a people fear from a breach of the penal code? Punishments here are scarcely more than nominal; and may well suggest the question to a more civilized community, whether it is always the severest punishments that have the best effect in reclaiming offenders.

Modern day commentators have made similar observations as to the advanced and liberal nature of Métis law. Duke Redbird (1980: 10-11) has pointed out that rules of the hunt were often misconstrued as being similar to a white institutional process (para-military), whereas the Métis process was always one of including all of those that the decisions were to affect.

"The fact is that the Métis utilized a task force process in the selection of their leaders. The individual best suited for a particular job was democratically selected to assume authority for a limited time period —usually until the task for which he was selected to lead was accomplished. The basis for this type of democracy was from the Indian form and not an imitation of white concepts."

George Woodcock analysed the laws of the hunt in his biography of Gabriel Dumont:

What one immediately notices about the punishments decreed in the rules of the hunt is their relative mildness. Physical sanctions seem to have been regarded as the last resort, to be used only against the habitual offender and against the worst crime of a hunter, which was to break order and risk scaring the buffalo herd prematurely. For the most part, reliance seems to have been placed on the moral effect of public ridicule among a proud people who found losing face more difficult to endure than losing possessions. The same sense of a community ruled by opinion embodied in a few simple and generally accepted moral rules emerges from Ross's descriptions of the gatherings of captains and elders at the end of each day's travelling or hunting, when they would sit tailor-fashion on the ground to hold council....

(The) Métis (were) members of an egalitarian community influenced deeply by the kind of primitive and direct democracy which existed among the great Indian tribes of the plains, where the authority of the chief depended always on the revocable consent of his braves (Woodcock, 1976:34-35).

NEGOTIATIONS WITH THE UNITED STATES GOVERNMENT

On September 20, 1851, a treaty was signed by Alexander Ramsey, Governor of the Minnesota Territory, and members of the Red Lake and Pembina Bands of Chippewa. Some 250 Indians and several hundred Métis were present during the negotiations. According to Ramsey the councils for this treaty were held at Pembina simply because the majority of the Métis resided in that area. Ramsey's position during the negotiations was that the Chippewa of Red Lake and Pembina should cede some of their territory to provide land on which "their Half-Breed relatives" and the non-Native immigrants could settle and engage in agriculture (Ramsey and Morrill, 1863:3).

Ramsey noted that the half-breeds approached him prior to the treaty council and asked to be included as it was they who, in their view, were the true occupants of the country and were the ones who defended it against enemies (referring to the Dakota). He replied that he could not treat with them as they were only quasi-citizens of the United States (Ibid). Ramsey did use two Métis men, Rev. James Tanner and Joseph Nolin, as interpreters for the treaty negotiations.

Although the Métis were not specifically included in the Treaty, Article 2 called for the United States to pay the Indians $30,000 "to enable them to make provision for their half-breed children" (Ross, 1856:411). According to Ramsey, this article was urged upon him by the Chippewa (Ramsey and Morrill, 1863:286).

Although the treaty was completed and signed it was never ratified. Alexander Ross observed that:

....the terms of the treaty have proved a sad disappointment to the poor half-breeds, after their long struggle to obtain a settlement, in the belief that they themselves would have been recognized by the

American Government as the rightful owners of the disputed lands of Pembina (Ross, 1856:411-412).

Ramsey, however, continued negotiating a land settlement in this part of the territory. A treaty of October 2, 1863, was negotiated near what is now Crookston, Minnesota, involving the US government, the Chippewas from Red Lake and Pembina, the Métis from Red Lake and Pembina-St.Joseph, and several Chiefs from Leech Lake. The Red Lake party included 579 Indians and 24 Métis, while the Pembina party rostered some 352 Indians and 633 Métis (Ramsey and Morrill, 1863:31).

Although Ramsey was still not willing to sign a treaty with the Métis, Article 8 pertained directly to them. It provided that each Métis related by blood to members of either the Red Lake or Pembina Chippewa Bands, and who had adopted the habits and customs of "civilized life" and who was a U.S. citizen, could obtain a homestead of 160 acres of land, on land not previously occupied (Kappler, 1903:653-655).

Alexander Ramsey and A. C. Morrill (1863:74) outlined the relationship between the Chippewa Indians and the Métis:

> Today the Pembina Indians arrived, bringing in their train nearly twice their own number in Half-breeds from Saint Joseph, who insisted in regarding themselves as individually and collectively the guardians and attorneys of the Pembina Chippewas in all matters touching the disposition of their landed interests... (they) came unbidden under color of their relationship to the Indians. The messenger or agent who had been authorized to furnish subsistence for the Pembina Indians on their way to the treaty ground gave as his excuse for bringing so large a number of uninvited guests that the Pembina Indians are completely under the control of their half-breed relatives, and could not have been induced to come unless accompanied by the latter, who having long been accustomed to consider themselves, to a certain extent, the real owners of the soil, and as having even a greater interest in any treaty for its purchase than its far less numerous or powerful aboriginal occupants.

Voegelin and Hickerson (1974:173) summarized the dynamics that were of concern to the US government:

> Actually, the Chippewa were able to extend their hunting enterprises south and west of Fort Garry as the half-breeds increased in numbers and intensified their own hunting. The half-breeds were acknowledged by authors in the 1840s and succeeding decades as the "owner" or "occupants" of the Pembina-Sheyenne-Devil's Lake-Missouri Coteau-Souris River area. The

1851 treaty itself received much of its impetus from the desirability, as expressed by such authorities as Belcourt, Wood, Ross, and Ramsey, of settling the half-breeds on United States soil, and thereby reducing tensions that arose as a result of their "encroachment" on American land from British territory.

The 1863 treaty ceded a 30-mile-wide strip on each side of the Red River (5,634,820 acres in North Dakota and 4,156,120 acres in Minnesota). The balance of Indian and Métis traditional hunting territory, approximately one million acres, was ceded in what became known as the "ten cent treaty" because one million dollars was paid for ten million acres of land. This formally titled "McCumber Agreement" (1892) was eventually negotiated by what became known as the Committee of 32 (16 full-blood Indians and 16 mixed-blood Mechif). It was ratified in April, 1904. The roll compiled by Senator McCumber "consisted of 1,739 mixed-blood and 283 full-bloods but it was said the remainder of the 1,476 mixed-bloods (including those considered white Canadians) and others, were not considered eligible and left out many who were eligible" (Turtle Mountain Indian Reservation, 1986:93).

This treaty had allotments of 160 acres for each adult on the roll. The allotments located on the Turtle Mountain Reservation were given to the older full-blooded Indians and some of the older mixed-blood Mechifs. The remainder of the lands were allotted on the public domain in Montana and western North Dakota. As with most negotiations with Aboriginal people, this agreement was not implemented immediately as McCumber's roll was not accepted. When it was finally completed and approved in 1943, it consisted of 7,317 members, 160 of whom were full-blood Indians.

THE LAWS AND REGULATIONS ESTABLISHED FOR THE COLONY OF ST. LAURENT ON THE SASKATCHEWAN

The first Métis community on the plains west of what is now the province of Manitoba that made attempts to codify a set of laws and set out rules of governance was St. Albert, near Edmonton. Discussions towards this were held at Edmonton House and were recorded in the Hudson's Bay Company Journal entry for April 29th, 1867, as follows:

A number of Halfbreeds from St. Albert came here today to express a wish that some steps should be taken to institute Laws to allow for the good Government of the Colony &c &c —told them to embody their request in the form of a petition signed by the inhabitants which should be presented to the Governor and Council—the subject of Laws in the plains in the Halfbreed Camp was also talked over. The majority of the people are well disposed and would wish to have Laws and order at home and in the plain camp when off to the Buffalo hunt, but there are no leading head men among them capable of laying hold and carrying out their plans.[6]

The Métis at St. Laurent were more productive in their efforts, largely due to the leadership provided by the Dumont family. A condensed report of the December 31, 1871, meeting of Métis winterers at the Mission of St. Laurent near Carlton exists.[7] At this meeting, Lawrence Clarke, a Hudson's Bay Factor, was voted chairman, Joseph Emilin was elected vice-chairman, and Father Alexis André was elected secretary. Excerpts from the minutes of this meeting included the following:

Lawrence Clarke said that the honour of being voted chairman... was not an isolated instance of their respect and esteem for the Company's officers; at the large and important Métis Settlement of St. Albert near Edmonton; Mr. Chief-Factor Christie had been chosen by the people there, as their president, to counsel and advise, with a Committee representing the whole population of the settlement, to form a code of Laws for the self-government of the Colony...(he)would further assure the meeting that whatever steps they took to form themselves into a permanent colony, they would have the best wishes and sympathies of the Chief Officer of the Hudson's Bay Company in the country Mr. Donald A. Smith... (who) will give his hearty assent to any measures which shall have for their object the fostering and development of the resources of the country, the opening out new and extended commercial intercourse and business relationships with all the inhabitants present and future, but more especially with the Métis Hunters of this great prairie country. Joseph Emilin said that..." he trusted that the words spoken there this evening would not be *inutile,* but that they the Métis would show that the stain cast upon their character as a people, of being unstable in their pursuits was a reproach they thrusted back upon their slanderers. He had the honour of knowing His Excellency the Lieutenant Governor, and felt certain that whatever measures they adopted to found a French Métis Colony in this section of the Saskatchewan would meet with his approbation...he would impress upon them that unity is strength, and so long as we are a dispersed people we can never become a nation, but must be lost in the future populations of this vast territory.

Several others of the patriarchs of the Camp spoke "...all agreeing that it was desirable in the interests of their families to change their nomadic life and have a fixed habitation and a home."

A committee made up of Father André, Alexander Hamilin, Jean Dumont Jr., Jean Dumont (*dit* Chakaska), Isidore Dumont (*dit* Ecapoo), Joseph Emilin, Philip Gardupine, Joseph Paranteau Sr. and Louison Letendre, was chosen to examine, choose and allot a claim near Carlton for the proposed French Métis colony.

Subsequently the committee selected a site at St. Laurent and the colony went about setting up its own unique set of laws. At a public assembly held on December 10, 1873, in the winter camp on the Saskatchewan River, the Métis updated and formalized the old laws of the prairies into what came to be known as the *Laws of St. Laurent*. This written document set out the civil rules for the life of the community established there. It also contained a section called *Laws for the Prairie and Hunting* which had 25 articles for the regulation of all aspects of the buffalo hunt. For all these laws the council was to act as a judicial tribunal which had a mandate to settle differences between people by way of arbitration as much as possible. It is significant, too, that the council recognized contracts written "in French, English or Indian characters even if made without witnesses."

According to these laws, and Métis custom, the punishment for most offenses was quite lenient, usually only a fine. Several changes in punishment provisions are evident when one compares these laws with the rules of 1840. Corporal punishment was removed and punishment by ridicule was replaced by monetary fines, likely due to the development of a cash economy. The crimes specified in the laws were those which were most likely to disrupt community life: horse theft, dishonouring young girls, lighting prairie fires in summer, failure to restrain horses or dogs and defaming the character of others. As more violent offenses are not mentioned, it would appear that the goal of the community was to establish a set of laws which would be most likely to reduce incidents which could be used as excuses for violence.

The Laws were drawn up during the Assemblies of 1873 to 1875, in the absence of any other government presence in that area. The initial decision of the assembly was to have the *Laws of St. Laurent* administered by an elected president and council. A translated copy of these laws is contained in a letter to Colonel French from the St. Laurent priest, Father Alexis André, who added his own commentary and interpretations. This letter was date-stamped by the Department of Justice in Ottawa on October 2, 1875, and is now on file with the Public Archives of Canada.[8] Because so many Métis people have indicated that they have not seen these laws and regulations in their entirety, the full text of Father André's letter is presented here:

The inhabitants of St. Laurent held a public assembly to draw up laws and regulations for the peace and tranquility of their community. In the absence of any form of government among them to administer justice and to judge the differences that may arise among them, they have thought it necessary to choose from among their number a Chief and Councillors invested with the power to judge differences and to decide litigious questions and matters affecting the public interest.

The Chief with the members of his Council is elected for one year and during this term of power, the President and the members of Council are empowered to judge all cases that shall be brought before them. The chief, by the advice of his Council, can convoke the general assemblies of the public, in order to submit for their decision matters of higher consequence, concerning which they would hesitate to pass orders without knowing the opinion of the majority of the public.

It is well understood that in making these laws and regulations the inhabitants of St. Laurent in no wise pretend to constitute for themselves an independent state but the actual situation of the country in which they live, obliges them to take some measure to maintain peace and union amongst them, knowing that so large a society as theirs can exist only under some sort of organization to preserve mutually their rights, but in forming these laws, they acknowledge themselves as loyal and faithful subjects of Canada, and are ready to abandon their own organization and to submit to the laws of the Dominion as soon as Canada shall have established amongst them regular magistrates with a force sufficient to uphold in the country the authority of law.

In the Assembly held on the tenth of December 1873, in the winter camp, Gabriel Dumont was elected President for one year. The following were chosen as members of Council:[9]

> Alexander Hamelin
>
> Baptiste Gurriepy [Gariepey]
>
> Pierre Gurriepy [Gariepey]
>
> Abraham Montour
>
> Isidore Dumont Jr.
>
> Jean Dumont Jr.
>
> Moyse Walet [Moise Ouelette]
>
> Baptiste Hamelin

After the election of the president and the members of Council, the Assembly, on the motion of a certain member, expressed a desire that President and members should take an oath before Father André their missionary to faithfully perform their duties in the honesty of their conscience without exception of anyone and to judge the cases brought before their tribunal. The President and the members consented to take the oath on condition that the persons who had chosen them should likewise swear to support them, not only with their votes but also to aid them to maintain the laws they might make and to execute the sentences they might pronounce.

Father André having explained to them the nature of the oath, and having made them understand that it was in his capacity of minister of the Gospel, and not as a civil officer that he received their promise to fulfil their engagements, all the members of the assembly came on their knees to kiss the Holy Bible, calling the Divine Word to witness their firm resolution to support their laws according to justice and to punish those who would infringe them.

Article I. On the first Monday of the month, the President and members of his Council shall be obliged to assemble in a house indicated before hand by the President in order to judge the cases that may be submitted to their arbitration.

Article II. Any Counsellor who, unless by reason of illness, or impossibility shall not be present at the indicated place shall pay a fine of five Louis.

Article III. The President, who, by his own fault shall not meet his Councillors in the indicated place, shall pay a fine of three Louis.

Article IV. Any captain refusing to execute the orders that he shall receive in the name of the Council shall pay a fine of three Louis.

Article V. Any soldier, who shall refuse to execute the orders of his captain shall pay a fine of one Louis and a half.

Article VI. Any person who shall insult the Council or a member of the Council in the public exercise of his functions shall pay a fine of three Louis.

Article VII. Any person who shall be guilty of contempt of any measure of the Council or of one passed in a general Assembly, shall pay a fine of one Louis.

Article VIII. Any person wishing to plead shall inform the President beforehand and shall deposit with him as security, the sum of five shillings.

Article IX. In every case the plaintive shall deposit two Louis, five shillings with the president to renumerate him and the members of the Council for their loss of time, but at the termination of the case, the person losing it shall pay all the costs and the plaintive if he gains shall receive back the money deposited.

Article X. Any person who shall call the Assembly together shall pay five shillings to the president and to each member; should he come to a compromise with the other side and abandon the prosecution of the case.

Article XI. Every witness in a case shall receive two and a half shillings a day.

Article XII. Any case, once brought before the Council can no longer be judged by any arbitration outside the Council.

Article XIII. Any person judged by the Council shall be allowed ten days to make arrangements with the person with whom the quarrel is, at the expiration of that term the Council shall cause its order to be forcibly executed.

Article XIV. Any person, who only has three animals, shall not be compelled to give up any one of them in payment of his debts. This clause does not apply to unmarried men, who shall be compelled to pay even to the last animal.

Article XV. Any person who shall be known to have taken another person's horse without permission, shall pay a fine of two Louis.

Article XVI. Any contract made without witnesses shall be null and void and its execution cannot be sought for in the Council.

Article XVII. Any bargain made on a Sunday, even before witnesses, cannot be prosecuted in court.

Article XVIII. Any bargain, any contract, any sales shall be valid, written in French, English or Indian characters even if made without witnesses, if the plaintive testifies on oath to the correctness of his account or contract.

Article XIX. Any affair decided by the Council of St. Laurent shall never be appealed by any of the parties before any other tribunal when the government of Canada shall have placed its regular magistrates in the country, and all persons pleading do it with the knowledge that they promise never to appeal against the decisions given by the Council and no one is is permitted to enjoy the privileges of this community, except on the express condition of submitting to this law.

Article XX. Any money contribution shall not exceed one Louis and every public tax levied by the Council shall be obligatory for the inhabitants of St. Laurent, and those who shall refuse to submit to the levy shall be liable to pay a fine, the amount of which shall be determined by the Council.

Article XXI. Any young man, who, under pretext of marriage, shall dishonour a young girl and afterwards refuse to marry her, shall be liable to pay a fine of fifteen Louis: this law applies equally to the case of married men dishonouring girls.

Article XXII. Any person who shall defame the character of another person and shall attack his honour, his virtue or his probity shall be liable to a fine in proportion to the quality and rank of the person attacked or to the degree of injury caused.

Article XXIII. Any person who shall set fire to the prairie from the 1st August and causes damage shall pay a fine of four Louis.

Article XXIV. On Sundays and obligatory festivals the river ferrys shall be free for people riding or driving to church, but any person who shall cross without going to church, shall pay as on ordinary days.

Article XXV. All the horses shall be free, but he whose horse causes injury or annoyance, shall be warned and should he not hobble his horse he shall pay a fine of 5 shillings a day from the time he was warned to look after his horse.

Article XXVI. If any dogs kill a little foal, the owner of the dogs shall be held responsible for the damage done.

Article XXVII. Any servant who shall leave his employer the expiration of his term agreed upon, shall forfeit all right to his wages; in the same way, any employer dismissing his servant without proper cause, shall pay him his wages in full.

Article XXVIII. On Sunday no servant shall be obliged to perform any but duties absolutely necessary, however, on urgent occasion, the master can order the servant to look after his horses on Sundays only after the great mass: he shall never prevent him from going to church, at least in the morning.

Public Assembly held at the winter camp of the Métis the Tenth February 1873.

The following resolutions were passed in this assembly.

Resolution I.

In order to put an end to the difficulties that arise concerning the limits and boundaries of lands between neighbours, the Council shall appoint a Commission of three competent persons to examine the lands and enquire into the matter: but he who shall have caused the difficulty by wishing to encroach on his neighbour's land shall pay the three Commissioners at the rate of five shillings a day.

Resolution II.

Every chief of a family shall not have the right to take a tract of more than two miles in length and a quarter of a mile in breadth but every chief of a family can take a tract of land for those of his boys who shall have attained the age of twenty years.

Resolution III.

Every individual shall possess an exclusive right to the hay and wood on his land and which may be found up to the end of the two miles of his claim, and no one shall have the right of cutting wood or hay without the permission of the proprietor.

Resolution IV.

To have a right to a claim, wood must be placed and it must be occupied within six months dating from the present decree, at the expiration of this term if the land be not occupied, the first comer can take possession of it.

Resolution V.

In order to prevent the useless destruction of wood it is decreed that no one shall fell more trees than they can use for work for two weeks, otherwise he shall use (sic) all right to the wood, and should he leave any trees in the wooded tract on the ground without cutting off the brush, the first comer can take the wood without the other being able to reclaim it.

Resolution VI.

Any man who has established himself on a land as fit for cultivation shall not be able to claim another tract of land beyond the limits of the first, as a land which he reserves on account of the utility which he thinks to draw from it on account of the wood that may be found on that land: the lands solely covered with wood and not fitted for cultivation shall be common to all the inhabitants established at St. Laurent.

Assembly held at St. Laurent, 10th December 1874.

A year after the establishment of law, the inhabitants of St. Laurent, assembled in the church. The president and the Councillors told the people that the year of their functions had expired, and that they returned into their hands the power with which they had invested them: that they begged them to choose another president and other councillors: as to themselves they would be content to be released from their duties which caused them a great loss of time: that they were, however, all aware of the salutary benefits of these laws which they had established and that, thanks to this organization they had lived in peace and without the slightest disturbance.

Father André, their missionary, addressed to them a powerful exhortation to press them to maintain their laws and to preserve their confidence in the men who had watched over their interests with so much devotion during the year that had just passed; he recalled to their minds the wholesome measures that had been passed: the hatreds, quarrels, disorders that had been avoided by the establishment of these laws and of the government amongst them. The following were chosen as President and Councillors.

Gabriel Dumont was unanimously re-elected President.

Councillors:

Alexander Hamelin

Baptiste Boyer

Abraham Montour

Moyse Walet [Moise Ouelette]

Jean Dumont Jr.

Isidore Dumont Jr.

Baptiste Hamelin

The President and the Councillors were confirmed in all the rights that had been conceded to them and the general assembly ratified the measures that they had thought fit to pass in the course of the year for the public welfare: they received new assurance from the public of support in case of need, on every occasion.

27th January 1875. Resolutions passed by the President and his Council.

The President and his Councillors having assembled on the 27th January of the present year; considering that the people of St. Laurent had invested them with the power of making such laws as they should judge conducive to the welfare of the parish of St. Laurent, considering moreover that at the time of their election, the public had authorized them to levy a contribution for the public good, not exceeding one Louis sterling, the following measure was unanimously passed: the want of a school being greatly felt in the Parish of St. Laurent, all the heads of families of the said Parish, are taxed one Louis each to build the school house; this contribution shall be paid in money, provisions, or in labour according to the wish or convenience of each man, but no one is exempt from this contribution unless he comes and proves before the Council his inability to pay. One month is allowed for each man to pay the contribution to Mr. Moyer Vallet, who is empowered to receive contributions for the erection of the school house.

LAWS FOR THE PRAIRIE AND HUNTING

Article I. Every spring at the end of April, a general public assembly shall be held in front of the church of the Parish of St. Laurent to fix the time of starting for the prairie.

Article II. No one, unless authorized by the Council can leave before the time fixed for departure.

Article III. Any one infringing the provisions of Article II shall be liable to a fine, amount of which shall be determined by the Council.

Article IV. Should a certain number of men conspire together to evade the provisions of Article II and start secretly, the president shall order the captains to pursue them and bring them back: and these breakers of the law shall pay the wages of the captains and soldiers occupied in their pursuit, at the rate of five shillings a man.

Article V. The Council shall be able to authorize the fixed time of departure to be accelerated for those who, by reason of want of provisions wish to go to the prairie to seek for means of living, but a certain point shall be fixed beyond which they shall not be allowed to go, and they shall be obliged to wait for the great brigade of hunters at the place fixed for the rendez-vous of the whole caravan.

Article VI. Those persons, who, having obtained permission to start in advance shall profit by it to push ahead and to hunt without waiting for the big caravan shall be liable to pay a large fine which Council shall fix according to the damage caused by them.

Article VII. Whenever the caravan of hunters has arrived at the place of general rendez-vous, the camp shall be organized, the captains, the guides for the roads, hackers for the animals shall be named, and the prairie laws shall be in full force.

Article VIII. In the morning no one shall start before the guide gives the signal, and every one shall stop his carts and pitch his tents in the place pointed out by the guide.

Article IX. All carts shall be placed so as to form a circle and every day the captains and soldiers shall go round the camp to see if there be any break in the line of carts forming the circle.

Article X. It is expressly forbidden to fire when the animals are announced in the neighbourhood: a person infringing this law is liable to a fine of five shillings.

Article XI. Any person, who in the morning when the camp is raised, shall fail to extinguish his fire, shall pay five shillings: a captain shall be told every day to visit all the fires as soon as the camp is raised.

Article XII. The Council shall indicate the hour and time at which the animals shall be chased, and also the herd if there are several herds.

Article XIII. If in the course of the hunt a man is accidentally wounded, the person who wounded him shall work for him until he be cured.

Article XIV. If a man while hunting, kills another man's horse, he shall pay the value of the horse; should he wound a horse he shall lend another until the wounded horse is cured.

Article XV. After a run, if new animals appear, no one shall run them without permission from three captains.

Article XVI. He who, after killing a beast abandons it on the plain, shall pay a fine of one Louis.

Article XVII. If any person, or party of persons shall steal away secretly in order to run a herd of beasts they may have discovered, they shall pay a fine in proportion to the damage caused.

Article XVIII. Any one starting before the signal is given by the captains shall pay a fine of one Louis.

Article XIX. If a soldier, whose turn for sentry duty it is, shall fail to go to his post, he shall pay a fine of ten shillings: if the offender be a captain he shall pay a fine of one Louis.

Article XX. A soldier sleeping at night on his post, shall pay a fine of ten shillings - if the offender be a captain, ten and a member of Council, one Louis.

Article XXI. If a captain, knowing the faults of his soldiers does not report them to the Council, he shall pay a fine of two Louis.

Article XXII. No person or no party shall be allowed to leave the camp without leave of the Council: any one so doing shall pay a large fine.

Article XXIII. If a party under pretence of independence and of living in perfect freedom, resides in the neighbourhood of the great caravan: the Council of the great camp shall first warn these people not to run the beasts beyond the time fixed by the Council of the great camp: if they infringe this prohibition the Council of the great camp shall take measures to oblige these people to join the camp: should they not be willing to do so, they will oblige them to do so by force. (Note: this custom has always been prairie law as far as the Métis are concerned; the savages have enjoyed full liberty unless they were in the camp of the Métis, in which case they could no more separate from the camp than could the Métis.)

Article XXIV. Where owing to a scarcity of animals, or one (sic) the opinion of the camp is divided about the direction the camp shall take; one side voting for one direction in which they hope to find more animals, and the other for the opposite direction, the Council shall call a general assembly and according to the majority shall pronounce for one direction. The minority shall be obliged to submit to this decision.

Article XXV. The period of return, when every person shall be at liberty to go where he pleases, shall be also determined by a general vote.

COMPARISON WITH INDIAN CUSTOMARY LAW

It is difficult to find written examples of specific rules of law in Indian cultures because the rules of social control are often of a religious nature or are part of an unwritten system of beliefs learned from childhood in the course of everyday instruction. Guiding devices are also considered to be "legal" forms of behaviour.

Indians as a group are generally not legalistic or litigious and when a wrongdoing is committed it is generally acknowledged as a wrong by the wrongdoer. Furthermore, the distinction between legal and moral guilt is not a part of the Indian tradition. Neither is the adversarial system considered a valid approach in resolving disputes (Canada et.al., 1985:12).

It is clear that the organization of hunting and the penalties imposed for transgression of the laws of the hunt, as reported by Alexander Ross (1856) and Father André (above), are based upon the organization and rules customary to the Plains Cree and the Plains Ojibway hunters.

Howard (1977:24-25) reports that the Plains Ojibway generally conducted their great hunts in the summer and late fall. The chief and council would meet and select one member of the band to act as hunt chief. His appointment would last for the duration of that particular hunt. The hunt chief would then select several men to act as police *(okitsita)*. Their duties were to keep order during the march, to watch for enemies and, most importantly, to prevent the younger men from rushing ahead and frightening the herd by firing in advance of the main party and thus spoiling the hunt for the whole band.

Those caught firing in advance of the main party were punished by having their belongings seized and their tipi cover slashed to shreds. They were also subject to flogging. If the offender submitted to these punishments without defiance, his belongings were usually returned, either by the police directly or by a collection from other members of the camp.

However, if he remained defiant, this restitution was not made. For a second offence the offender could be banished from camp, while for a third he might be shot.

Theft was uncommon, but neighbours would usually identify the thief to the complainant who would retrieve his belongings from the thief. "Public ridicule constituted the thief's only punishment (Ibid:83)." Quarrels were usually settled by the *okitsita* forcing the disputing parties to smoke a pipe and accept arbitration. Alternatively the lance bearers would thrust their lances in the ground between disputants and force mediation of the issue.

The two underlying principles of Plains Ojibwa justice seem to have been conformation to tribal mores for the general good and restitution to the injured party. Even murder could be redressed with gifts or by the murderer taking the dead man's place....Secondary sanctions included ridicule (in the case of theft or stinginess) and the use of magic. Members of the Midewiwen and Wabano societies were particularly feared for their magical prowess, and fear of this power was often an active deterrent to theft and violence.[10]

Howard (1977:78) in his studies of the Turtle Mountain Chippewa Band and Métis community notes that the government of the Métis was similar to that of the Plains-Ojibwa. Indeed, they often shared the same main chief *(le chef)* and had several secondary chiefs, the secondary officer being called *le premier*. The Métis had a general council and an *okitsita* policing organization call *la garde*. Unlike the Indians, *le chef* was not a hereditary position, but an elected one.

Mandelbaum (1979:115) reports that among the Plains Cree, policing functions were one of the duties of the Warrior *(Okihtcitawak)* societies. The Warrior Chief (distinct from the Chief proper) was selected by the Warriors and directed policing operations. As with the Ojibway and the Métis, individual hunting in advance of the main party was one of the more serious offences. Offenders were subject to immediate slashing of their tipi and destruction of their other possessions. If the offender took his punishment in a composed manner, then four days later the Warriors would gather and each would contribute an article until there was ample restitution for the guilty man's losses. Mandelbaum reports that offences such as theft were rare among the Plains Cree, and usually the consequence of a thoughtless act by a young man. The custom was that when the boy's father learned of the theft, the parent would immediately return the stolen article to the owner.

THE APPLICATION OF COLONIAL LAW TO THE METIS

In the case of the Métis, the Hudson's Bay Company used the law as a flexible tool. The first policing device of the Company was simply to criminalize all those who worked against its monopoly. The penal and temporal civil code of 1838 reflected this intent. As law, its major characteristic was discretion. As the Company was the dominant party in selecting appointments to such legal offices as Recorder, the legal system mirrored Company interests.

Permissive statutes ensured that relevant cases were decided in favour of the Company by the Company's nominee judiciary. Alexander Ross pointed out that the discretionary powers economically enslaved both Métis and Indians, as well as incoming settlers:

Their being legally disqualified by Mr. Thom's interpretation of the Charter from trafficking in furs with the Indians is the greatest of all grievances: furs are the only circulating medium the country affords, beyond the limits of the colony (1856:378).

Knafla (1986:38), after reviewing the records of the Quarterly Court of Assiniboia, notes that the law was not only constructed unfairly, but applied unfairly:

Thom exceeded his judicial authority in hearing cases over which he had no jurisdiction, expressed a dislike for English common law and allowed Company officials to use illegitimate means in dealings with others... [and] had little regard for the Métis or for the French language, often giving arbitrary judgements and excessive sentences against them: Thom was in fact a racist.

The Métis challenged both the composition of the policing system and the core of the criminalization process. In 1843, the Métis petitioned for either a reduction in the numbers of police or a change to make the membership subject to democratic election.

In both 1835 and 1845, the Métis unsuccessfully demanded the removal of the criminal sanction from free trading practices. On the latter occasion, a group of Métis petitioned the Governor of Assiniboia, Alexander Christie, for a clarification of their legal rights and status. They clearly recognized that discretionary law meant Company law. This had led, they said later "....to the utter impoverishment if not ruin of the Natives" (Cooper, 1988:297).

It was inevitable that the community law of the Métis would come into conflict with the law of the Empire as enforced by the Hudson's Bay Company. In 1875, a number of Métis hunters, bound by the St. Laurent constitution and led by Peter Ballendine, an employee of the Hudson's Bay Company, left for the annual hunt in advance of the main party.[11] The St. Laurent community, acting according to its own laws, sent its President, Gabriel Dumont, and the Métis captains, acting as the police of the settlement to apprehend the violators.[12] They were then fined according to township law. Ballendine complained to the Hudson's Bay Company Factor, Lawrence Clarke, who was also the local magistrate.[13] Although Clarke had chaired the 1871 community meeting that set the colony and its regulations in place (his intent being economic exploitation and control of the labour force)[14], he now implored the Mounted Police to intervene and supplant Métis law and its enforcement.

On July 10, 1875 Clarke wrote to Lieutenant Governor Morris with outrageous allegations:[15]

(they)...have assumed to themselves the right to make such laws, rules, and regulations, for the...colony and adjoining country of a most tyrannical nature which the minority of settlers are perforced bound to obey....This [St. Laurent] court pretends further to have the power to enforce their laws on all Indians, settlers, and hunters, who frequent the Prairie country in the lower section of the Saskatchewan, and have levied by violence and robbery large sums of money off inoffensive persons who resort to the buffalo country for a livelihood... unless we have a certain protective force stationed at or near Carlton the ensuing winter, I cannot answer for the result. Serious difficulties will assuredly arise and life and property be endangered... I have thus presumed to address you not as an officer of the Hudson's Bay Company but in my magisterial capacity.

Clarke's letter was perfidious for a number of reasons. He had worked closely with the Métis men he was now labelling as insurgents. He had served on their Council and, along with Father André, had supported the development of the *Laws of St. Laurent*. Further he was well aware that Ballendine's actions were a serious threat to the community and well knew that his portrayal of the Métis threat was overly alarmist. The subsequent investigation carried out by Major General Smyth and Colonel French ascertained that these claims were overblown; and in fact they implicated Clarke as a conspirator with Ballendine. When Dumont returned from the annual hunt and was finally brought before Magistrate Clarke, he was given only a small fine. The effect of this case, however, was to delegitimize the laws and regulations of the Métis colony and to end their effective use. Thus the Métis were criminalized under the laws of the central state through the agency and double-dealing of the Hudson's Bay Company Factor. Colonial law usurped prairie law and community law.

At the same time, the government of Canada was supplanting the rule of the tribal chiefs. Sir John A. Macdonald had suggested that elected councils be set up to determine municipal law and further that these councils be presided over by a functionary such as a Reeve or, in the initial stages by the Indian Agent.[16] However, as Stanley (1936:240-241) has pointed out, the power of the Chiefs under the treaties was only nominal anyway, as Indians were subject to the government's laws and the government's courts. Local affairs were regulated by the Indian Agents, not the tribal council. As well, the government had assumed the power to depose chiefs by refusing recognition under the treaties. Many of the time-honoured practices and customs of social order were being abandoned under government pressure. For example, the Mounted Police often withheld provisions as a method of discouraging such traditional practices as feasts and dances, practices which served as major unifying features of many Indian groups. It is clear from the historical records that while the Métis were establishing their own law on the prairies, Sir John A. Macdonald had been making plans since 1869 to send in a federal police force. The North West Mounted Police was created as a national force by an Act of Parliament in the spring of 1873. It was to be a para-military group centrally controlled in Ottawa without reference to the people of the territories. It was originally to have been a multi-racial force with Indians and Métis serving on it (a copy of policing in India), but this idea never came to fruition. It was derivative of the British Imperial model of the Irish Constabulary, a force which was set up to control social unrest in Ireland. Lieutenant-Governor William McDougall had such a force in mind when he was appointed to administer the North West in 1869. A North West Mounted Police Commissioner, D. R. Cameron, was appointed in 1870, but before his force could move west, the Manitoba Act came into force. This Act left the administration of justice and the police in the hands of the province. What is clear is that earlier petitions for a locally controlled and staffed policing system were ignored. The customary law developed on the plains, a hybrid of Indian and Métis custom, was also disregarded, although customary family law survives to some extent to this day, recognized in the common law of Canada (Morse, 1980).

The Métis sociologist, Ron Bourgeault (1983:71), described the demise of Métis social control mechanisms:

> After re-organization of the Company in 1862, the internal politics and economic structures of Assiniboia began to crumble. Elements of the labouring class were becoming radicalized: reduced wages, unemployment and over-work increased their suffering. Strikes were more numerous among the voyageurs: the La Loche boat brigades engaged in work shut downs every summer throughout the 1860s.[17]

The influx of Anglo-Canadian migrants from Ontario had Orangist political leadership. They were "racist, anti-Indian, anti-French and anti-Catholic." However with the return of Louis Riel in 1868, "a more radical democratic wing emerged," set in a broad political base comprised of voyageurs, plains hunters, small landowners, freighters and the poorer merchants. They believed that all the mechanisms of British colonialism, both political and economic, were useless and oppressive.... fundamental change could only take place with the establishment of responsible democracy and the creation of a state over which they held political power (Ibid.:72). This led to what Bourgeault termed a "national liberation struggle". To lose this battle would lead to, in the words of Louis Riel, "extermination or slavery." This struggle continues today.

NOTES

1. Research for this chapter was supported in part by a grant from the Manitoba Law Foundation.
2. Report from the Select Committee of the House of Commons.

3. 43, George III, cap 138, Statutes at Large, Vol. 44, p. 916.
4. Ekstedt and Griffiths (1988:15-65). For a brief review of the Canadian penal system up to 1900, see The Sub-Committee on the Penitentiary System in Canada (1977: 11-12).
5. In 1851, the population of the Red River Settlement was 2,417. This rose to 11,400 in 1871, of whom 9,800 were Métis, almost evenly split between French- and English-speaking Métis (Stanley, 1961:13).
6. Hudson's Bay Company Archives. B 60/a/36, Journal of Daily Occurrences at Edmonton House, April 29, 1867.
7. Glenbow Institute, Hardisty Papers, GA1A, vol. 2, file 34, condensed report of a meeting at St. Laurent Dec. 31, 1871, author unknown, report signed "Blaireau".
8. PAC, RCMP records, R.G. 18A1, vol. 6, no. 333, Father A. André writing to Colonel French, sometime after January 1875, the letter is date stamped in Ottawa by the Department of Justice October 2nd, 1875.
9. This Council was made up of men who had close ties to each other and to the politically active families back in Manitoba.
Pierre Gariepey: son-in-law of Cuthbert Grant
Abraham Montour: related to Nicholas Montour, a clerk of the North West Company
Isidore Dumont Jr.: Gabriel Dumont's brother
Jean Dumont Jr.: Gabriel Dumont's cousin
Moise Ouelette: Gabriel Dumont's brother-in-law
Baptiste Hamelin: a member of the family of Salomon Hamelin who was appointed in 1871 as a member of the Manitoba Legislative Council
For a further discussion of the close family ties in the Batoche area and the use of nicknames to distinguish any extended family with the same names see Payment (1990).
10. Howard, (1977: 83). For a detailed account of the practice of having an offender take the place (within the family) of a murder victim see Ross (1856:324-330). Ross details a set of treaty negotiations between the Métis (represented by Cuthbert Grant) and the Sioux in November and December of 1844. This type of reparation was suggested by the Sioux to compensate for the deaths of a number of Sisseton and Yankton Indians at the hand of some Métis.
11. This hunting party was made up of three Métis members of the St Laurent community; Baptiste Primot (Primeau), Alexandre Cadien, and Theodore Convenant. Two others were English Métis, Peter Ballantyne (Ballendine) and William Whitford.
12. Before pursuing these men, Gabriel Dumont first sent them a letter by courier (June 17, 1875) (all spelling shown as in the original) PAM, MG 12 B1, No. 1040:

My friends,

We are not satisfied that you go so before us, and you are hunting in our contry.

Therefore all the people of Métif of Carlton pray you to come all at once to our camp. If that agree not to yourselfs, all the cavaliers wil go and bring you to our camp; and if you cause dommage to ourselfs you will pay. That concern especialy the Metifs of your camp.

We write to you as friends to advice you. If you wil not believe us, certainely you will pay all the cavaliers who will go and bring you.

Farewell,

Your servants,
all the people of Metifs of Carlton
camped in the plain,
Gabriel Dumont.

13. PAM, MG12, B1 No 1040 Alexander Morris, Lt. Gov. Collection; letter from Peter Ballendine to Lawrence Clarke. July 12, 1875.
14. Lawrence Clarke to Donald A. Smith, Chief Commissioner HBCo., Glenbow Institute, Hardisty Papers, G-AIA-vol.2, file 34, Jan. 15, 1872.
15. PAC: R.G. 18A1, vol. 6, no. 333.
16 Canada Sessional Papers, 1881, Macdonald to Lorne, n.d., Vol. III, No. 14.
17. This study was based on research carried out by the Association of Métis and Non-Status Indians of Saskatchewan.

THE RISE AND FALL OF THE WESTERN METIS IN THE CRIMINAL JUSTICE PROCESS

Mike Brogden

Métis history within the territories which became nineteenth century Canada includes a narrative dominated by continuing attempts by the state to utilize legal process as a means of repression. Through a focus on the processes of criminalization and law enforcement, a rather different history of the Métis (and by implication, of other Native people) can be glimpsed than that which appears in orthodox accounts of the Canadian frontier. This chapter offers a reconstruction, from the perspective of a criminologist, of the early commitment by western Métis to legal process and of the consequences for them of that legal struggle.

This chapter has three objectives. First, it seeks to show that legitimate claims by Métis people against the authorities of the day were often represented as challenges to the rule of law. Second, it argues that the corpus of criminal law used against the Métis people was imaginative, flexible and permissive. At various times in their history, Métis people were defined as economic, political and social criminals, legal labels that reflected more the strategic imperatives of their opponents than any intrinsic characteristics of the Métis. Third, in the course of this representation we need to reflect upon the legitimacy accorded to particular bodies of law and of law enforcement machinery. "Law and order" may have very little to do with the practices of wearers of scarlet and gold. Just because Métis people disproportionately appeared in the nineteenth century courts—variously accused of breaking economic laws, of political insurrection and later of vagrancy—does not of itself demonstrate their criminality. Criminals were what the Canadian state and its predecessors made of them. Criminality was a social artifact, a device through which Métis rights to act according to their own laws could be denied.

THE METIS AS ECONOMIC CRIMINALS: THE STRUGGLE WITH THE HUDSON'S BAY COMPANY

The label of economic criminality was the major legal weapon used against the Métis in their developing struggles against the Hudson's Bay Company at Red River. In a relatively homogeneous economy, at the periphery of the complex economic and political relations of Imperial Britain, the legal problem of the Company derived from the economic problematic, such that criminalizing certain Métis practices was a prerequisite of maintaining an economic monopoly.

In attempting to maximize the profitability of Assiniboia, the Hudson's Bay Company was faced with two major contradictions. First, while the Company required a pool of surplus labour to be seasonally available, it neither wished nor needed to sustain that labour pool out of season, that is in the fall and winter. Although that seasonal labour was an asset in keeping down the wages of indentured servants, the labourers had little stake in the system and little reason for abiding by rules from which they obtained few benefits.

Second, given the nature of the terrain, the Company required entrepreneurial contact with the Indians. As long as there was only one outlet for products of the chase and hunt (the Company trading posts), all such goods had to be funneled through the Company for shipment to England at Company prices. With the appearance of competing purchasers across the American border, venturesome Métis were encouraged to sell outside the monopoly.

Aspiring Métis entrepreneurs, debarred from rising in the Company's hierarchy, much like the surplus labour of the Red River Settlement could only survive through independent commerce. The development of those alternative markets, however, meant infringing the economic monopoly of the Company (Bourgeault,1988).

The major response by the Hudson's Bay Company was simple and direct: it was to criminalize the competitors. In this endeavour, the Company drew upon the all-encompassing powers granted by the British state, powers which embodied tight controls over economic life. Initially, authority had been given:

....to the Governor and Company to seize any of his Majesty's subjects who (without leave of the Company) trade in their territory (2. William & Mary, c.23, 1690).

This legislation was reinforced in succeeding years—especially with regard to the fur trade (1, & 2. Geo. IV, c.66, 1821; 7. William, IV; 1. Vic. c.73, 1837). Ancillary legislation followed as, for example, in the Penal Code of Assiniboia of 1841. This law specified the right of the

Company's court to try the inhabitants of Rupert's Land, including Company employees, European settlers, Métis and Indians.

In the face of this legal weaponry, between the 1820s and the 1830s, the French Métis traders created a livelihood, an economic stake in the colony, by the illicit trading of furs into the United States (Morton, 1956). With highly discretionary legislation and nominated magistrates (such as the Recorder, Adam Thom) at its disposal, however, the Company was able to protect its economic prerogative through the criminal law. Occasional seizures of the goods of free traders were interspersed with passive acceptance when resistance proved too great (Glueck, 1965). Discretionary justice, arbitrary seizures and company nominees acting as magistrates and police, ensured a measure of respect for Company law. The Recorder might act as counsel, witness and judge, all in the same case (Gibson & Gibson, 1972). He could improvise law and prerogatives where there was no specific mandate, give prior credence to the evidence of Company officials, disallow the French language of the Métis and impose excessive sentences (Knafla, 1986). Repeated missives were directed to suppress the American and Métis trade with the Indian bands (see, for example, Oliver, 1914). Land grants were tied to injunctions against free trade (Howard, 1952) and furs were sporadically seized from free traders' houses (Tremaudan, 1982).

Successive Company policing institutions were formed to enforce partisan law by partisan officers. A small police force had been created in 1825:

> ....mainly recruited from the Scottish population, whose more stable character and proven loyalty to the Hudson's Bay Company made them superior to the other groups.[1]

It was re-organized a decade later,[2] and again in the early 1840s[3] before it was finally disbanded in 1845, due to a combination of apparent inefficiency and accusations that the police themselves were engaged in illegal trading in furs (Giraud, 1986:388). A reactive—thief-taker—piecework system followed,[4] reinforced initially by a troop of dragoons who were in turn later replaced by a corps of unwilling military pensioners.[5] Judging by the court records, the reports of free trading, and the turnover of personnel, the policing system of the Hudson's Bay Company was generally ineffective and partisan. Its occasional sallies to arrest free traders met with little success in repressing the trade (Giraud, 1986).

The legal institutions of the Red River Colony were skewed against Native people. Legal statutes, legal procedures and legal personnel combined to criminalize the free traders and to stifle independent trade among Indian hunters, Métis entrepreneurs and American buyers. On other occasions legal restrictions were complemented by price-fixing devices, by bribes to the American competitors and by licensing stratagems (Glueck, 1973).

The power to criminalize the Métis competition was the central edifice of the Hudson's Bay Company's economic ascendancy. Furs were the only circulating medium in the Colony, and the denial of access to that trade was a major grievance (Ross, 1972). Métis rights to economic survival encountered the barrier of the criminal law. The combination of discretionary justice and partisan personnel ensured criminal justice was Company justice. In the endeavour to safeguard the Company's economic monopoly, the stability of social order in the Red River Colony was maintained partly by criminalizing those who attempted to trade independently and partly by direct economic constraints.

By the 1850s, when the Company's power was under attack from several sides, it still held a monopoly of economic and legal power. Criminalizing the ascendant Métis remained a residual political weapon.

RESISTING CRIMINALIZATION

The criminal label process was not accepted passively throughout that quarter century, however. Free trade was only intermittently interrupted. There were increasingly overt challenges to the policing and law enforcement system. Opposition to the criminalization process was a continuing feature of Métis-Company relations between the 1820s and the 1850s.

By the early 1820s, for example, illegal cross-border trade was already flourishing (Glueck, 1965). Ten years later, subversion of the monopoly had expanded with horn cattle, horses, furs and small articles of colonial industry being exchanged across the border for cotton goods, groceries, ammunition and tobacco (Gunn and Tuttleworth, 1880:286). Contraband traffic continued as did independent transactions with the Indians (Giraud, 1986).

More directly, the Métis challenged the legitimacy of the policing system and of the Company courts. In 1822, Governor Bulger complained that the Métis showed disrespect for the Company's laws, and "....openly defied the magistrates."[6] Free traders petitioned the Company in 1835 and again in 1844 for the right to hunt furs and buffalo and to sell the products to the highest bidder (Glueck, 1965). The laws, it was claimed, had led "....to the utter impoverishment of the natives" (quoted in McLean, 1985). In 1846, what Factor Christie described as a "near-revolt" occurred over the free trade issue. The Métis affirmed their conviction that they could trade and hunt as they sought fit and "....put in question the entire economic and political sovereignty of the Hudson's Bay Company" (Giraud, 1986:232).

In one of the best-recorded acts of resistance against criminalization, an 1848 meeting of Métis demanded free trade in furs and the abolition of existing laws respecting trade with America and criticized the partiality of the Recorder, Adam Thom. By this time, prosecutions by the Company had become desultory but remained symbolic in their attempt to maintain the legitimacy of Company rule (Giraud, 1986:244). The token prosecution of four Métis in 1849 signified the effective termination of these attempts to use the criminal law to resist Métis aspirations. This particular criminal trial was metamorphosed into a political confrontation, after the formation of "committees of the people" by the Indian and Métis (Bourgeault, 1988). What was portrayed as economic crime by the Company was given an alternative political construction by the Métis. The fact of free trading was not denied but rather was regarded as legitimate (Ross, 1972:372).

The defendants were formally found guilty—but no penalty was levied—in the face of a threatening demonstration by the Métis. Even though some minor cases were to follow in succeeding years (Giraud, 1986:249), the trial had serious consequences for the administration of justice in the Red River Colony (Gibson and Gibson, 1972:35). Given that its local economic strength depended upon such criminalizing practices, it was the final symbolic nail in the Company's Red River coffin. The label of "economic criminal" was summarily rejected in a communal statement of the right to buy, sell, and exchange furs without Company permission (Tremaudan, 1982:47).

This event did not take place in a vacuum. It reflected the diminution of the political and economic power of a trading company faced with external pressures—the emergent forces of industrial capitalism from the banks of Upper Canada, and from the United States—and internally with the rising consciousness of the Métis as a political and cultural entity, such as the 1849 formation of a Council of the Nation to demand free trade and responsive government (Bourgeault, 1988). The label "criminal" was successfully rejected after a long process of struggle. Further surrenders of power included the dismissal of Company nominees from the judiciary (Stubbs, 1967), and the inclusion of some Métis representation on the governing Council of Assiniboia (Giraud, 1986:248).

POLITICAL CRIME

The critical phase of the Métis experience with the criminal justice process lay in the interregnum between the decline of the Hudson's Bay Company and the rise of the settlements heralded first by the North West Mounted Police and later by the Canadian Pacific Railway. This was a period when several Métis communities developed sophisticated municipal, legal and political structures, and thus provided local alternatives to the structures of the central state. In the larger political context, such structures could be interpreted as threatening, a political challenge which could only be met by political criminalization.

Community Law on the Saskatchewan: The legitimacy of Métis criminal justice processes prior to 1885

Métis communities were not the first to develop complex democratic legal structures with humane notions of mediation and reparation. Most writers have traced the institutional structures of Métis democratic law to the rules of the buffalo hunt and have concentrated upon the French Métis to the exclusion of the Scots. But there is at least one other source of the popular justice of the Métis.

Similar traditions were part of the inheritance of the Scots Métis. Many of the initial Hudson Bay traders had been recruited from the Outer Hebridean island of St. Kilda (Bourgeault, 1988). St. Kildan society practised forms of communal justice described by one 1831 commentator (quoted in Steel, 1975): "Their government is strictly a republic...." with an emphasis upon the sharing of goods, services, and responsibilities. A daily communal meeting aimed to resolve infractions of the informal rules. All St. Kildans, male and female, had equal rights to speak and to vote (Steel, 1975). At Red River it is possible that this particular Scots tradition converged with the Native tradition of the buffalo chase.

The continuity of the latter was apparent. In the 1840s "committees of the people" had been instituted including both Indian and Métis members (Bourgeault, 1988). "Their ideal would have been a purely elective government, where the magistrates as well as the councillors would have been designated by popular suffrage" (Giraud, 1986:223). These developments had given rise in the late 1860s to democratic legal and political processes. Following from prairie tradition, groups of families formed local communities, each electing a captain. The captains chose a principal leader and he presided over the council of captains, the body which set the regulations and met each day to handle offenders against the community's laws.

The first organized opposition to Ottawa's land surveys had occurred through the medium of such democratic structures. In 1869, at a meeting in St. Norbert, the election of the younger Louis Riel to coordinate resistance, and the formation of Métis resistance groups, was based upon the buffalo hunt model (Sprague, 1988). Similarly, the short-lived Métis provisional government of Red River had followed that democratic path with a demand for the election of all law officers. On Red River "....the traditional organization of the hunt gave the Métis a political structure with which to resist the surveys" (Sprague, 1988:79). Even after the decline of the hunt, that political organization had a continuing social significance.

The same political and legal tradition survived after the dispersal of so many of the Métis across the western plains. In several prairie townships —originally wintering quarters for the buffalo chase—legal constitutions were fashioned according to the traditional rules of the buffalo hunt.[7] In Qu'Appelle, the Métis constructed their own community constitution and criminal laws. Similar developments were apparent over the American border on the Milk River (Giraud, 1986:405). A complex legal system, embodying political, legal and land tenure rights, was enunciated in the Township of St. Laurent in what is now Saskatchewan.[8]

The St. Laurent constitution required that the President and councillors be subject to annual election, and be responsible for formulating the rules of the hunt and the municipal laws. The traditions of the hunt in which "....the dixaines formed a veritable police force...." (Giraud, 1986:361) were applied to the community. As a body of civil and criminal law, the township's legal process was progressive and democratic.

This new system was sophisticated. Its predominant feature was that of mediation, of settling disputes with minimal harm to both parties, rather than of adjudication, of findings of guilt combined with punitive sanctions. Community law was concerned with the restoration of the integrity and harmony of the community, not with the stigmatization of individuals or families through convictions. A central principle was that of restitution. Article XIV, for example, passed on January 27, 1875, provided for the replacement for any horse wounded by another man. Restitution was combined with reparation. Article XIII, passed on the same date, required that where a personal injury was inflicted, the aggrieved party would have the services of the other until the wound was healed. It was a compassionate, pragmatic body of law. St. Laurent Law was not in the business of transforming those convicted of crimes into paupers and dependents. According to Article XIV, for example, passed at an Annual Assembly on December 10, 1873, "Any person who only has three animals shall not be compelled to give up any one of them in payment of debts."

Contractual relations between two parties, irrespective of their ethnicity, were to be certified by community law. Article XVIII, again passed at the Annual Assembly on December 10, 1873, stated that "Any bargain, any contract, any sales, written in French, English or Indian characters, will be upheld, even if made without witnesses, if the plaintive testifies on oath to the correctness of his bargain or contract." Community law also dealt with character defamation and provided penalties for men "dishonouring girls". In recognition of the dependence of the community upon natural resources, it contained penalties against waste of timber and animals, and for the protection of the prairies from fire. As far as males were concerned, it treated all who came before the St. Laurent Council acting as a court, as equals, whether servant or master, Métis, Indian or European settler. Physical punishments were not contemplated.

Prevention, not retribution, communal integration and equilibrium, and mediation rather than conviction, were the central principles. Justice was not about punishment. Its central concern was utilitarian, that of restoring communal welfare at minimum cost to individuals and to the community.

The St. Laurent Métis risked conflict with the colonizing power and their encroaching Dominion law when they constructed this legal system. The subsequent destruction of their evolved legal process is symbolized in one incident, a clash over the timing of the annual buffalo hunt.

The St. Laurent constitution specified a common start to the chase in order to give all hunters equal opportunities. In 1875, this law was broken in a hunt apparently encouraged by the local Hudson's Bay Company Factor, Lawrence Clarke. Gabriel Dumont, the St. Laurent President, and several *dixaines* pursued, arrested and fined the malefactors according to community law. What was legitimate under community law, however, could be construed as illegal under the laws of the Dominion of Canada.

One of the accused, a Company employee, complained to Clarke who, along with many other Company Factors, had become the local agent for Imperial law in his capacity as a magistrate. In a heated protest to the Commissioner of the newly-formed North West Mounted Police (NWMP), Clarke sought a political-criminal label for the community police:

> (they)…have assumed to themselves the right to make such laws, rules, and regulations, for the…colony and adjoining country of a most tyrannical nature which the minority of settlers are perforced to obey….This (St. Laurent) court pretends further to have the power to enforce the laws on all Indians, settlers, and hunters, who frequent the Prairie country in the lower section of the Saskatchewan, and have levied by violence and robbery large sums of money off inoffensive persons who resort to the buffalo country....[9]

Clarke pleaded for a force of police to deal with the St. Laurent hunters and "....to make law and order present." The dual role of Clarke as Company Factor and Government Magistrate conflated the interests of Company and law. His request met with some scepticism from the Dominion government, a state whose financial and industrial interests transcended those of the declining mercantile interests. Ottawa had to choose between the costs of immediate military action and the possibility of peaceful pacification and incorporation.[10] State reluctance to act punitively resulted in Dumont receiving only a small fine and a caution from

Clarke (McLean, 1985). Despite the minimal penalty, the result was to undermine the legal process of the Métis community. A North West Mounted Police post was established nearby, symbolizing the extension of Dominion law and the denigration of communal justice.

After Dominion rule had been affirmed across the plains, a series of petty measures increased legal marginalization, through such devices as the denial of requests for French-speaking juries and for a magistrate of French or Métis origin (Giraud, 1986:435). In future, enforcing community legislation would represent a political denial of the sovereignty of the Dominion, as the popular legitimation of Métis authority was challenged by the rational legitimation of the Dominion. Dominion (really Imperial) law usurped popular justice and determined that those who maintained the latter were in breach of the authority of the central state, that is, were political criminals. The St. Laurent incident illustrates the manner in which the informal criminal justice process of the Métis was gradually denied legitimacy by the central state. Legal process which did not accord with that of Ottawa would henceforward be perceived as a political challenge, a threat which could only be met by making such practices illegitimate, a process of political criminalization.

Pax Mountie Versus Pax Métis — Did Popular Justice Continue?

The St. Laurent incident did not signify the termination of Métis popular justice and community law. The criminal justice institutions of the Canadian state were not accepted automatically. However, the North West Mounted Police, as part of their national Imperial mission, denied any possibility of an alternative to their authority. "Is it to be wondered at that the French half-breed is restless and unsettled, that he looks with regret and longing on his old life which was one of freedom...untrammelled by laws...."[11] On the one hand was the informal system of dispute resolution of the Métis settlements of the South Saskatchewan, in which the rules and sanctions were derived from traditional forms of mediation and reparation. On the other hand was Pax Mountie, the encroaching enforcement system of the federal government, committed to adjudication, conviction and punishment. For the Métis, in the period leading up to the events of 1885, community social order was maintained according to their own traditions, and in spite of the St. Laurent incident. Informal justice rather than Canadian justice seems to have prevailed.

The evidence for this thesis is limited. It is deduced from the flexible and adaptive qualities of Métis law as reflected by the transformation of the democratic traditional rules into the progressive rules of a small integrated township. What else could survive one major economic transformation, could adapt beneath, albeit temporarily, the cultural, linguistic, and legal impositions of an alien order? Canadian legal institutions (as epitomized by the implanted and ubiquitous NWMP posts) and civil law (symbolized by the land surveys) concerned the externalities with which the Métis were forced to abide. The internal informal rules, the traditions of social justice, continued at the community level.

Circumstantial evidence of the continuity of the Métis system of popular justice derives, paradoxically, from the yearly returns of the policing agency of the central state. The Annual Reports from the North West Mounted Police posts in the region throughout the 1880s and early 1890s repetitively state: "There has been a total absence of crime in this district. No information of any kind has been brought to my attention."[12]

That no signficant crime was reported on the Indian reserves and in the Métis settlements, for nearly a decade spanning the 1885 resistance, is curious. It seems that, rather than there having been "no crime", given the evidence of the sophisticated structure of law and policing in the 1870s, the institutions of informal justice still prevailed. External legal institutions were complied with at the margins. The Métis had been accustomed to maintain order in their own settlements without resort to outsiders. Métis police, as part of the larger communal kinship system, wore no uniform and were literally indistinguishable from the community. If elements of traditional law were maintained despite the denunciation of communal justice institutions such as that at St. Laurent, then tranquillity may have been the norm despite —rather than because of—the presence of the North West Mounted Police. To those settlements of French-speaking Métis, the North West Mounted Police was itself illegitimate. It is possible that no crime was reported to that agency, especially after the 1885 resistance, because the government force was seen to be irrelevant to community needs. The alien Mounted Police, the symbol of the Imperial state, had no legitimacy, merely coercive power. Pax Métis seems to have existed, not Pax Mountie. Crime was a phenomenon dealt with by Métis legal process.

Political Criminalization Through the Construction of Treason

In an account of earlier risings (the Papineau revolts in Lower Canada in 1837 and 1839), Greenwood (1984) has suggested that where the state has the capacity to treat acts by dissidents as either criminal or political, decisions over prosecution have little relationship to the gravity of the particular case and more to the perceived needs of the social audience. On such occasions, state perception and the concern for its own legitimacy determines the choice of legal charges, not the specific merit of the case.

The critical factor affecting the prosecution decision is the reaction of the different communities to which, in part, the state is itself a hostage.

Where the political charge is constructed, the criminal process has a symbolic quality. The rebel is on trial but so is the state's own legitimacy. In the Papineau example, the trial represented:

....treason as the mother of all crime by dramatizing the Chartrand atrocity...For a few hours in a packed Montreal courtroom, the prosecution and defence staged a morality play in which the passions generating insurrection and repression engaged once again in pitiless combat.... (Greenwood, 1984:129).

The word *treason* has an especially emotive meaning, a label which denotes pejoratively the final assault on the legitimacy of the state.

In the Papineau and the Métis struggles for autonomy, the state reacted in different ways. A relatively relaxed use of law in the first instance was followed by a deliberate decision to politically criminalize the resistance in the second. The 1869 declaration in the Red River Settlement was met with a mixture of indulgence and a relative lack of recrimination. Although Riel was later to be refused admission to Parliament, under threat of arrest, there was no overt attempt to politicize the rebellion through public trial. The state, unsure of its own strength and unity, feared to dramatize the offence, adopting instead a relatively conciliatory approach.

But in the second case, in 1885, the stage was set in a quite different way. First, a confident central state could, through the use of an emotive legal process, dramatically reinforce its own authority while permanently degrading the supporters of the resistance. The political construction of the Saskatchewan Métis, not just as erratic malcontents but as pathological criminals, was established through legal discourse in the celebration of military victory, in the formulation of charges, in the preparation and enactment of the trial, in the form of execution, and finally in the lessons publicly read into the event by the government and by its supporters.

The returning militia were given a triumphant welcome celebrating an allegorical victory of good over a pathological enemy. For example, the Winnipeg Light Horse was met with "....the most tumultuous cheering from fully ten thousand people...waving handkerchiefs, and throwing of bouquets...." as they marched under a triumphal arch. They were eulogized by their commander "....Canada could well congratulate herself on the bravery of her sons...." and received such newspaper tributes as "....the bronzed Canadian heroes."[13]

This political manifestation of victory served the function of uniting the developing nation-state of Canada around its very own "armed forces." Anglo-Canadian nationalism was celebrated for its triumph over the "anti-nationals." As the first battle fought by a Canadian army, it signified a catharsis in the relationship between the eastern provinces and the western settlements and thus contributed to a symbolic unity. As well, the discourse of the six charges against Riel rang repetitiously with the language of political vilification and of social degradation:

....being moved and seduced by the instigation of the devil as a false traitor...and being then unlawfully, maliciously and traitorously assembled...(Riel) did levy and make war...against our said Lady the Queen.[14]

As a presumed traitor, Riel and his allies had challenged the legitimacy of Imperial rule. Only a public scourging in the Dock of the Regina Court could drive out that bodily corruption.

This attempted degradation of Riel as the representative and symbol of the Métis nation was pursued through the humiliation of Riel as the defendant. Alternative labels were available, for example, the claims that Riel was "mentally ill" (because of his messianic protestations) or "wicked." The latter choice fitted state requirements most neatly. Mental illness, after all, involves granting the patient the recognition of having been sane at some time. An inferior race was not entitled to that assumption. It also neatly fitted the pathological perspective held by most non-Native Canadians of Native people as inferior and amoral. Further, when "....any evidence... regarding the prospect of the "Republic of Saskatchewan" is adduced, roars of laughter follow. Riel does not appreciate the merriment...."[15]

The most graphic demonstration of the political criminalization of the Métis and Indian leadership was contrived through, and culminated in, ritual punishment. Of the execution of the Indian Chiefs who joined the rising, Greenland has commented: "....there can be no doubt that the savage punishment of the Indians was a calculated act of terrorism instigated by Prime Minister Sir John A. Macdonald" (1987:415). The hanging of eight Chiefs, before a lamenting audience of their kin in the dim Regina dawn, surrounded by a large contingent of Mounted Police, was an act of theatre designed to serve the political purpose of cowing both Indians and Métis, as non-Natives celebrated the demise of inferior races.

The execution of Riel and the Indians was a ritual delegitimation of their cause, of their defence of the customary laws governing their townships and landholdings. The Métis resistance had been construed as a challenge to the legitimacy of the emerging Canadian state. The staging of the trial and subsequent executions vindicated the authority and unity of the new nation-state, a dramatic purging of antithetical elements. The political criminalization of Riel and his companions was a critical step in the establishment and legitimation of Canadian sovereignty in the prairie provinces. With one fell swoop, the Métis traditions of local democratic rule and of popular justice were denied. Political crime was a label imposed according to the requirements of the central state. The Métis had been transformed from economic criminals under the Hudson's Bay Company to political criminals under the newly sovereign Ottawa government.

THE METIS AS SOCIAL CRIMINALS

After 1885, Métis peoples engaged in a similar diaspora to that of the early 1870s, but with one difference. After the Red River episode, there had been a place of retreat for many. Post-1885, social fragmentation and marginalization were substituted for geographical dispersal. Physical retreat was replaced by a social atomization as culture, livelihood and —critically—legal status were consigned to a residuum in which the Métis, like many plains Indians, became the social property of an occupying police force seeking to establish its own legitimacy.

Many western Métis were degraded economically into a marginal class outside the primary economy of railroad and agricultural settlements. This degradation was accompanied by a new personal and legal straitjacket. The older settler perceptions of the Métis as pathologically inferior, as a society fit only for an earlier stage of social evolution, were given new life by the settlement of the Great Plains. They were legally ennobled as citizens of the Empire while at the same time receiving the harsh inquisitorial reality of the English legal process. They were to be controlled by an occupying army which both coerced and fed.

In this process of degradation, a legal process—the criminalization of the western Métis—played a major part. Law became the straitjacket of social degradation through which many western Métis and plains Indians were consigned to the oblivion of a marginal class under the "parental tutelage" of a "superior" white civilization. As the major agency of state administration on the plains, the North West Mounted Police used two weapons to marginalize the Métis people. Permissive laws allowed a form of inquisitorial justice to prevail in relation to the Métis. Famine and poverty resulting from the combination of climate, of military depredation and of settlement, gave the North West Mounted Police the power of life and death over many Métis. The carrot and stick of food in return for forced labour created a legal and social dependency class.

Dominion Law: the Inversions of Criminal Justice

The depredations of 1885, the succeeding bad harvests, the decline of transport occupations as the railroad extended further across the prairies and the implantation of settler colonies had major effects on the legal status of many western Métis. They were turned into a kind of social criminal, the marginal group without effective civil and social rights, to be helped or criminalized according to the policies of Ottawa and of its local policing agents.

The North West Mounted Police approached the task of dealing with the western Métis and plains Indians informed by a Darwinian ethic of the evolutionary superiority of white civilization. Adoption of Christianity by the Indians was considered to be a necessary part of this process.[16] It was necessary to establish tutelage over races who were considered patently unfit to govern themselves. The perceived alcohol problem served to illustrate the general inferiority of the indigenous races:

> It is said that those dangerous days are now past, and the present population should hold in their own hands the regulation of the liquor traffic. This may be true as a matter of principle in an old established country, where all the people are civilized and subject to the controlling influences of civilization; but this country cannot yet be said to be inhabited by people, all of whom are fit to be their own guides and a law unto themselves, I speak of the half-breed and Indian population.[17]

It was considered the responsiblity of the North West Mounted Police, as a surrogate parent to those children of the plains, to instruct them in the ways of civilized values and work discipline. They became the equivalent of "....police property when the dominant powers of society...leave the problems of social control of this category to the police" (Lee, 1981:53-54).[18]

As part of an historically and structurally formed residuum, social criminals as police property lose all effective rights and are subject to the broadest interpretation of discretionary legislation. They are penalized by the law for what they are, rather than for what act they have committed. Race and gender are blurred as the individual loses all personal identification characteristics and is subject to generalized negative stereotyping. However, different modes of segregation and marginalization may be practised. For the plains Indians, location as social criminals entailed a Reserve existence where the combination of a pass system and vagrancy laws entailed a physical segregation.[19] The prairie Métis after 1885 had a different experience of social criminality. As children in the eyes of the parental North West Mounted Police, they were considered to have no need, or indeed understanding, of civil rights.

They were subjected to discriminatory forms of policing and of criminalization. As social deviants, law was no longer a protection but a weapon to be used against them. They had lost their own legal institutions with no compensatory gains.

This social and legal degradation was generally accepted. Although there were some occasions when prairie Métis communities protested against their treatment,[20] humiliation and legal subordination without recorded resistance were common. The position of the Métis in relation to the central state and to the legal process had changed dramatically. Before the resistance, their significance as a potentially formidable and resilient opposition had been recognized.[21] But once the tinder had been soaked, the new Dominion's Imperial powers were untrammeled. Only when Native people ceased to obstruct the implantation of settlers by eastern finance capital was there a shift in the attitude of the police, so that persuasion was replaced by coercion (McLeod, 1976). Cajolery was unnecessary. A combination of factors reduced many of them to a marginal condition outside the pale of both incoming European settlers and the reserve status of the Indian bands.

The land question was settled decisively for many western Métis. As social criminals, as a marginal class outside the primary relations of production, the Métis had few possessions. The right to a homestead and to the products of labour from the chase and from the soil had disappeared. Those who had claims to scrip but could be shown to have taken part in the resistance lost all. Those who retained scrip found that its value was often halved, and were often forced to sell it to survive (Giraud, 1986:456ff). Not merely were the legal rights to land and property lost, but the physical depredations of the resistance[22] and natural calamities had left them property-less dependents.

Given the ideological, institutional and economic hegemony of the young Dominion, lower class Métis, like the plains Indians, were socially structured as a dependency class so that after the resistance of 1885, they served as cheap agrarian labour for the incoming settlers (Bourgeault, 1988:67).

With political and economic aspirations frustrated, the Métis formed that residual pool from which police forces have traditionally culled petty crime. Repetitive North West Mounted Police reports document the destitution and squalor, with the fruits of the household economy being replaced by qualified relief from the North West Mounted Police.[23] They were forced into the desperations of the secondary economy, a reserve army of labour for the ascendant capitalism in transportation and construction. Traditional occupations had disappeared with the advent of the railroad.[24] It was a subsistence economy ranging from meagre fishing to selling buffalo horn to train passengers,[25] and with a paucity of work utensils.[26]

Where the Hudson's Bay Company store still monopolized a township, prices paid for the rewards from the disappearing hunt were too low to permit an investment in agricultural tools. The basic necessities for homesteading were at a price beyond the reach of many prairie Métis. They assumed the features of a social group subsisting on the margins, and accessible for police culls under the wide discretionary powers of English common law. In this final stage, as new social criminals, the Métis were subject to two forms of police discipline, legal and economic.

Criminalizing through the Vagrancy Act

The Métis were controlled under that wide body of legislation that has traditionally been used against marginal groups in the social history of the Imperial legal process (Chambliss, 1969; Brogden, 1984). The new non-Aboriginal rule of law made several distinctions. For the plains Indians, legality entailed carefully structured inferiority. For the Métis, it led to the label of criminal, and the criminalization of people with an extensive history of democracy and justice. For most, however, the rule of law meant protection for social status and property.

Legal degradation was the major feature of that discipline. That discretionary omnipotence affected both Indians and Métis. Both proactive and reactive powers were available. The width of the Vagrancy Act, introduced to the prairies in 1883, represented an omnibus power.

Idealized English due process law was based upon several assumptions, including innocence until proven guilty, trial by one's peers, and the separation of the executive function of apprehension from that of judicial disposition. Vagrancy law—very much like several other common law powers—inverted these assumptions. Vagrancy was in the eyes of the beholder, be it Mounted Policeman or European settler. The magistrate —often, in the remoter townships, a Hudson's Bay Company employee— had little in common with those individuals, Natives and itinerant non-Natives, who appeared before him. In other townships, the local Mounted Police commander combined both police and magisterial functions in his office. In particular, the vagrancy law (and its associated legal euphemisms such as "reasonable suspicion") concealed subjective colonial assumptions. "Normal", "non-suspicious" citizens of the Empire, the non-Native settlers, had two primary social characteristics; they had a fixed abode and they maintained an approved occupation.

Intinerant Métis (Payment, 1985) often did not meet the first criterion. Similarly, survival strategies, such as selling buffalo bone, did not constitute a "real" occupation. The magistrates were culturally askew of Native people, uncomprehending these subjects of the Empire. In their eyes the Métis were quite properly, as a result of the contortions of English and Canadian due process law, guilty until proven innocent.

But the vagrancy law, and its associated stop-and-search powers, were more important as a threat than an action. In practice, relatively few Métis and Indians appeared in Court on vagrancy charges after 1885. It was unnecessary. As legal powers, they gave Mounted Police Officers the authority to 'move on' those they regarded as 'different', at will. Local superintendents interpreted the Act as was intended—"....the terms of the Vagrant Act recently extended to these territories, stating that no body of men would be allowed to remain idling about the country...." [27]—forcing the Indians onto reserves, and the landless Métis to keep moving. In the words of Superintendent Crozier's report "....there are always a great many disputes and difficulties satisfied to the satisfaction of justice without going through the legal process and consequently of which no record is kept." [28]

His report can be read in two ways. On the one hand, it implies an informal process of dispute resolution (as was apparent under Métis township law). In this context, it demonstrates the power of the policing agency (evident throughout the colonies of Imperial Britain in the nineteenth century [Brogden, 1990]) to move on, and otherwise dispose of, those whom they regarded as being abnormal, or a nuisance, according to the conventions of a European quasi-military army of occupation.

These powers gave the Mounted Police unilateral rights of disposal "....the Vagrant Act has been found, in the West, to be very efficacious. Suspicious characters who have been in the habit of loitering about with no apparent means of gaining a livelihood, notwithstanding that in some cases they have been well supplied with money...have been given 24 hours to quit the place, and as a rule, they have promptly availed themselves of the invitation." [29]

On the other hand vagrancy law was a flexible tool. Métis, for example, like Indians were arbitrarily moved from secondary occupations dependent upon the railroad under threat of arrest. [30] The names of itinerant Métis were noted and passed from one police post to the next. [31] Law enforcement against the Métis contained little of the baggage of due process. They were guilty of criminal intent unless they could prove otherwise, subject to arbitrary arrest "....if not personally known to some member of the detachment." [32]

In the web of an inquisitorial legal process, the Métis were subject to all the discretionary and discriminatory powers which had been suffered by other marginal groups incurring the displeasure of the British Raj over the centuries. The Vagrancy Act was a powerful piece of legislation with which to marginalize those at the foot of the social hierarchy.

Policing by "Sturdy Beggar" Controls

Not all of the discipline imposed upon the western Métis and the plains Indians by the North West Mounted Police was exercised through legal process. The authoritarian state insisted on politically-coerced labour, a process in which lower class Métis were required to cooperate in their own dependency. Authority was exercised through compulsory work schemes in return for sustenance, indeed often exercised more reliably than through the Vagrancy Act. Given the post-resistance impoverishment of many Métis, obtaining basic foodstuffs, especially during the winter and spring, was a major problem,[33] one which made many susceptible to a tight social discipline.

English social history has coined the term "sturdy beggar" to highlight some of the moralizing and disciplining features of that type of relief provision. Traditionally, English workhouses were instructed to distinguish between the deserving and the undeserving poor, the latter to be sent on their way (often, in Elizabethan days, with a whipping). Those who were fit to labour and had possible means of subsistence—the pathological, the incorrigibly idle—should be left to fend for themselves. Charity to such people, in a Calvinistic ethos, would do harm both to giver and to receiver. The latter in particular would be discouraged from self-endeavour, discouraged from pulling themselves up by their own bootstraps if they found charity too easy to come by. Discouraging the improvident poor was a moral duty both to society and to the poor. "Sturdy beggars" were to be discouraged or, at the very least, made to appreciate their dependent status through honest work.

But there was a secondary motivation for control of labour through "sturdy beggar" channels in the prairie territories. For European immigrants, this was pioneer territory, lacking the infrastructure necessary for the smooth running of public administration and the maintenance of Ottawa's public order. Bridges had to be built, barracks constructed, roads laid. The use of conscripted labour for such purposes has been noted since feudal days. In providing relief to many western Métis, therefore, the Mounted Police commanders combined a moralizing injunction with a utilitarian work ethic. The "sturdy beggar" theme dominated:

> I directed the Sergeant to make free issue of provisions to two widows. Finding that they had grown-up sons... I discontinued the issue and offered work.[34]

Cheap or unpaid labour was essential to the construction of early public works. Relief was granted in return for work and appropriate behaviour.

Last winter considerable suffering existed.... They .
largely by freighting the lumber for the police barracks at Battleford.... As far as possible, the needy half-breeds only were employed.[35]

Instructions from Ottawa, including moralizing injunctions, were combined with a judicious recognition of the value of labour:

In preference to giving assistance, those able, be employed in getting our logs for stockades, hauling gravel or work of some kind. If rations are issued now they will have to be continued till next May which encourages idleness...the extent of distress is exaggerated.[36]

Given the pathological image of the Métis held by non-Aboriginal official eyes, it was their "fecklessness" and apparent inability to adapt to the new work norms of the settler community, that was the problem:

It will naturally be asked why it is in a well-wooded fertile country a large percentage of the people, who are native to the country, should be in such an unhappy condition. The answer lies in the customs and habits of the Métis. They are unaccustomed to hard work and are improvident. Their means of living has been narrowed to farming, which they cannot do. They are ignorant of the persistent and persevering labour required to farm... While they have plenty, they live on plenty, not caring for the morrow.[37]

Disciplined work was considered by non-Aboriginal authorities to be essential to the Métis future, to mould them to the work ethic and labour practices of settler Canada. Forced labour was considered good for primitive people with a weak and amoral nature. The North West Mounted Police had a moral duty to undertake that supervision and to direct local Métis onto the path of righteousness.

There are many half-breeds in this section in poor circumstances ... Many are idle and have no settled occupation, and if they get money, waste it in drinking and gambling.[38]

Forced labour practices were noted at many police posts.[39] At Battleford, for example, road works were the chosen labour. In a revival of the old Hudson's Bay Company tradition, the North West Mounted Police sometimes granted provisions and seed grain against a mortgage on future Métis crops.[40] The "sturdy beggar" thesis underpinned these disciplining practices, with any suspicion of the existence of able-bodied relatives leading to the immediate discontinuation of this social assistance.[41]

Local Superintendents were exhorted to avoid creating long-term expectations of relief.

There was no distinction by sex or by age, as policing linked with colonial education to create a pathology of the Métis people. Métis women were seen as especially debased "...being in themselves in that debatable land between savagery and civilization." [42] There was an opportunity with the young, however, for whom manual training schools were encouraged to train plains Indians and Métis for either subsistence production or marginal employment for the developing economy.

All these practices were in the service of an ideology which insisted upon the superiority of European, and especially English, civilization (from law to education), the benefits which it could bestow and the evolutionary inferiority of the Aboriginal people of the Canadian prairies. Such police work embodied a missionary zeal for social reconstruction through the work ethic. The so-called natural characteristics of plains Indians, embodied in subsistence through the hunt, were channelled into labour. The work autonomy of the prairie Métis was to be coerced into subordinated labour. As a marginal class, the Métis were deemed to require authoritarian work structures.

Pathology and Legal Marginalization

By the 1890s many western Métis had been successfully reconstructed as an underclass through the twin disciplining powers of the Vagrancy Act (and associated legislation) and the "sturdy beggar" controls. In particular, their assumed pathological incompetence had been reaffirmed through the policies of the North West Mounted Police. "In the average half-breed, the Indian nature largely dominates.... It is not in their nature to be provident, and doubtless by the time midwinter arrives many cases of absolute destitution will present themselves as deserving aspirants for Government aid." [43]

Drawing upon North West Mounted Police records for the second half of this paper has highlighted the paradox at the heart of the Métis legal experience in western Canada in the nineteeth century. In the language of Ottawa, they were a species lower in the human race than the incoming European settlers. In Darwinian theory, their evolution had not kept pace with social change. They were considered to be out-of-joint with the times for their innate weaknesses had not allowed them to adapt to the disciplines of settler economics. This unfortunate backwardness was evident in their perverse inability to recognize the benefits of the state's legal process.

But these were the words, the conceptions and the predispositions of the conqueror. In a tradition which Sprague has documented, the western Métis were portrayed by a non-Aboriginal colonial government as some lower form of human species, people who required legal tutelage if they were to adapt to the new order. As people with a primarily oral tradition, the Métis were outflanked in the historical reconstruction of the legal process by their oppressors, whose histories drew upon the written word. The "facts" of Métis legal history are produced in such official discourse as the Hudson's Bay Company records and the North West Mounted Police Reports. These objective accounts denied the possiblity of alternative systems of law and justice to any people in the Imperial state.

In fact, Métis peoples throughout the nineteenth century were committed to democractic legal structures. Drawing upon their own traditions, they were committed to a progressive form of justice. Because the informal, representative, legal process of the Métis could not be recognized by lawyers and police officers trained in Imperial traditions, Métis claims for an historic autonomous legal tradition were—and continue to be—discounted. The Métis practised forms of law (albeit in small communities) superior in many ways to those of their colonial oppressors. Where these forms disappeared, it was because of the overwhelming supremacy of the "law and order" institutions of the Empire, not through any moral superiority.

By the end of the nineteenth century, now labelled social criminals, the francophone Métis of western Canada enjoyed few protections. They had lost the defences afforded them by their traditional process of informal justice, but had received little in return from the North West Mounted Police to whom they apparently afforded little legitimacy. Their new social status made them susceptible to arbitrary, indeed inquisitorial, legislation. Their poverty and social dislocation allowed the Mounted Police to enforce a variety of legal and administrative controls over them. From the pinnacle to which they had ascended in 1869, prior to political criminalization and the delegitimation of their legal institutions, the Métis had fallen to the social scrap-heap outside the safeguards which the Imperial legal process afforded to the non-Native settlers. Their designation as social criminals was a surface manifestation of the deeper economic relationship which they had with the new Dominion of Canada.

Legal institutions are not the prerogative of a central state. Changing economic relations can encompass a plurality of legal processes. Practices of traditional informal justice may have more value in influencing social relations than the imposed standards of external authorities. Law and order did not suddenly arrive on the South Saskatchewan River with the entry of Commissioner French and the North West Mounted Police. The civilization of which the officers of the police were wont to speak was little more than the imposition of repressive legislative standards over indigenous tradition, as part of the wider Imperial intent to marginalize and segregate those Aboriginal people—western Métis and plains Indians—who hindered the thrust of eastern Canadian and European capitalism.

NOTES

1. H.B.C. Records A/17 1826:14.

2. Assiniboia Council Minutes, 1835:269.

3. Assiniboia Council Minutes, 1843:307ff.

4. Assiniboia Council Minutes, 1845:315ff.

5. H.B.C. records Series a. 12/4.

6. Selkirk Papers, p. 7726.

7. See Ross, 1972 and Steele, 1972, on the traditional rules of the buffalo hunt.

8. Public Archives of Canada. André, Vol. 6, no. 333, Fr. André to Col. French. January 1875.

9. PAC, R.G. 18 A1, Vol. 6, no. 333, Clarke to Morris. July 10, 1875

10. "The Hudson's Bay Company officals...have shown the greatest possible hostility to this force since they found out that it is being organized totally independently of them...the interests of the Hudson's Bay Company will not usually run in the same groove." Ibid.

11. NWMP Prince Albert Report, 1887.

12. NWMP Report Prince Albert, 1888.

13. The British Weekly Whig, 23rd July, 1885.

14. Daily Intelligencer, 13th July, 1885.

15. Ibid, July 31st, 1885.

16. NWMP Prince Albert report, 1888.

17. Report, 1888, p. 98.

18. The latter term was an accepted police discourse within the NWMP —for example, Commander Herschmer refers to 'Irish Ruby' as being the "common property of the police" (letter, Regina, 25th December, 1888). For a further elaboration, see Brogden et al, 1988.

19. For the Indians, on the reserves, the Pass system was judiciously combined with the Vagrancy Act. Although the Pass system had no legal standing, it was, in the practice, normally supported by the powers of the Vagrancy Act. An Indian off a Reserve without a Pass was deemed to be a vagrant thus making the Pass a de facto legal authority.

20. There were several incidents of apparent later resistance recorded in Batoche—see the NWMP Prince Albert, letter-books for 1888 and 1889, and NWMP Report, Prince Albert, 3rd December, 1888.

21. For example, PAC, R.G. 18, Vol. 2229, p. 185.

22. See Major Boulton's memoirs — Reminescences of the North West Rebellion, 1886; 289-90; and especially Father André's letter in *The British Weekly Whig,* 20th August, 1885.

23. NWMP Batoche Report, 1889.

24. NWMP Calgary Report, 1889; NWMP Prince Albert Report, 1893.

25. NWMP Maple Creek Report, 1889.

26. For example, using an 'ice-battery' to thresh oats — NWMP Batoche letter-book, 12th July, 1889.

27. NWMP Maple Creek Report, 1883:16.

28. NWMP Fort Walsh Report, 1879.

29. NWMP Commissioner's Annual Report, 1884:19.

30. NWMP Maple Creek Report, 1883.

31. NWMP Fort McLeod Report, 1888.

32. NWMP Annual Report, 1886:23.

33. For example, the petitions on fishing in the closed season NWMP Batoche letter-book, 7th October, 1893.

34. NWMP Battleford letter-book, 4th December, 1888.

35. NWMP Batoche Report, 1889:108.

36. NMWP Commissioner's telegram, 21st October, 1888.

37. NWMP Prince Albert Report, 1888.

38. NWMP Annual Report, 1888:49.

39. For example, NWMP Prince Albert Report, 1893:133.

40. NWMP Battleford letter-book, 30th March, 1888.

41. Ibid, 4th December, 1888.

42. NWMP Annual Report, 1888:49.

43. NWMP Prince Albert Report, 1892.

1. Métis hunters camp, 1874. Public Archives of Canada, C-81767

2. Unidentified Métis hunter, mounted, ready to hunt buffalo, 1890s.
    Glenbow Museum File No. NC-22-33

3. Gabriel Dumont, Métis leader c. 1880s, Glenbow Museum
   File No. ND-1177-1

4. "Opening the Ball at Batche", 1885. From Capt. Peter's Album, PAC-C-3464 (Provincial Archives of Manitoba)

5. Métis Council, in shackles, as prisioners in Regina, 1885 (Provincial Archives of Manitoba)

6. North West Resistance aftermath, Métis refugee camp at Fort Pitt, 1885, from newspaper front page (Provincial Archives of Manitoba).

7. Stony Mountain Penitentiary c. 1892. Provincial Archives of Manitoba N7943.

8. Scrip buyer, Mounted policemen and Métis on the Nelson River, 1910, Provincial Archives of Manitoba A. V. Thomas Collection (90) N8164

Part Two

The Twentieth Century

INTRODUCTION

Lawrence J. Barkwell

Historically, the Canadian legal system has been an instrument to establish the economic and political goals of the dominant society. Threats to the authority of the colonizers have been suppressed through the agency of justice officials and the "just-us" system, as it is called by many Aboriginal people.

The Métis remember only too vividly that when their forefathers assumed political control of the Red River Settlement in 1869 and established their own judicial system, retribution was the reflexive response. When promises of land and language rights were made in 1870, these were quickly abrogated. When the Métis of St. Laurent on the South Saskatchewan established their own laws in 1873 and then tried to enforce those laws in 1875, retribution by the Hudson's Bay Company Factor and local magistrate was the reflexive response. When the Métis moved to protect their land at Batoche in 1885, retribution was reflexive and swift and cruel.

Any attempt to give an overview of crime and criminality among Aboriginal people is inordinately difficult because of a lack of published research. Official data usually deal only with registered or Status Indians. Few data exist with regard to the Métis. Little is known about differences in crime patterns among Aboriginal communities.

Prior to the 1960s, there were few studies documenting the impact of the justice system on Aboriginal people. The first major report was done in over two decades ago (Canadian Corrections Association, 1967). This report, and subsequent studies, presented what can only be characterized as substantially shallow analyses of reality. As these studies either ignored history or relied upon distortions of history, they assumed explanations for criminality among Aboriginal people based upon the observed correlations between Aboriginal crime on the one hand and alcoholism, family violence and social disorganization on the other hand. It is only in the last few years that researchers have realized that in this area we are reaping the rewards, and seeing the logical outcome, of the neo-colonial policies of segregation and assimilation. As Harding (1990) has noted, previous analysis was rooted in a vague concept of "Native criminality" or the "Native offender." rather than the fact that Aboriginal people were placed in a dependent position by a dominant group which insisted upon its own world view. This world view was enforced through a unilateral relationship. What is now clear is that paternalistic authoritarianism has failed.

All Aboriginal organizations have now issued a clarion call for meaningful law reform, Aboriginal self-determination and a separate parallel justice system based upon custom and tradition. This position is now supported by the Canadian Bar Association which has recommended sectoral shifts of control into Aboriginal hands. Most thinking people have now rejected the view that Aboriginal offenders are simply people who cannot adjust in modern day society or, alternatively, are merely part of a pathological sub-group which by nature exhibits extensive social and personal problems. What is also clear is that simply tinkering with the status quo is not a solution which is acceptable to the Aboriginal community.

Since the advent of the Aboriginal Justice Inquiry in Manitoba, the Manitoba Métis Federation Inc. (MMF), through research conducted by its Justice Committee, has been trying to rectify this situation.

After one year of work, a number of statements can be made in characterizing the justice system from a Métis point of view:

1. In the development of Canadian law, law reform efforts have not taken Métis people and their customary practices into account and there has been minimal consultation with Métis people in this regard.

2. Canadian society's reflexive response to antisocial behaviour and delinquency within Métis communities has been to increase the amount of effort and money spent on social control, but not to increase the effort with regard to social development.

3. Substantive law and the law enforcement system discriminate against Métis people. The attitudes and methods of the system are culturally alien to Métis people.

4. There is qualitative and quantitative inadequacy of legal representation for Métis people. This is characterized by inaccessibility, under-utilization, lack of outreach and preventative educational programs, as well as linguistic and cultural barriers.

5. Administrative and policy control of the legal and justice systems are highly centralized with the result that planners are neither aware of nor capable of responding to the real community needs of Métis people.

6. The discretionary powers of the police and of provincial and federal correctional officials are exercised according to criteria which penalize Métis people.

7. This dramatic lack of adequate assistance simply means that problems which are dealt with by social and psychological counselling for other Canadians are pushed into the youth and adult justice systems for Métis people. This in turn leads directly to higher incarceration rates as less intrusive alternatives are either never considered, or if considered, are not readily available.

The Chapters in Part Two contain rewritten and expanded discussions of the Manitoba Métis Federation research that formed the basis of the MMF submission to the Manitoba Aboriginal Justice Inquiry. As well, some of this work was presented at a 1990 consultation sponsored by the Prairie Justice Research Centre on "Strategies to Reduce the Over-Incarceration of Canada's Aboriginal Peoples", held in Prince Albert, Saskatchewan.

The theme of these sections is to draw the linkage between the devaluation of a people who have low status in Canadian society and the subsequent dehumanizing prejudicial treatment they receive. Federal and provincial government correctional and court programs are examined to determine whether they are achieving their stated goals. A factual basis is presented for the contention that Aboriginal people receive court dispositions on the extreme end of the punishment scale. Evidence is brought forth which reveals that while much of the rhetoric of correctional and court officials focusses upon community-based programming, the reality is that the greater part of correctional funds and manpower are invested in incarceration.

Although most Aboriginal people feel that descriptive studies of over-incarceration and systemic discrimination have been "done to death", the MMF research reveals few research efforts that actually evaluate the justice system with a view to holding it accountable for its failures—failures in program planning, implementation and evaluation. As long as the planners and policymakers of the justice system are allowed to rationalize its failures by pointing to, and blaming, large and vaguely-defined "social problems," and claim that these are factors beyond control, they will continue to sidestep questions of relevancy and will continue to feed the syndrome of blaming the victim.

DEVALUED PEOPLE: THE STATUS OF THE METIS IN THE JUSTICE SYSTEM[1]

Lawrence J. Barkwell
David N. Gray
David N. Chartrand
Lyle N. Longclaws
Ron H. Richard

In July of 1988, the Government of Manitoba set up a Public Inquiry into the Administration of Justice and Aboriginal People.[2] This Inquiry was established to examine the impact of the legal system on the Indian, Inuit and Métis population of Manitoba and to produce a final report for the Legislature with a conclusion, opinions and recommendations.[3]

The Inquiry was given broad scope to examine issues including all components of the justice system. A mandate to determine the extent to which Native and non-Native persons are treated differently by the justice system, and to consider whether or not there are specific adverse effects against Aboriginal people in the criminal justice system including possible systemic discrimination.

The objects of this paper are to review the general effects subtending to Aboriginal people as a devalued group, and to then examine the status of Métis people within the provincial correctional system. This paper presents research evidence that Métis and other Aboriginal peoples are differentially impacted by the operation of the justice system as it now exists, that the effects are adverse, and that systemic discrimination is prevalent.

The lack of recognition of the social viability of Native communities — and a corresponding failure to permit Native people to address their own needs and to manage their own affairs—is rooted in the history of Manitoba. The basis of this colonization is, of course, economic exploitation. The devaluation of a people and their culture renders it more acceptable to the colonizing group in its rationalization of the exploitation, for when people are seen as less than human, interference with their lives is seen as more palatable. We contend that the effects of the dehumanization are translated to the present day situation where Native people are over-represented as victims, witnesses and of course the accused of the justice system. This then becomes a self-perpetuating cycle because the dehumanizing treatment received from the justice system further erodes self-esteem.

Aboriginal youth get into conflict with the law at a younger age than do non-Aboriginal youth, and for them, life is confusing and dislocating. There is less success in school and there are fewer work and recreation activities available. In Manitoba, Métis youth are admitted to probation at a (mean) age of 15.6 years, compared to 16.1 years for non-Natives. Over one-third (34.4%) of Métis youths admitted to probation are not living with their parents, compared to 25% of non-Native youth. The average age of first conviction for Métis children is 14.2 years, compared to 15 years for non-Natives, and 56.8% of Métis youth have less than Grade IX, compared to 34.4% for non-Native youth. If one combines these factors with the observation that many Métis youth come from communities with less than adequate social services, it is not surprising that their success rate on probation supervision is only 34.9%, compared to a 52.1% success rate for non-Natives and 42.8% success rate for Treaty Indians living on reserves.

During the course of the public hearings throughout Manitoba in 1988 and 1989, a number of people appeared before the Aboriginal Justice Inquiry and blamed Aboriginal individuals or communities for justice system problems, in effect, asserting that Aboriginal people are the sole authors of their own misfortune. These arguments are flawed both from a lack of understanding of complex societal interactions and because they are founded upon that historical inaccuracy and distortion which are often used to buttress such arguments. This has generated a number of different reactions within the Aboriginal community and within the wider community.

This paper will deal with complex societal interactions and leave historical distortions to be dealt with at another time. The paper will present a paradigm which goes some way to explain what occurs in the lives of devalued people and outline the evidence that these factors are in play within the justice system.

In a presentation to the Aboriginal Justice Inquiry (Barkwell, 1988), the senior author dealt at length with factors which tend to dehumanize both those who are processed by the justice system and those who have responsibility for administration of the various branches of the system (the employees). Those arguments need not be presented here, but do serve as useful background to this presentation.[4]

Devalued People

Historically, devalued people are those who are racially different, physically different, or behaviourally different from the majority. The basis for the "differentness" resides in accidental or chance factors which are not the making of the individual. For people who are in any way different from the norm, there is a risk that they will experience low status within the larger group. They will remain low status within the community unless a number of other significant factors are present in their lives.

If the individuals draw strength and support from traditions, spiritual resources, a strong family network, or a strong community network (within the context of a shared language), the chances are very good that they will not experience the detrimental effects that usually subtend to persons of low status.

The only other counters to low status are tremendous inner reserves of coping skills or alternately to have very powerful or high status people on one's side (a process of inclusion).

If there is no counterbalance as noted above, there are a number of outcomes from being low status and devalued. There are four things these individuals will experience: rejection, low personal autonomy, negative imaging and involuntary poverty.

Rejection: Rejection leads to the creation of distance by the process of either congregation or segregation. Within the earliest communities, banishment was a practice. However, this occurred only as a last resort and was an ultimate disposition as the individual was so dependent upon the community as a whole for survival. In the criminal justice system, those who refuse to adhere to social norms are segregated from the community, often for relatively minor offenses. Unfortunately, they are also congregated in large deviant subcultures.

In any event, rejection leads inevitably to the experience of discontinuity, both physical discontinuity (being moved from place to place), and relational dicontinuity (being moved or separated from family, friends and social network). This in turn results in personal insecurity and the consequent loss of the ability to trust others.

Negative imaging: Often the person who is identifiably different is described in a pejorative way, and at the same time is suspected of multiple deviance. From personal experience, everyone can recall instances where they have almost reflexively ascribed additional negative attributes to those they perceive as being different. Although we are not discussing stereotyping, the process clearly does lead to stereotypical views.

Low personal autonomy: Low personal autonomy leads to being controlled by others. Low status devalued people are most often viewed as being incapable of managing their own affairs. Most people find this demeaning and find it difficult to maintain their own self-esteem in the face of this pressure. Higher status persons often patronize devalued people, or think they have an inherent right to order them around.

Involuntary poverty: If one is viewed as incapable, the larger community is unlikely to entrust one with communal resources. This involuntary poverty leads to the impoverishment of experience. This, in turn, leads to anger and/or depression, low energy, low self-esteem, feelings of not deserving success and, ultimately, self-rejection.

The four factors listed above lead to social interactions where the devalued person is prone to being on the receiving end of psychological or physical brutality. Quite understandably then, these people come to see themselves as a source of anguish. When an individual has been cycled through this process a number of times, the result is most often dissipation. At a minimum, the devalued person comes to distrust those in positions of authority.

A major additional problem arising out of poverty, hopelessness, and the sense youths have that to be Indian or Métis is to be a failure, is that according to a self-esteem model of deviance, juveniles may become involved in delinquency as a response to negative self-attitudes and high self-esteem needs.

Recent research by Wells (1989) tested that self-derogation theory which predicts that low self-esteem motivates youths to try out delinquent activities aimed at restoring self-esteem. He found significant evidence that this is indeed the case:

> The effects are pronounced for more substantial forms of delinquency (theft, vandalism, and fighting)....The enhancing effect of delinquency is showing up significantly and most consistently in persons whose level of self-derogation are extreme...such persons have less to lose by getting involved in socially disapproved deviance and a lot to gain psychologically, since their self-esteem cannot get much lower. (Wells, 1989:248-249)

The effects were found to be persistent, enduring undiminished for one and one-half to three and one-half years. Thus, there is extremely good research evidence that the more a group is devalued or denigrated for its own conditions or status, the higher the likelihood of deviant behaviour from youth of that group.

Even a cursory examination of the front page of the newspaper will reveal reports of this process:

> Manitoba and Saskatchewan residents blame Natives for their own problems and are less likely than other Canadians to support

Aboriginal rights, an Angus Reid Group poll has found...Pollster Angus Reid said yesterday the most troubling of all the findings in the national poll is the tendency of Manitoba and Saskatchewan residents to blame Canada's Native people for the problems that confront them. (McKinley, 1989)

The public responses to a recent article in Canadian Social Trends (Statistics Canada, 1989) are most instructive in this regard:

Spokesmen for Native run social agencies who were interviewed yesterday blamed poverty and hopelessness, as well as conditions that go beyond economics; a sense that Native people must assimilate to survive, and that to be Indian or Métis is to be a failure. Alcoholism, child abuse and family murder are all "symptoms of a basic deprivation of a place in the world", said Martin Dunn, senior advisor with the Native Council of Canada, in Ottawa. (Fine, 1989)

The Globe and Mail was also able to document poignant self reports of Native leaders expressing the view that they had feelings of self-rejection and a sense of themselves as a source of anguish.

Virtually we grew up to hate what we were. We used to watch cowboy and Indian movies and we'd be rooting for the cowboys as they killed off the Indians (Fine, 1989).

The end result of the interaction of these factors is that custody rates for youths in Manitoba are 57.4% higher than the national average, custody rates for adults in Manitoba exceed the national average by 26.5%, and adult sentences are twice as long as the Canadian median sentence (61 days compared to 30 days).

This devaluation is present across Canada. However, because the proportion of Aboriginal people in the population is largest in Manitoba, Saskatchewan and the Northwest Territories, the results are more immediately obvious in these jurisdictions. This effect amplifies the rates of incarceration for the population as a whole. This is documented by the fact that the over-representation of Aboriginal people in the justice system creates a larger general rate of incarceration in Manitoba than the national average. Statistics Canada (1989) reports the following comparative figures for 1988-89:

	Canada	Manitoba
Youth custody rate per 10,000 youth population	18.3/10,000	28.8/10,000
adult custody rate per10,000 adult population	8.85/10,000	11.2/10,000

Figure 1: Canada/Manitoba Incarceration Rates

A review of the Statistics Canada Key Indicator Reports reveals that the same trend exists in all provinces and territories with significant Aboriginal populations. Most provinces report that Aboriginal people are over-represented in custody. It is noteworthy that Alberta recently set up a commission of inquiry to determine why almost one-third of that province's prisoners are Indian or Métis.

TABLE 1: YOUTH CORRECTIONS REFERRALS
Manitoba: 1987 Admissions
Métis and Aboriginal Admission Rates

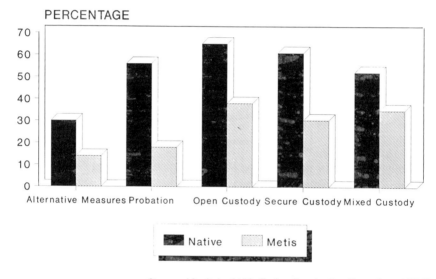

Source: Manitoba Métis Federation Justice Committee (1989)

Status Of Métis People In Provincial Corrections In Manitoba

As illustrated in Table 1, Métis youth constitute:

*   14.0% of those receiving diversion from court;
*   17.9% of those receiving probation;
*   30.4% of those receiving secure custody;
*   34.8% of those with mixed custody dispositions; and
*   38.0% of those receiving open custody.

Métis admissions to open custody since the implementation of the Young Offenders Act (1984-1987) exceed all non-Native admissions and Treaty Indian admissions when compared individually. Métis youth are also severely affected by mixed custody admissions (34.8% vs 17.4% for Treaty Indians, and 47.8% for non-Native). The percentage of Métis admissions to secure custody is only 8.7% less than the percentage of all non-Native admissions.

TABLE 2: YOUTH ADMISSIONS TO CUSTODY
Manitoba 1984 - 1987

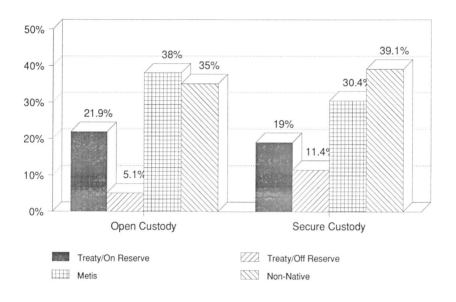

Source: Manitoba Métis Federation Justice Committee (1989)

As one moves from diversion from court to more secure custodial sentences, Métis youth are more severely impacted. Métis children are committed to youth institutions at twice the rate they are diverted from court. This is true for Native youth in general but nowhere are they more unfairly treated than in the pre-court process. In 1989, a survey by the Native Caucus of Probation Officers revealed that the remand cottages of the Manitoba Youth Centre were basically full of Native youths:

- 92.8% of the girls held on remand were Native; and
- 47.0% of the boys held on remand were Native.

There is a large number of secure and open custody beds at the Manitoba Youth Centre. The survey revealed:

- 87.5% of the girls and 55.5% of the boys held in the open case custody units of the Manitoba Youth Centre were Native; and

- 100% of the girls held in secure custody at the Manitoba Youth Centre were Native.

There is good evidence that it is considered acceptable by correctional authorities to treat devalued people in a substandard fashion. Recently in Manitoba there were as many as twenty-six youths held in cottages designed to hold fifteen. This exceeds the Canadian Criminal Justice Association standards for minimum cell size by so much as to make a mockery of the standards. We believe that it is only because Native youths are without strong advocacy that this situation has not been brought to public attention and has been allowed to continue over the years. We believe that the effect of this overcrowding is a reinforcement of the devaluation. These youths can be clearly identified as a group that is primarily Native, and this situation has, we reiterate, the effect of devaluing these people as individuals. There is also a widespread belief—in both the Aboriginal and non-Aboriginal communities—that if the majority of those locked up were from a white, middle class family background, the over-crowding would not be allowed to continue.

In Manitoba, and indeed across the country, there is great variation in designating open custody facilities. Of the fourteen open custody homes throughout Manitoba, five are operated by Aboriginal families, two in Thompson, one in Gods Lake Narrows, and two in Winnipeg (normally licensed for two beds each). At the other extreme, four cottages within the grounds of the Manitoba Youth Centre and one cottage within the grounds of Agassiz Centre for Youth are designated as places of open custody.

There also appears to be considerable variation in the use of custody facilities. Recent Statistics Canada figures show that while Saskatchewan has only three juvenile girls serving custody sentences, Manitoba has sixteen (almost all Aboriginal) in custody institutions, yet the two provinces have similar population bases and demographics.

In the case of the Manitoba Youth Centre, an appeal of an open custody disposition resulted in that designation being overturned in *Re F v the Queen et al* (1984).[5] Subsequently, after some juggling of placements by the province, the Court of Appeal[6] suggested that the Lieutenant-Governor in Council has authority to define what constitutes open custody, as long as the definition falls within one of the generic descriptions of the Young Offenders Act. As a result, the characteristics of a custodial sentence received by a youth may vary more according to where the youth lives than on the basis of the offence for which he or she has been convicted (Caputo & Bracken, 1988). Open custody placement is mostly dependent upon availability of governmental and non-governmental resources in a particular community and, further, a youth is more likely to receive culturally appropriate services if he or she is fortunate enough to be placed in an open custody home in the community.

The Native Caucus of Probation Officers (1989) assessed institutional programming for Aboriginal youth as inadequate and piecemeal, inadequately linked to the community, and providing education which is below community standards, all within a context in which there are few, if any, Native persons as staff.

The concerns of the Native Probation Caucus are borne out by a report of the Ombudsman of Manitoba to the Manitoba Legislature. He documented the following criticisms of youth custody programming (1989:37-40):

1. The Positive Peer Culture program at Agassiz Youth Centre is geared to adolescents, yet approximately 30% of the population at the Centre is over eighteen years of age.

2. Given the diverse cultural backgrounds of the residents (high number of Métis and Indian), he questioned whether the program could meet the variable needs of the residents.

3. The Ombudsman questioned the use of quiet rooms and containment at Agassiz.

4. The report noted that the optimum Positive Peer Culture group size is nine residents and one staff, whereas at Agassiz the ratio ranged from 13:1 to 15:1.

5. The report called for program review to determine the effectiveness and quality of the program being delivered.

6. The Ombudsman commented that the Agassiz school program was not affiliated with the local school division and appeared to be operating with a much lower budget than a public school. The available resource materials and teaching aids were not comparable to those of a public school.

7. The Ombudsman expressed the opinion that the living units at Agassiz required maintenance and upgrading, and recommended that the Fire Commissioner's Office inspect the facility to ensure compliance with safety standards.

Métis parents have told researchers (Manitoba Métis Federation Justice Committee, 1989) that they feel pressured to provide clothing for their children after the youths are committed to custody sentences, even though the parents' welfare issue is reduced after the youth is placed away from home. Youths report to the MMF that they are required to purchase clothing and some toiletry articles out of allowances or earnings while serving their sentence. The alternative is to wear used institutional clothes (including used underwear). Youths also complain that when their clothes are stolen or disappear, the institutions claim they cannot guarantee security of personal possessions and the youths must replace these items themselves.

Youths also note that the institutions do not pay for phone calls to family or social workers, and they must either phone collect or pay for the calls at pay phones. It is clear that Aboriginal youth would be better served if large secure institutions had never been designated as places of open custody, and if there had been more dispersal of open custody beds by way of designation of open custody homes throughout the province.

The argument that these conditions apply to all youth, and thus race is not a factor, simply does not reflect the reality of the situation. First, as we have documented, there is a large over-representation of Aboriginal offenders in the justice system. Second, the economic station of those affected makes the measures more drastic to most of the Aboriginal youth. This leads to the logical conclusion that the function, if not the purpose, of these rules and policies, is to further the devaluation process.

We note as well that a high proportion of the youths so jailed are entirely removed from their communities, which are in some instances 600 or more miles away. They are then placed in a restrictive and culturally foreign environment. They are placed in "open custody", which in fact is a very secure jail. All of these factors lead to greater, not to lesser, devaluation, and thus cannot be considered rehabilitative in any sense.

Métis youth and the system in general would have been much better served if the Department of the Attorney-General of Manitoba (now the Department of Justice) had acted on the advice given by its own Research, Planning & Evaluation Branch (Latimer, 1986); that is:

a) Too many young people become too involved in the criminal justice system for relatively minor offences.

b) The criminal justice process in Youth Court is markedly slower and more intrusive than in Adult Court.

c) Provisions in the Young Offenders Act intended to protect the rights of young accused are not being applied (e.g. Section 30, Review Board provisions).

d) Custodial rates under the new legislative regime have increased; the consistency of the application and intent of the provisions must be ensured.

Research done for the Manitoba Métis Federation (Manitoba Métis Federation Justice Committee, 1989) reveals that alternative measures are less frequently used for Métis youth than for others. There is also provision in the Young Offenders Act, under Section 3(d), for no measures to be taken against youth for minor infractions and this Section is not being used at all.

The Manitoba Métis Federation submission to the Aboriginal Justice Inquiry (1989) documented the high custody rates for Métis youth and the lack of implementation of the legislative intent of open custody. The submission noted that provisions for intermittent sentences under the Young Offenders Act have never been implemented for youths in Manitoba. However, given current practice, they were of the opinion that intermittent sentencing would only widen the net for catching Métis youths.

Adults

For adults in the provincial correctional system, the picture is similar, as can be seen in Table 3:

TABLE 3: ADULT CORRECTIONS REFERRALS 1987
% Native vs. % Non-Native

Source: Manitoba Métis Federation Justice Committee (1989)

Métis adults constitute:

- 13.19% of those on probation;
- 12.60% of adult jail admissions; and
- although no remand figures are available, we believe that they parallel the youth experience.

83

Brandon Correctional Institution, Dauphin Correctional Institution and the Winnipeg Remand Centre do not fund, nor directly provide, programs or services exclusively for Native inmates. The mechanisms in place for the resolution of inmate complaints are infrequently used by Native inmates throughout the adult correctional systems. On the other hand, there appears to be a higher representation of Natives involved in disciplinary hearings compared to non-Native inmates. Correctional officials also report that Native inmates at the pre-trial stage are less likely to receive bail or to apply for bail under the current system (Attorney-General of Manitoba, Report to the Aboriginal Justice Inquiry, April, 1989).

These trends for the incarceration of Métis people are cause for grave concern. There is evidence that these problems will get much worse before they get better. The non-Native population of Manitoba, unlike the Native population, has experienced a declining birth rate and if the incarceration rates for Aboriginal adults (Métis and other Natives) follow what we are now seeing in youth corrections "the demographic changes alone would cause Native admissions to rise to about 80% of all admissions, while the absolute number of non-Native admissions could actually decline" (Hylton, 1981). Of particular concern is that 80% of the provincial corrections budget is spent on locking up people, a practice that seems to be disproportionately reserved for Aboriginal people.

Research indicates that each year the corrections allocation budget differs from actual expenditures by some $2 million. Expenditures always come in higher, because the department obtains spending warrants during the fiscal year to cover cost over-runs in institutions. This fact is only revealed if one closely examines the Public Accounts of the Province of Manitoba. The government agreement with Manitoba Government Employees Association requires them to put more staff on the floor at institutions as the inmate population rises. The same is not true for community caseload increases or for increased needs for open custody homes in the community.

The community based workers we interviewed deplored this policy as it skews the system to favour institutional dispositions while holding community expenditures down, in the face of rising demand. It is known that recidivism will increase as probation caseloads rise and less differential programming and supervision is available.

It is apparent that other major interest groups, such as government employees, are given a seat at the decision table, while at the same time the group most drastically affected are not even consulted. Indeed, many in the system believe their views to be inconsequential! In the words of the famous Métis rights activist Malcolm Norris, "To be ignored is more vicious perhaps than to be oppressed" (Dobbin, 1981:231). While the trends of increasing incarceration for Métis youth and adults are clearly documented within the correctional system, the Manitoba Métis Federation has never been provided with the data, nor consulted about the causes of the trends or possible methods of reversal.

It is instructive to note the degree to which this lack of community consultation and lack of resource development affects adult admission to custody for bail and probation violations. The Solicitor General (1985:17) reported that in 1980 to 1982:

In:

British Columbia	26% of all bail/probation violators jailed are Aboriginal.
Alberta	35.3% of all bail/probation violators jailed are Aboriginal.
Saskatchewan	73.7% of all bail/probation violators jailed are Aboriginal.
Manitoba	73.9% of all bail/probation violators jailed are Aboriginal.
Ontario	8% of all bail/probation violators jailed are Aboriginal.

Thus, the broader picture is that, during those years, while Aboriginal people made up about 40% of the adult probation caseload in Manitoba, they constituted 73.9% of the program failures resulting in custody. The figures given above reflect the state of things at that time, which was before the institution of fine option programs in several of these jurisdictions. The failure rates have been considerably ameliorated since the advent of fine option programming.

Compare the 1980-82 figures with the results after implementation of a Manitoba fine option program, a program which is widely available and which is regionalized with Aboriginal carrier groups. Currently, although 60.2% of all Manitoba fine option registrants are Aboriginal, only 11% default. It is clear that the decline in breach rates is rooted in the nature of the program, its availability, and its cultural appropriateness. The effect of Aboriginal people enforcing the punishment, as well as enabling the participant, cannot be minimized. When the major instruments (and reinforcers) of devaluation are removed (that is, social control imposed by others, labelling as failure by the system, and meaningless dispositions), not only are Aboriginal people less devalued, but the success rate is in fact higher than the norm! It is noteworthy that Nova Scotia does not have such programming and Recommendation 17 of the Royal Commission on the Donald Marshall Jr. Prosecution was: "We recommend that the Government

85

immediately proclaim the Alternative Penalty Act, S.N.S. 1989, c.2..."
(1989).

Alternative Measures

Our research reveals that only 14% of alternative measures participants are Métis, whereas Métis youth constitute 17% of the youth probation caseloads, and from 30.4% to 38% of the youth custody population (Tables 1 and 2). Only 25% of the Métis communities which are served by local fine option and community service order programs are also served by local youth justice committees.

TABLE 4: YOUTH REFERRALS 1987
Alternative Measures vs. Probation

Source: Manitoba Métis Federation Justice Committee (1989)

This lack of diversion for Métis youth is due to a number of factors. Research recently completed by Ryant and Heinrich (1988) found that differences in community characteristics are a significant variable:

Highly disorganized and disintegrated communities tend to experience a greater number of offences by young people, but outside Winnipeg, they are also less likely to have formed youth justice committees. In these communities, the challenge of providing social services through community based intervention is greatest; these communities are often geographically isolated and constrained by having to negotiate separately with federal and provincial bureaucracies regarding Native self-government.

On the other hand, communities in relatively prosperous rural areas which have the resources, time and tradition of community participation, have formed committees whose main challenge is to maintain the motivation of their membership in that referrals are so infrequent. Ryant and Heinrich (1988) also point to inconsistency in community dispositions, the claims of some committees that cases are being withheld from them, and the lack of data base to guide selection of the most effective dispositions, as areas of administration in the youth justice committee system in Manitoba that require improvement. Ryant and Heinrich (1988) note that on reserves the support of the Band Council is integral to the operation of youth justice committees. They note that no committee could operate without at least pro forma approval of a Band Council, but their study revealed that Band Council support was minimal, as was overt interest in the communities. Their study makes no comment on Métis communities. This appears to be a serious omission in this federally funded study.

In November of 1989, the Manitoba Métis Federation held three justice workshops at their 21st Annual Assembly. Delegates (195) attended from every region of the province and 72 delegates completed justice questionnaires, which specifically asked about knowledge and involvement in alternative measures, justice committees and community service dispositions (Barkwell, 1989). The delegates indicated that few Métis communities had been approached to participate in youth diversion programs. The specific question asked was:

Have you or your MMF local been approached by provincial or federal corrections to participate in community corrections services?

	Affirmative answers
Fine Option	43.0%
Community Service Work	19.4%
Youth Justice Committees	5.5%
Alternative measures	1.4%

At the same time, 88.9% of the respondents indicated they would like more information about the justice system, and 59.7% felt there was enough interest in their community or local to warrant a justice issues workshop. One can only conclude that part of the reason for lack of diversion from court for Métis youth is a lack of outreach and education to these Métis communities as to the diversion provisions of the Young Offenders Act.

Fine Option/Community Service Order Program

Manitoba Corrections has contracts for Fine Option and Community Service work centre operations with 24 Métis communities (Community Councils and Local Government Districts), four Manitoba Métis Federation locals, and four Indian/Métis friendship centres, as well as 54 contracts with Band Councils.

In all, 85 of 135 Métis communities (63%) in Manitoba are served by Fine Option Program/Community Service Order community resource centres, operating directly in their area, and 54 of 62 Indian Bands (87%) are served by Band Council operations.

The participating MMF locals are:

- MMF Northwest Métis Council
- The Pas, Manitoba Métis Federation
- Vogar, Manitoba Métis Federation
- Leaf Rapids, Manitoba Métis Federation

The participating Indian Métis Friendship Centres are:

- Swan River Friendship Centre
- Dauphin Friendship Centre
- Lynn Lake Friendship Centre
- Ma-Mow-We-Tak Friendship Centre

Most of the remaining friendship centres participate in the program by serving as work locations.

Aboriginal adults and youth made up 4,450 (60.2%) of the 7,393 registrants for fine option in 1987. The successful completion rate remains high (around 70%).

Of fine defaulters admitted to jail in 1988:

- 23.6% of Métis admissions were for fine default;
- 21.5% of other Aboriginal admissions were for fine default; and
- 20.9% of non-Native admissions were for fine default.

Comparing registrations with defaults, we find that 11% of the Aboriginal people who register default, whereas 13.6% of the non-Aboriginal registrants default.

Overall, the Fine Option/Community Service Order Program seems to serve the Treaty Indian/Métis/Non-Status Indian community quite well. High use is made of the program by Aboriginal people, their completion rate is better than average, and the jail admissions for default are not out of line with default admissions from the non-Aboriginal community. The slightly high rate of Métis admissions may be explained by the fact that community resource centres are directly serving only 85 of 135 Métis communities, whereas 54 of 62 Bands are served by Band local resource centres, operated by Band Councils.

TABLE 5: ADULT JAIL ADMISSIONS 1987
Fine Default vs. Other Admissions

Source: Manitoba Métis Federation Justice Committee (1989)

We also note, as one example, the case of one Native young offender who was given a Community Service Order and was charged three times with a breach of probation for failing to complete the order. In an interview with a Native probation officer, the accused offered no reason for this failure. The probation officer set new terms and asked the young offender if he understood. He said, "yes". Because of suspicions aroused by certain contextual references, the probation officer asked the youth to name the months of the year in English. The youth could not! The probation officer then explained the obligations in Saulteaux and the youth completed his obligation in one week. This graphically demonstrates that if a program is to be effective and efficient, cultural awareness is essential.

Nonetheless, this program stands as an example of extensive effort on the part of correctional officials to involve local Indian and Métis governing bodies in the delivery of service, and to provide extensive regionalization. The program is diverting people from jail and it produces default admission rates where Aboriginal people are not disproportionately represented. Manitoba Métis Federation research has indicated that Métis women are less likely to complete Fine Option/Community Service Order work. There has been no study or research of this, but we are told that the obvious problems of lack of child care, low incomes and lesser accessibility are primary causes.

The Status Of Métis Women In Corrections Manitoba

The Portage Correctional Institution (PCI) is a provincial jail for women in Manitoba with a capacity of 43 inmates. Sentences up to two years are served there, and women sentenced to serve federal terms at Kingston, Ontario are held at PCI during their appeal period. Alternatively, they can serve federal sentences there under a federal/provincial transfer agreement.

The majority of admissions are Aboriginal women, 68.4% in 1987 (Table 6). Of federal prisoners transferred to Kingston during 1987, 100% were Aboriginal women (four). This incarceration rate for Aboriginal women mirrors their arrest rate. Over the last decade, Winnipeg City Police have indicated that about 70% of the women arrested in Winnipeg are of Aboriginal descent.

TABLE 6: PORTAGE WOMEN'S JAIL
1987 Admissions

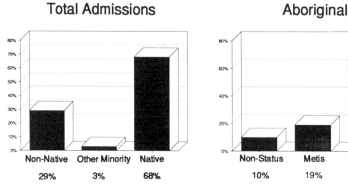

Source: Eleanor Robertson (1988)

In the latest figures available to us (Robertson, 1988), Métis and Non-status Indian women made up 30.3% of the Aboriginal admissions to PCI. The majority of these women are sole support parents from male dominated environments. The majority of Indian Bands in Manitoba are headed by male Chiefs and male mayors head most Métis and non-status communities. The superintendent of PCI is a man. The Native liaison worker at Kingston Prison for Women is a man.

Portage Correctional Institution operates a program whereby newborns are not separated from their mothers. However, because of the location of PCI, most inmates lose regular contact with their older children (Robertson,1988).

While the research on infant-parent bonding would support the practice of not separating mothers from infants, running the program in a jail as austere as PCI, rather than in a halfway house, is questionable.

In federal corrections nationally, Aboriginal females made up 14.2% of the women in federal prisons. Indians were 11.4% and Métis 2.8% of this female inmate population. All but two were held at Kingston (Solicitor General of Canada, 1989).

The Aboriginal Womens' Justice Committee (1988) reports that the personal histories of Native women in conflict with the law are set in a socio-political system where they have no status except through a husband, and where they feel compelled to keep silent on the violence within their lives.

Liaison workers who visit Aboriginal women at the Portage Correctional Institution for Women report that every woman they have visited has, at one time or another, been a victim of sexual or physical violence.

They surveyed offenders as to the stress factors that led to the commission of crimes and came up with the following list in order of frequency mentioned:

Reason for Crimes	% mentioning this reason
Alcohol and drugs	70.0%
Physical abuse	53.0%
Sexual abuse	42.8%
Poverty	29.8%
Lack of education	28.5%
Single parenthood	25.9%
Boredom	19.5%
Because they are Native	6.5%
Retaliation	3.9%
Lack of self-esteem	2.6%
Culturally appropriate	1.3%
Desperation	1.3%
Rebellion	1.3%
Loneliness	1.3%
Mad at life	1.3%

The committee noted, with interest, that the Aboriginal women surveyed were least familiar with programs that should have been the most relevant, such as the Awasis Agency, a northern Indian Social Service Agency, the Department of Indian Affairs, Medical Services and Court Communicators services.

It was their assessment that Aboriginal women are not only challenged by social and economic inequities, but must also cope with the devaluation of their culture, religion, traditions, and life-style. These concerns are only exacerbated when Aboriginal women leave rural areas to escape all of the negative factors in their lives. Furthermore, Aboriginal women caught up in the criminal justice system have a documented victimization rate far in excess of the general population.

The feelings of worthlessness which so many incarcerated Aboriginal women indicate, are only reinforced by the jail system. They are separated from their children, and children visiting them are often subjected to the indignity of "strip" searches for contraband, as are the women themselves upon returning from temporary absences in the community.

A Métis woman who used to work in liaison at the Portage Correctional Institution noted that even when she was able to take older children out to visit their mothers, this had unsatisfactory results, because the visiting area is crowded and inadequate, and the jail has no provision for private visiting with families.

The women also report that they must wear used institutional under-clothing if they do not have money to buy their own. This has also been confirmed by the executive director of the Elizabeth Fry Society when she questioned, in an interview, the amount of time and money this private agency had to expend in trying to provide the basic necessities for jailed women. The Elizabeth Fry Society also confirmed that most Aboriginal women in jail are a significant distance from family, friends and support networks. Because they are poor, the cost of visiting or even making long distance phone calls on the pay phone is prohibitive.

In its 1989 submission to the Aboriginal Justice Inquiry, the Manitoba Métis Federation recommended that because of the geographical distribution of women incarcerated in the Portage Correctional Institution and the Kingston, Ontario, Prison for Women, accommodation must be made for them to meet regularly with their families and adequate bed space must be contracted within Aboriginal receiving groups for the release of Aboriginal female offenders on temporary absence and day parole.

The Manitoba Métis Federation Inquiry report agreed with the Native Probation Caucus (1989) assessment that, " the criminal justice system is not sensitive to Native women", and institutions for these women make little effort to aid transition to the community.

Conclusion

It is our assessment that there are clearly a number of factors which interact to produce the overrepresentation of Métis people as offenders (with high re-involvement rates). These same factors interact to make Métis people more susceptible to victimization.

1. There has been an historical repression of Métis custom and tradition, social structures and support systems.

2. The Métis have little discretionary time or money available to respond as a community to the problems of crime.

3. Official responses to the problems documented above are usually framed in terms of social control rather than social development.

4. Aboriginal people as a visible minority have been denigrated and their history has been conveyed in a distorted way. In youths this leads to self-derogation, feelings of helplessness and alienation.

5. The intended child welfare remedies have not worked for Métis children.

6. Official justice system interventions have been culturally alien or irrelevant and poorly understood by the Métis community.

7. The Métis have been effectively denied participation in the creation and administration of law.

8. The official justice system has acted in ways which engender disrespect and cynicism within the Métis community.

9. In many instances correctional and other related services have been denied or not made available to the Métis.

When a people are weakened by these factors, which we view as additive as well as interactive, the symptoms of devaluation of which crime is but one, are inevitably found to be in ascendancy.

We have, we think, been able to demonstrate the collective effect on Aboriginal people of the phenomenon of devaluing a group. We would also like to demonstrate some individual and specific effects of this behaviour. In particular we want to note certain specific behaviours of devaluation that have resulted in negative consequences either to Aboriginal individuals or to groups of Aboriginal people.

One instructive case can be found in the Aboriginal community of Shammatawa, Manitoba. In that community there had been an outstanding agreement between the Band Council and Justice officials to hold Provincial Court in the Band Hall. This agreement continued for a period of time until a new school was built in the community.

It is interesting to note that for a number of reasons, the Justice officials then insisted upon holding Provincial Court in the new school gym. They did this without discussing the issue with the Chief and Council who clearly had jurisdictional control over the reserve. The primary reasons given by the court officials appear to have been a lack of space for interviewing in the Band Hall and access to better bathroom facilities in the school. The argument contrary to this, advanced by the community leaders, was the inappropriateness of students seeing the perpetual run of persons in the court. They felt this exposed them to the negative and unsettling effects of the legal process. This would tend to lead these students into thinking less of themselves as Aboriginal people. This was particularly true in those cases where persons would be incarcerated, as incarceration cases would be served a substantial distance away from the community. The effect would be, it was thought, a reduction in respect for social control.

The court party, however, was unmoved. Rather than taking up a concern with the appropriate leaders, that the facilities for the court party were inferior and should be improved, the officials simply wanted to move to the newer school facility. They did this presumably on the basis that while the Band Hall and its deficiencies were adequate for the Indian people living in the community, they did not meet the superior hygienic and other standards of the mostly non-Aboriginal persons who travelled with the Provincial Court to dispense justice in Shammatawa. In the end, the Court quit sitting in the community of Shammatawa until they were allowed to hold sessions in the new school. The result was that persons charged with offences from Shammatawa had to travel by air to Thompson for appearances on relatively routine matters. In a community where, as in many northern reserves, nine out of ten family incomes included social assistance, this caused extreme hardship. The individuals were then, if they could not afford to travel, subject to further criminal sanctions and a vicious cycle was started.

We have not escaped the effects of this devaluation as a society either. Examples of this abound. We find that in recent studies, most notably an Angus Reid Poll conducted in September 1989, the Manitoba and Saskatchewan response demonstrated the highest rate of negative opinion to Native self-determination. In addition, there was various evidence in similar polls that elements of racism, as evidenced by devaluing other people, are hardening, particularly in Manitoba. Evidence of this within the system is more difficult to ascertain. This is perhaps because the system has long tolerated the devaluation of people. A noted example (Native Probation

Caucus Report to the Inquiry, 1989) is that one official, well known within the Manitoba Department of Justice, continued to deride Aboriginal people with negative stereotypical terms. He continued to do this throughout the Aboriginal Justice Inquiry, despite the fact that it was widely known in the Department. This was allowed to continue despite its effects, known to be traumatic to the individuals to whom he dispensed his from-the-lip justice.

Another example of this type of behavioural devaluation was exhibited by Sheriff's officers during the course of the Aboriginal Justice Inquiry. It was observed that several youths were manacled together and taken through a public place. A guard, in a voice loud enough that others could hear, said to the youths, most of whom were Aboriginal, "[alright you guys get going, let's do] the Sheriff's shuffle". The effect of this upon the youths involved can only be subject to speculation, but it does not take much imagination to recognize that it can only decrease the self-esteem of those individuals.

We also draw upon the case Regina vs. Ross (Provincial Judges Court, Norway House, Manitoba, 1989). This court case was cited in the Manitoba Métis Federation Justice Committee (1989) presentation at the Manitoba Aboriginal Justice Inquiry. The facts in short are that an accused was charged with a sexual assault after being encouraged by another man to have sex with his wife while she was sleeping and under the effects of alcohol. When she became aware of this she objected and asked that the individuals be charged. They subsequently were.

In appearing in court, counsel for the defence advanced as mitigation the suggestion that it was common amongst Aboriginal people of the north to so share their women. Far from jumping up and objecting, the Crown Attorney sat silently by and allowed this ludicrous statement to go unchallenged. The judge similarly, rather than challenge the statement, made the comment that:

I accept what your lawyer tells me, that you honestly believe that if the husband said it was okay, it was alright to have sex with her.

He then reinforced this incredible perception with the following statement:

...It's because of this honest belief (sic), because there may be some belief in the community, that the man can control the situation....

Again one can only speculate that the effects of devaluation upon the individuals experiencing this would be heightened rather than lessened. We believe that such speculation is valid.

This paper would, we think, be incomplete without recommendations as to change. We therefore recommend the following (the substantive body of these recommendations is contained in the Manitoba Métis Federation presentation to the Aboriginal Justice Inquiry (1989)). We suggest that the implementation of these recommendations would have the effect of reducing the devaluation of people that has occurred, and which continues to occur, and would enhance the role of Aboriginal people in the justice system.

It is apparent that these solutions require a committed effort on behalf of the people who make up the system and on behalf of Aboriginal people. It is further apparent that failure to introduce changes will result in further damage to the Aboriginal people of Canada.

We propose that a separate but parallel, alternative Aboriginal justice system would be a major step in alleviating the dispossession that people feel as a result of the current infliction of the system. We suggest that such a system based upon, as it would be, traditional values and norms would devalue people less and would allow them to "buy into" the system more readily. This would have the end result of enhancing the respect which people have for the law and would achieve the social control that is clearly the function of all law. This, of course, was supported by, amongst others, the Canadian Bar Association in a report issued in September, 1989. In particular we feel that the following changes are important:

1. that Aboriginal communities have the opportunity to divert cases out of the conventional justice system; and

2. that Aboriginal communities and organizations be encouraged and supported in the establishment of separate correctional and after care facilities with specific focus on appropriate treatment, bearing in mind cultural and social norms of the Aboriginal offender; and

3. that the provision for appropriate spiritual, religious and traditional activities be made for Aboriginal offenders and that planning for this take place both in the separate system and in the traditional system.

Additionally we suggest, especially for remote and other predominantly or exclusively Aboriginal communities, that police functions be turned over to Aboriginal agencies which can be more responsive to the needs of the citizens. It is felt, based upon the current situation in the limited operation of the Dakota Ojibway Tribal Police and the Navaho Police, that this is a crucial next step. The comments of Police specialists before the Aboriginal Justice Inquiry in 1989 that racism among City of Winnipeg Police officers is in fact increasing are a startling revelation and suggest that separate police forces, where practical, would be an appropriate measure.

Similarly we recommend that for others within the system (such as police officers in traditional forces, judges, lawyers, clerks, jail guards, probation officers, and all others), a substantial course be provided in the area of Aboriginal cultural awareness. It is crucial that all players in the system at least begin to understand the Aboriginal societies and values in order to comprehend the characteristics of Aboriginal offenders, victims, and witnesses. In addition, Aboriginal witnesses and victims will be, we suggest, better treated. A greater understanding of Aboriginal peoples will, we suggest, decrease the inclination of justice personnel to devalue these "faceless people".

As well, we recommend that advocates for Aboriginal people be available at the earliest opportunity, and in particular that the functions of court communicators and other like agents be committed to ensuring that Aboriginal people involved with the justice system receive appropriate and fair treatment. In particular, we suggest that there is a need for persons involved in the system to be held accountable. A knowledgeable and paid advocacy service for ensuring that Aboriginal people are treated appropriately should thus be established. It is noteworthy, as well, that the Manitoba Law Enforcement Review Agency has not had a substantial overhaul since its inception some four years ago. We suggest that it has proven to be a dismal failure and that substantial changes be made to the system to allow for the better resolution of complaints against police officers with respect to treatment that is not of a suitable standard.

Additionally we suggest that substantial law be amended to provide for a criminal, or a quasi-criminal, offence for persons either advancing or acquiescing in the advancement of racially motivated statements or actions within the justice system. In particular we suggest that comments such as those noted above in the Ross case should be the subject of disciplinary action through either criminal or quasi-criminal action.

Perhaps most importantly we suggest that the number of Aboriginal people employed in this system must begin to approximate the numbers of persons who are Aboriginal within the general population. To this end we suggest that Aboriginal people be hired on a priority basis at all levels of the justice system to increase sensitivity in the criminal justice system. We suggest, as well, that in hiring Aboriginal persons there be substantial supports provided for those Aboriginal persons. It has been a some-time practice that Aboriginal persons, once hired, tend to become a part of the current system. This would, we suggest, not alleviate the problems identified in this paper but would in fact increase them. If this is the case, then we suggest that support systems which would allow Aboriginal workers to maintain their role within the system, but not sublimate their own culture, would be an appropriate adjunct to increased hirings.

We suggest that the whole issue of removal of persons from communities needs to be reviewed. A study of the location and existence of programs should be made a priority. We suggest that no new incarceration facilities be constructed but that instead we begin the process of spending dollars on community based alternative programs. These programs would begin to attack the cycle of devalued people and would begin to alleviate some of those concerns.

Tied to this, but not reasonable to study because of the length of the subject matter, would be increased economic opportunities for Aboriginal peoples, particularly in their home communities. This has long been a problem and was advocated as long ago as 1972 by the Manitoba Métis Federation Inc. and the Manitoba Indian Brotherhood. We submit that tying intervention in the current pattern of devaluation to increased economic opportunity is the only reasonable approach to beginning to break the cycle of problems that have been identified within this paper.

We suggest further that if the preceding recommendations, or some reasonable facsimile of same, are not implemented in due course the chronic problem of devaluation within our system will become in fact terminal. We suggest further that modern society can still learn from traditional systems and we note that in the 19th century the Métis, particularly, maintained social control by the mildest of means. In fact, some commentators have remarked that the current system was far less enlightened than that system and certainly the present results, as the statistics set out herein demonstrate, are far more tragic to Aboriginal people in general.

The system can be changed only through a genuine commitment to change which addresses the need for the Aboriginal control and operation of Aboriginal social control and correctional systems. An existing correctional service with the three strikes of massive discrimination and racism, almost wilful ignorance of Aboriginal people, cultures and communities, and a refusal to address systemic problems—such as cross-cultural recognition and major shortcomings in the staffing arena—clearly cannot cope with the present situation. What, then, will happen in the future, if the present trend of increasing overrepresentation of Aboriginal people continues?

NOTES

1. The Canadian Journal of Native Studies IX, 1 (1989):121-150. Reprinted with permission.

2. The opinions expressed herein are those of the authors, and do not necessarily represent those of their employers.

3.   Portions of this paper were first researched and presented as the Manitoba Métis Federation Justice Committee submission to the Aboriginal Justice Inquiry. The original MMF research and report was supported in part by funding from the Government of Manitoba. Copies of those reports can be obtained by writing to W. Yvon Dumont, President, Manitoba Métis Federation Inc., 408 McGregor Street, Winnipeg, Manitoba, R2W 4X5.

4.   The senior author acknowledges personal communications with David Wetherow (Association for Community Living: Winnipeg) and Dr. John O'Brien (Responsive Systems Associates: Atlanta, Georgia), as well as the workshops and written work of Dr. Wolf Wolfenberger, for the concepts which form the basis for the discussion of devalued people.

5.   *Re F v the Queen et al.* (1984), 14 Canadian Criminal Cases (3d) 161 (Man. Q. B.).

6.   *C. F. v R* (1984), 2 Western Weekly Reports 379 (Man. C. A.).

THE CURRENT STATUS OF METIS PEOPLE IN THE FEDERAL CORRECTIONAL SYSTEM

Lawrence J. Barkwell
Lyle N. Longclaws

Aboriginal people comprise 2.5 per cent of Canada's population but are represented at three and one-half times that rate in Canada's prisons.[1] The Ministry of the Solicitor General of Canada has stated many times that even this figure is an under-estimate of the Aboriginal incarceration rate. There are a number of reasons for this: the estimates are based upon self-identification and many non-status and Métis individuals are reluctant to declare Aboriginal roots upon admission for fear of encountering prejudice and/or because of a sociological identification trauma. In addition, the Ministry has noted some inaccuracy in data collection.

Aboriginal prisoners fill nine per cent of the cells nationally, but make up over one-third of the prison population in the prairie region (see Table I).

TABLE 1: PROFILE OF FEDERAL ABORIGINAL OFFENDERS
Solicitor General of Canada Task Force (1990)

Region (Men)	Total Inmates	Aboriginal Inmates		Indian	Métis (% Total Aboriginal)	Inuit
Prairies	2379	730	(36.1%)	64.9%	30.8%	4.1%
Pacific	1818	246	(13.3%)	84.1%	15.4%	0.4%
Ontario	3736	147	(3.8%)	93.1%	6.2%	0.6%
Atlantic	1039	34	(3.0%)	79.4%	5.8%	14.7%
Quebec	3887	35	(0.7%)	68.5%	14.2%	17.1%
(Women)						
Canada	154	16	(14.2%)	75.0%	25.0%	0.0%

All figures are from Correctional Services Canada December 31, 1990 Profile Report

As outlined, the trend for Aboriginal people is towards even greater over-representation rather than less. The number and proportion of Aboriginal prisoners being admitted is rising. As well, Aboriginal offenders tend to serve more of their sentence inside prisons; they are less likely to receive day parole, full parole, or half-way house placement. The facts delineated in a 1989 task force report on Aboriginal people in the federal correctional system are as follows:

1. The total number of male inmates serving federal sentences fell 1.3% between 1985 and 1987, but the Aboriginal inmate population grew by 3.5%.[2]

2. In the prairie provinces Aboriginal inmates make up 32.7% of the federal prison population.

3. Only 8.1% of Aboriginal inmates are in minimum security facilities compared to 15.6% of non-Aboriginal inmates.

4. As of December 31, 1987, 74.1% of the male Aboriginal inmates in Canada were Indian, 23.3% were Métis and 2.4% were Inuit. On the prairies, the figures were 69.3% Indian, 28.7% Métis and 1.9% Inuit.

5. Aboriginal women made up 14.2% of the 164 women in federal prisons. This was a decrease of 4% over the last survey in 1982-83. Currently, Indians comprise 75% and Métis another 25% of the Aboriginal women in prison. Provincial governments across Canada report an increase in the proportion of Aboriginal women in provincial jails, from 18.2% in 1982-83 to 25.3% at the end of 1987. Officials in both the federal and provincial correctional systems feel that these numbers for both men and women are underestimates.[3] It is clear that the over-representation recognized in the provincial correctional systems is repeated in the federal correctional system, although the full extent of this overrepresentation is not yet known.

6. Aboriginal inmates in federal institutions tend to come from smaller communities than non-Aboriginal prisoners; 20.4% of Aboriginal inmates were born in communities of over 10,000 population, and 36% were born in communities of between 100 and 10,000 population; 28.5% were born in communities less than 25 kilometers from a centre of more than 100 people. A further 15.3% were born in isolated rural communities. Clearly these inmates have their origins in smaller and more isolated communities.

7. Transition to urban centres is a complicating factor. At the time of admission to prison, 67.2% of Aboriginal offenders lived in centres of over 10,000 population, although only 20.4% were born in communities of this size.

8. Aboriginal offenders are less likely to be released on parole. In 1986-87, 79.5% of the Aboriginal applicants were denied full parole versus 62% for non-Aboriginal applicants. This represents an increase of 5.1% in denials to Aboriginal applicants over the prior year. It is worth noting that the Parole Board does not actually interview provincial prisoners who apply for parole. Thus, these inmates have no opportunity to counter any negative appraisal forwarded by the Parole Officer.

   The reasons for the bias against the Aboriginal parole applicant have been known for many years.

   In an extensive study of parole decision making Demers (1978) found statistically significant bias in the process.

   > Although race exerts no direct impact on (parole) board decision in the selection process indians (sic) and metis (sic) candidates are less likely to receive favourable officer recommendations than their white counterparts. In fact the analysis indicates that parole officers differentiate between racial groups in selecting and weighing information when formulating paorle evaluations. Thus it would appear that officer assessment can indirectly produce racial inequalites with reference to parole selection (Ibid.: 206-207).

9. Aboriginal offenders are less likely than other federal inmates to be released on parole instead of mandatory supervision. During 1987, only 18.3% of Aboriginal prisoners were granted release on full parole, compared with the 42.1% of non-Aboriginal offenders granted release on full parole. The cumulative effect of this practice is that as of May 1988, only 10.2% of Aboriginal offenders were serving their sentence on full parole, compared with 23.9% of non-Aboriginal offenders.

10. A 1980-83 study found that while 16% of Caucasian offenders were released from prison after serving 36% or less of their sentence, this was true for only 4% of Aboriginal applicants over the prior year.

   Two other factors operate to increase the number and proportion of Aboriginal inmates in the federal correctional system. Although the Correctional Service Task Force Report did not collect data on these two factors, waivers and "gating", our research indicates that they are significant elements in maintaining the over-representation of Aboriginal people in the inmate population. These two practices can be considered systemic in the sense that they represent common practice in the treatment of Aboriginal offenders, and relatively uncommon practice for non-Aboriginal offenders. They are thus sociologically systemic factors which discriminate largely against Aboriginal inmates.

11. If an inmate waives the right to a Parole Board hearing the Board is not obligated to study the case. They may, however, review the file material without meeting the inmate. If parole is then denied on the basis of a file review alone, re-application can only be made after six months. It may then take a further four months to get a hearing. Evidence was presented to the 1989 Task Force on Aboriginal peoples in Federal Corrections that many staff, and Aboriginal inmates in particular, do not understand the waiver process. Further, many Aboriginal prisoners say that case management officers either openly or subtly encourage them to waive the right to parole hearings. We understand that waivers by Aboriginal inmates occur at a much higher rate than for inmates in general although no specific figures are available. Thus, either lack of understanding or case management influence may be artificially suppressing Aboriginal parole applications and thus reducing the number of Aboriginal applicants. The ultimate result would be a lower number and proportion of Aboriginal inmates released on parole.

12. "Gating" is the practice of detaining prisoners due for release on mandatory parole based upon internal assessments of risk and dangerousness. While the federal practice was thought to be illegal given recent court decisions, we understand from interviews that the practice is still in effect (although now the affected individuals are called "detainees"). Our research reveals that over 60% of those in the prairie region due for release on mandatory supervision in the community but "detained", are Aboriginal inmates.

13. Correctional Service of Canada officials indicate the cost per inmate in the federal prison system is $48,000 per year. Staff to inmate ratio is one-to-one. The estimated expenditure for assisting parolees in the community is $1,000 per offender per year. Staff to offender ratios are in the vicinity of one to forty.

> How is rehabilitation and reintegration to be effective when most of the budget goes to lock-ups and so little is expended in the real world where risk to the community is highest and offender assistance would be most meaningful?

There are also some institutional systemic barriers to release for Aboriginal federal inmates. When an inmate submits a request for a parole, a community assessment is conducted. The parole officer will then interview family, friends, potential employers, or other members of the community to determine community support for the inmate. In practice, Métis community leaders are seldom, if ever, contacted.

> Police play an integral role in the decision making process. Officers are regularly required to undertake community assessments, especially in rural and isolated communities, and inform the National Parole Board about the community's acceptance of released inmates (Solicitor General, 1989:34).

The task force goes on to state that:

> Many of those consulted did not favour police involvement in pre-release community assessments. On the one hand, the majority of Aboriginal inmates expressed the strong belief that they could not get a fair assessment by the police... on the other hand, police often feel pressured by community leaders and the victim's family to write negative assessments. (Ibid.: 42)

A recent Manitoba Métis Federation (MMF) survey of selected Métis communities (Hourie, 1989) revealed no formal contact with Métis community councils in this regard. In fact, she could not document any approach by federal correctional officials to these councils, although the members did report extensive involvement in provincial correctional activities, and a willingness to become more involved. This information was recently confirmed (Barkwell, 1989) by polling the representatives of Manitoba Métis Federation locals at the Manitoba Métis Federation Annual Assembly in November of 1989.

A Manitoba Métis Federation vice-president confirmed that he could not recall one contact for community assessment in his fifteen years on a local council. The executive director of the Native Clan Organization, an Aboriginal service group active in the corrections field, reported that the same practice was true for reserves. Chiefs and Councils are seldom, if ever, contacted for community assessments. Further he indicated his belief that the police investigators normally put forward only their own opinions.

Another difficulty in the area of community re-integration is the inability of inmates to maintain contact with family and friends while in prison. The Stony Mountain Prison in Manitoba is somewhat isolated and is not located near public transportation. The only means many families had to visit their relatives was through a bus service provided by the Native Clan Organization. In 1990, they have had to discontinue this service due to a lack of funding.

Another systemic barrier to the release of Aboriginal inmates is a requirement that persons convicted of certain offences be screened for early release through psychological tests and assessments. To our knowledge, confirmed by a review of the standard manuals for tests and measurements (Burros), there are no psychological tests which have been normed for the Canadian Aboriginal population. This is compounded by the fact that psychologists conducting these tests are not required to have any particular cross-culture training with regard to Aboriginal people. The Task Force Report notes that the Ministry of the Solicitor General has no policies in place in this regard.

Native awareness training is provided at most institutions with substantial Aboriginal populations. However, systematic updating is not done and the allocation of fiscal resources through program agreements with the Aboriginal agencies who provide this training have remained static and at a minimal level.

The same lack of sensitivity and effort is noted with regard to citizen advisory committees. The Task Force found that despite the directive of the Commissioner of the Correctional Service of Canada Advisory Committees, the number of Aboriginal persons on these committees did not reflect the ethnicity of the prison population.

This lack of sensitivity permeates the system. The Task Force noted that because of security rules medicine and pipe bundles are often handled in a manner which is seen as desecration by Elders. They also note that, "despite the Commissioner's Directive on Native Offender Programs, Elders are sometimes not permitted into segregation or dissociation areas" (Correctional Service of Canada, 1989:52). Requests for the establishment of a Council of Elders and Spiritual Advisors have gone unmet in Manitoba. Correctional officials indicate this is due to budget restraint and priority.

The Correctional Service of Canada Task Force on Aboriginal People in Federal Corrections (1989) reported that:

> The practice of allowing traditional elders to perform spiritual services for Aboriginal inmates began in 1972 at Drumheller Institution. The practice has expanded across the country in varying degrees and has been supported by national policy since 1985. It is clear that the opportunity to engage in traditional spirituality has been seized enthusiastically by Aboriginal and some non-Aboriginal inmates. The practice of traditional spirituality includes solitary

pursuit as well as group ceremonies which must be led by a qualified practitioner.

The process of obtaining the right to practice traditional spirituality was not so easily or co-operatively acceded to as the federal government would have us believe.

Bill McKay,[4] a 38-year-old Treaty Indian from the Fisher River Band recounts the difficulties in having sweetgrass allowed in the federal penitentiaries.

Several years ago while I was an inmate in a federal prison (1982) I was charged, tried and convicted for possession of contraband, the contraband being several small particles of sweetgrass. During a routine cell search, prison guards found and confiscated the sweetgrass, even after I explained its purpose and role in the native religion. I was placed in solitary confinement and kept there for some time. I contacted a lawyer and after some inquiries and research the lawyer filed a notice of intent (court action) citing a section under the Canadian Bill of Rights, and later under the Charter of Rights and Freedoms, dealing with religious freedom. While that was in progress, I wrote letters to various Members of Parliament and the Chief Commissioner of the Canadian Human Rights Commission. The Human Rights Commission then took on the case.

In September of 1985 the case was settled at the Human Rights level. This involved the Canadian Human Rights Commission, the Correctional Service of Canada and myself signing agreements. It was agreed that the right to practise Native Religion would be extended to all Native inmates within all federal prisons Canada wide, and given equal recognition as that given to other religions. A letter of apology was drafted and sent from officials in Ottawa, apologizing for the wrongs committed against Native inmates by Corrections Canada officials.

Since that time, it is the authors' observation that when attending Stony Mountain (Federal) Institution to meet with the Native Brotherhood for traditional ceremonies, the guards allow entry without having to open medicine bundles or Medewewin bags. However, we have heard complaints that the sacred possessions of the inmates are not always handled with the same respect. The sweat lodge is not located in a place that affords privacy, and Aboriginal inmates are sometimes subjected to derision by staff and non-Aboriginal inmates regarding religious practices. While an Indian elder was briefly on contract at this institution during 1990, there has never been a similar contract for a Métis Elder and term funding to the Native Clan Organization for Elder services has now expired.

It is our observation that the Ministry of the Solicitor General sets meager targets for affirmative action in staffing. For the Correctional Service of Canada the target figure for Aboriginal staff is 1% and for the National Parole Board the target is 2% by 1991. We believe that these targets should have been set to reflect the racial mix of inmates (9%), or at a minimum the level of the Aboriginal population of Canada (2.5%). In this regard it is apparent that the federal government is not willing to hold its own correctional service to the same affirmative action targets that it applied to private corporations contracting with the government. The Task Force Report has a weak analysis as to the reasons for the lack of Aboriginal staff. They feel that there is a "we-they" dynamic in operation that deters people from applying. That is, Aboriginal individuals who might take jobs, or who do take jobs, are torn between the expectations of their correctional colleagues and the expectations of Aboriginal offenders. They also note that Aboriginal staff often resign early in their careers because there are few support mechanisms to deal with stress. In their analysis they deem that there are four types of potential Aboriginal employees:

a)   traditional persons;

b)   persons in transition from traditional life;

c)   bi-cultural persons; and

d)   assimilated Aboriginal individuals.

They then conclude that: "Aboriginal people considered bi-cultural are best suited for employment and should thus be the group targeted for recruitment by CSC" (Ibid:39). The task force discussion ignores the Métis. Interestingly, by this definition a Métis person would probably be the preferred employee!

This proposition seems preposterous and racist. First, how would one ever test out this thesis? Second, there are no similar or parallel criteria for non-Aboriginal persons, although it would certainly be helpful if they were required to have some cross-cultural awareness. Third, one can only imagine the hue and cry that would arise if the same test were applied to francophones in Canada and only those deemed "bi-cultural" and not traditional or assimilated were seen as fit for employment.

We suggest that there are two major reasons for the unwillingness of Aboriginal people to seek employment with the Correctional Service of Canada. The first is the systemic discrimination and racism which permeates this large institution. A second factor is one which is often neglected. The only entry point to the system is as a line level correctional officer or line level parole officer (if one ignores the few Native Offender program positions). Because many Aboriginal people gain their program and work experience elsewhere, who among them would give up such work to start at the bottom within the Correctional Service of Canada? In addition, because all hiring boards for management positions are by internal competition, working with this paradigm means that there will be few if any Aboriginal persons within the management hierarchy. The lack of Aboriginal women within the management ranks is particularly acute.

It is the understanding of the authors that the Correctional Service of Canada contracts for treatment services to parolees but does not provide these directly. In Manitoba, the only contract with Aboriginal groups is with the Native Clan Organization, but referrals are also made to the Native Alcoholism Council on a non-payment basis. In terms of cultural awareness programming we understand that the Native Clan program has now been supplanted by one that is run in-house by the person in the Native liaison position. Thus while an Aboriginal person has been added to government staff it has essentially not added to the available programming.

The Correctional Service of Canada Task Force on Aboriginal People in Federal Corrections did not consult with the Manitoba Métis Federation or any other Métis organization in Manitoba. We believe that this omission only serves to underline the fact that Métis issues are substantially overlooked within the correctional system. We are told that it was the initial decision of the Task Force to deal only with direct service providers because of logistics and time constraints. We would suggest that to talk only to groups who are dependent upon the federal government for their existence is unlikely to produce the most critical of analyses. Neither is this methodology likely to produce a lot of innovation.

Conclusions

As we have noted a disproportionate number of Indian and Métis are sentenced to federal prisons and once there, the procedures set up for release into the community while perhaps relevant for the mainstream institutional population seem to mitigate against the release of Aboriginal inmates.

1. Aboriginal inmates do not understand the parole process and have a higher rate of waiving their right to apply for parole.

2. Many come from small rural communities or are in transition to large urban areas. Our observation is that these inmates are in the most need of service, are under the most stress, yet have the least assets and community supports. Due to the lack of supports from their home communities and the complicated

logistics of administering such supports there is no substantial Aboriginal involvement in reintegration to the community. The Native Clan Organization involvement (in Manitoba), a program which is woefully under-funded, is only Winnipeg based, and has had to make service cutbacks within the past year.

3. The operation of an itinerant Parole Board based in Saskatoon has been criticized by many Métis people. This Board has to review both federal and provincial files. The process is inadequate as they arrive in Manitoba, complete the review in several days and quickly move on to the next location. They live out of a suitcase so that board members lose touch with the communities which they are expected to serve.

4. The Correctional Service of Canada officials we interviewed estimate that the expenditure per incarcerated federal inmate is $48,000 per annum, and the staffing ratio at these institutions is one-to-one. Contrast this with the forty-to-one caseloads in the community and the expenditure of about $1,000 per annum on community supervision and support. How is reintegration and rehabilitation to be successful with maximum expenditure on lock-ups and minimum expenditure on supports in the real world?

5. We have documented the fact that there is little contact with the Aboriginal community in the preparation of community investigations for release on parole. Neither are assessments conducted from an appropriate knowledge of Aboriginal culture. The McCaskill (1970:36) review of classification reports characterized these documents as "negative" personality assessments which revealed racist stereotyping of Aboriginal inmates. The majority of the reports defined Aboriginal personality as "immature, dependent, submissive, apathetic or primitive. It is obvious that (these) assessments reflect more the alien interview situation than the individual's personality." McCaskill recommended that all staff who work with Aboriginal inmates be sent to university level cross-cultural training. This is still not done some twenty years later.

6. To date requests for the establishment of a Council of Elders and Spiritual Advisors have gone unmet at Stony Mountain Institution. Officials indicate that this is merely a matter of lack of financial resources. While compulsory weapons training is firmly in place Native awareness training is hit or miss and is neither systematic nor given in a regularly updated form.

Allocation of fiscal resources through program agreements with agencies such as the Native Clan Organization have remained static and at a minimal level that accounts neither for workload increases nor inflationary cost increases.

7. It is obvious to all that the Correctional Service of Canada is not willing to hold itself to the same affirmative action targets that it sets for corporations contracting with the federal government. Perhaps the money spent in prosecuting these firms for failing to meet targets would be better spent improving their own affirmative action program.

8. In an attempt to counteract some of the negative factors noted above, Aboriginal agencies such as the Native Clan Organization in Manitoba and the Native Counselling Services of Alberta have been active in the delivery of parole supervision and half-way house services for many years. Their experience has shown that Aboriginal offender success rates can be increased. Currently as many as 78% of Aboriginal offenders under Aboriginal parole supervision complete their paroles successfully. This compares to the recidivism rates ranging from 70% to 80% (for 20-30% success rates) documented in 1969-70.

9. The effects of imprisoning Aboriginal women at Kingston Prison for Women are of particular concern to all Aboriginal groups. At a Prairie Justice Research Consultation (March 1990) in Prince Albert Saskatchewan, Adelle Ratt from the Iskwew Project documented the tragic suicides of three young Aboriginal women who had been incarcerated at Kingston. She attributed these deaths to the isolation from family and friends, the lack of community resources and the insensitivity of the prison system.

There have been two subsequent suicides by Aboriginal women at Kingston Prison for Women. The first was reviewed by a coroner's jury. "The jury criticized what it called systemic racism against natives of the facility."[5] The jury recommended that guards take courses in suicide awareness and Aboriginal culture (about one-quarter of the prison's inmates are Aboriginal). Last year the federal government announced plans to close this prison in 1994 and move the women to regional facilities.

Joan Lavallee, a Saskatchewan native activist and member of the government task force (which recommended the closing) said 'there seems to be a gross negligence about what's happening'. [6]

NOTES

1. The figures contained within this section are obtained from the Correctional Service of Canada, "Task Force on Aboriginal Peoples in Federal Corrections" (1989), clarification was obtained through discussion with Millard Beane, Special Advisor, Native Offender Programs (CSC). The 1990 CSC, profile report was used for Table 1.

2. Sentences of two years or more are considered federal sentences, and are normally served in the federal correctional system.

3. Interview with Curtis Fontaine, September 29, 1989.

4. Authors' interview with Bill McKay July 31, 1990 and written communications. Tragically, Bill McKay was killed in December, 1990.

5. Canadian Press, "Probe of women's prison demanded after suicide." Winnipeg Free Press, Feb. 9, 1991.

6. Ibid.

STATUS OF METIS CHILDREN WITHIN THE CHILD WELFARE SYSTEM[1]

Lawrence J. Barkwell
Lyle N. Longclaws
David N. Chartrand

In a national briefing paper prepared by the Métis National Council (1989), the position was taken that with few exceptions, the provincial child and family services and their supporting legislation are geared to urban areas and to values and concepts originally derived from Europe. Further, these services are delivered by staff who have little sensitivity to Métis culture or values. Neither are there observed plans on the part of the mainstream system to change this situation.[2]

The result is that a disproportionate number of Métis children are being taken into care, many for no reason other than the real-life Métis situation of living in poverty and overcrowded conditions. In effect, Métis children are frequently being alienated from their families, their communities and their culture for economic reasons. Such children often are condemned to a succession of foster homes, thus creating a terrible instability in their lives which defeats the reasons for taking them into care in the first instance (Manitoba Métis Federation, Inc., 1989).

Poverty has never been an acceptable reason for depriving children of their natural parents and their place in the extended family. The fact that the practice is so prevalent in Métis communities suggests the degree to which the Métis are a devalued people as well as the degree to which provincial family and child welfare institutions and Métis society are alienated from each other. Perhaps more importantly this type of intervention has tragic consequences for these Métis children, consequences illustrated by documented high rates of adoption breakdown, and suicide, as well as by high rates of juvenile delinquency (Barkwell et al, 1989).

The provinces so far have not taken any large scale measures to adapt their family and child welfare services to Métis needs. It was the judgement of the Métis National Council (Ibid.) that this was unlikely to occur, judging from past experience, without aggressive action on the part of the federal government. Provincial authorities, in the past, have tended to adopt the view that the very large numbers of Métis children coming into care are a result of inherent defects in Métis families, and not the outcome of serious shortcomings in their own operations.

In a 1989 submission to the Aboriginal Justice Inquiry in Manitoba, the Manitoba Métis Federation (MMF) developed an analysis which clearly demonstrated that of the many factors which interact to produce the over-representation of Métis people as offenders (with high reinvolvement rates), the single most highly weighted root factor was the treatment of Métis children within the child and family service system. In addition, all of the factors noted above interacted to make Métis people more susceptible to victimization.

The operant conditions for the perpetuation of this cycle are as follows:

1. There has been an historical repression of Métis customs, social structures and support systems.

2. The Métis have little discretionary time or money available to respond as a community to the problems of child welfare and crime.

3. Official responses to social problems within the Métis community are usually framed in terms of social control rather than social development.

4. Aboriginal people as a visible minority have been denigrated and their history has been conveyed in a distorted way. This leads to self-derogation, feelings of helplessness and alienation in young people.

5. The intended child welfare remedies have not worked for Métis children.

6. Official justice system interventions have been culturally alien and/or irrelevant and poorly understood by the Métis community.

7. Participation in lawmaking and the administration of laws, particularly family law, has been effectively denied to the Métis.

8. The official justice system has acted in ways which engender disrespect and cynicism within the Métis community.

9. In many instances child welfare, correctional and other related services have been denied or not made available to the Métis.

When a people are weakened by these factors which we view as additive as well as interactive, the symptoms of socially problematic behaviours are inevitably found to be in ascendancy.

It has been a long-held contention of Métis and other Aboriginal people that, due to the fact that they have no control over child and family services, and the fact that they are both poorly served and much devalued by the mainstream system, their children and youths are cast by default into the youth justice system.

This paper will review the over-representation of Métis children both in the child welfare system and the criminal justice system of Manitoba. It will also review how government policies and the implementation of those policies have exacerbated this over-representation. The authors will then show that this situation is founded upon a lack of concern for and awareness of Métis culture, and a consequent lack of community-based services for these people.

We have found compelling evidence that this is indeed what is happening. In the following section we will relate two instructive cases recently heard by the Manitoba Court of Appeal.

The Young Offender — Child Welfare System Link

The first case is the appeal application of a fourteen-year-old Métis youth against a one year sentence to secure custody by the Youth Court.[3] This youth was found guilty of four charges of break, enter and theft, one charge of possession of stolen goods, one charge of assault, and one charge of driving a motor vehicle without a licence. At point of disposition the youth was thirteen years old but three of the offences were committed when he was twelve. He had no prior record of offences. At disposition the Youth Court judge sentenced him to secure custody for one year on the break, enter and theft from a dwelling (the only charge on which he was eligible at his age for a custody sentence). He was also sentenced to two years of probation supervision following his release from custody, on each of the other charges.

The Appeal Court noted that, with respect to the most serious charges, other youths had also been charged as co-accused, but had received sentences of probation supervision.

The background information given to the Court of Appeal indicated that the youth came from a small rural town with a mixed population, Indian, Métis and non-Native. He lived as part of a single parent family. His mother, three siblings and four other relatives lived in the nine person household. His family described the youth as being beyond control. The local child and family service agency was active with the family but had not apprehended the young offender, despite the fact that he had been expelled from school. The school authorities described the lad as bad tempered, disrespectful, violent and defiant. The school had referred him to child and family services because of his behaviour and their concern over his intimidation of other students. The court was also told that the youth claimed to drink regularly and that he smoked marijuana when it was available. There was some indication that his associates left something to be desired and the lad himself admitted that disassociation from his friends was one way he could try to stay out of trouble.

The sentencing judge felt that the community and its institutions had not done enough, and that for the young offender's own welfare, he should not be allowed to remain in the environment within which his habits and attitude had developed. The sentencing judge had said:

> It's pathetic that the community could allow this to happen...I feel that we should nip whatever problem he has in the bud and get him the heck out of this community. If Child Welfare won't do it, the Court better do it....

Although the youth was under fourteen years of age and had no previous Criminal Code convictions, he was sentenced to a term of custody under the Young Offenders Act exception clause (Sec. 24 (4),a; "the offence is one for which an adult would be liable to life imprisonment").

Twaddle, J. A., speaking for the Court of Appeal, had this to say about the sentencing:

> Strictly the learned judge had authority for imposing this sentence, the lad having been found guilty of break, enter and theft in relation to a dwelling house for which an adult would have been liable to imprisonment for life... The learned judge did make reference to the protection of society and the seriousness of the offence. I do not suggest that society is not entitled to protection from burglary nor do I belittle the seriousness of the young person's participation in such a crime, but in comparison to the other offences of burglary this was amongst neither the most serious nor the most alarming. The judge took into account the totality of the lad's criminal behaviour, but that is not, in my view, the proper criterion in the case of a young person under the age of fourteen who has not been found guilty previously of a criminal offence. The judge also substituted secure custody for the care and control which the child

lacked and which the local child welfare agency had been tardy in providing.

The Court of Appeal then pointed out that even when the case first came before them for hearing there was still no plan proposed for the child's future care and control. They had then adjourned the hearing to give the boy's attorney the opportunity of presenting "....a plan which would offer guidance and assistance to the lad as well as provide for his care and control." This, they pointed out, was Counsel's duty. When the adjourned hearing resumed, the Appeal Court was advised that the child welfare authority was ready to apprehend and to take the steps necessary for the court's determination of his needs.

The Court then commented on the dilemma of "Hobson's choice" that had been offered to the sentencing judge: send the boy to custody or send him back to an inadequate home environment. It was clear to all that the youth required direction more than punishment, and help to find a purpose to his life "....rather than a mere temporary interruption of an existence without aim." Thus, the sentence to a term of secure custody had been clearly inappropriate:

> Where it is apparent that an accused young person is in need of protection, the child welfare authority should not wait until the court has sentenced the young person: such a delay prejudices the young person because there are then fewer acceptable options open to the court for dealing with the young person's conduct. The young person in such circumstances should be apprehended and proceedings for guardianship taken as soon as the need of protection can be identified and a youth court judge should adjourn proceedings, if necessary, to permit the child welfare agency to intervene. Although a sentence should reflect the young person's circumstances, it should not penalize him or her for want of a proper guardian.

Therefore, the Manitoba Court of Appeal reduced this youth's term of secure custody to time served, but directed that he comply with the terms of a probation order for two years.

Our second example is the case of a fifteen year old status Indian who was appealing his custody sentence, imposed upon conviction for setting fire to papers within two business premises. For these offenses he had been sentenced to eighteen months secure custody to be followed by six months open custody and one year probation supervision.[4]

The youth's background was described by the court as pitiful. He resided in a large urban centre as part of a seven person, single parent family. His father had been incarcerated for sexual assaults upon two of his siblings. Another sibling within the previous year had attempted suicide. The presentence investigation had revealed the youth himself had been the victim of physical abuse at home at the hands of parents who were described as having alcohol problems.

At the time of the offences the youth was attending, on an irregular basis, a special education program. He had been involved in altercations with other students and had previously been referred to probation services for setting a fire in his school. An assessment prepared for the Court by the forensic psychologist indicated that the youth was of borderline intelligence and had relationship difficulties. He was deemed to have poor judgement and comprehension and an inability to learn from experience. The forensic recommendation was for a lengthy period of secure custody to be followed by child welfare intervention "...since the need for child protection will continue."

In the words of the Court: "fortunately for the youth, he was referred by his counsel to Dr. Ellis, also a psychologist, who is on the faculty of the Department of Psychiatry of the University of Manitoba." Dr. Ellis noted that the youth seemed to have a lack of experience with anyone being interested in what he thought or felt. He exhibited concrete thinking and a lack of knowledge about relationships, feelings and normal family life expected of the average child. He did exhibit the capacity to learn and Dr. Ellis pointed out that he had been able to perform thirty hours of community work as a consequence for his referral on the previous fire setting. His response at that time had been described by the authorities as extremely positive.

Dr. Ellis noted that his delinquent career was of recent origin and coincided with a major family upheaval. Thus he assessed his current involvement as being reactive to major family stress. He commented "....it is no wonder that he did not perform well in a forensic assessment on a one shot basis with a stranger he did not know and experienced as potentially dangerous." He then concluded that, in view of the fact that the youth had never received treatment, he could not justify a term of custody which would deprive him of the appropriate treatment. Dr. Ellis also expressed the opinion that the child welfare authority had ignored the youth's plight both before and after his criminal involvement. They had been involved with his siblings due to the father's abusive behaviour, and thus knew of this lad's circumstances as well as his mother's inability to cope. After the youth was charged the court was informed that his attorney had contacted child welfare but was told that they did not wish to become involved until after he had been sentenced on the pending charges.

The Court of Appeal then ruled that in this case the sentencing judge had erred in imposing a custodial term totalling two years. They reduced the term of custody to six months with two years probation to follow. The

Court noted that the lower court disposition had obviously been influenced by the absence of a suitable guardian as well as the lack of a suitable plan for supervision and guidance. Undue weight had been given to protection of the public.

Twaddle, J. A. stated in the court's decision:

> There is, in my view, something wrong with a system that, in the case of a fourteen year old lad convicted of no heinous crime, with no previous findings of guilt on criminal charges against him and with this lad's disadvantaged background, confronts a judge with a choice between imposing a lengthy period of custody and returning him to oblivion....

> I am of the view that (the commission of these crimes) was a cry by the youth for help. The response of society should not be the imposition of a custodial term of two years....The protection of the public is a proper principle of sentencing young offenders, but the same public has a responsibility to prevent criminal conduct by young persons. It is not reasonable to ignore the special needs of a young person such as this lad....

These stories of a lack of needed child welfare services come from all parts of Canada. In an address to the Second National Métis Child Care Conference in 1988, Larry Desmeules, president of the Métis Association of Alberta, related the case of a Métis youth who had literally been cast out into the cold (Desmeules, 1988). This sixteen year old lad had been forced to wander the streets finding temporary shelter with friends and strangers. Although he was a permanent ward of Social Services, there was no permanency planning, for whenever he asked his social worker for help, he was referred to the Youth Emergency Shelter. In Desmeules' analysis:

> ...this young man didn't want just shelter. He wanted a home —a real home—and not just a room in an institution. He's been a ward of the government since he was two, and has been moved at least forty times between foster homes and institutions. Most recently, he lived with a youth worker who kicked him out after a disagreement. The longest he has lived in one place is one year. That is his tragic story as a temporary ward of the government for twelve years, and a permanent ward for the past two years. The system is failing this young man, and who knows how many others. Hopefully, he won't come to the tragic end of Richard Cardinal, who hanged himself at seventeen after a tragic life that included twenty-eight moves between foster homes and institutions.

Cardinal's death spurred creation of a new Child Welfare Act in Alberta that was to prevent further such tragedies. Obviously that isn't enough (Desmeules, 1988).

It is simply tragic that more often than not, Métis children have to come into conflict with the law before they are provided with any support services. The Manitoba Métis Federation child and family service workers have received scores of service requests from Métis families who have been denied service from the mainstream mandated agencies. Most often when they ask for help for a youngster who is behaviourally beyond their control, they are told, "He's not in enough trouble yet to justify our agency taking action." Then pathetically, mothers whose children are locked up on charges so serious that they cannot get them released on bail, are told that the child and family service agency wants to wait until the youth is sentenced before doing any planning.

From the stories and evidence as related above it might be surprising to learn that the over-representation of Métis youths committed to custody sentences by the youth courts (Table 1), mirrors the over-representation of Métis children brought into care by child and family services (Table 2). To us, the reason is quite evident. Simply put, preventive services are either not offered to Métis families, are offered only after problems have become severe, or are of such a weak intensity that the penetration into custody situations or removal from home is not averted.

TABLE 1: YOUTH ADMISSIONS TO CUSTODY
Manitoba 1984 - 1987

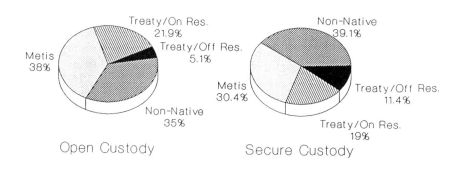

Open Custody   Secure Custody

120

TABLE 2: CHILDREN IN PLACEMENT: WARDS AND VOLUNTARY PLACEMENTS
Community Services Annual Report

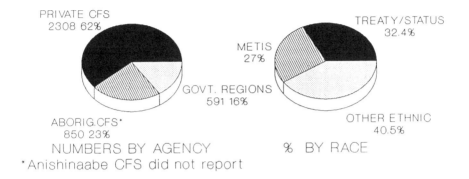

PRIVATE CFS
2308 62%

TREATY/STATUS
32.4%

METIS
27%

GOVT. REGIONS
591 16%

ABORIG.CFS*
850 23%

OTHER ETHNIC
40.5%

NUMBERS BY AGENCY   % BY RACE

*Anishinaabe CFS did not report

Critique of the Child Welfare System

It is our observation that those agencies mandated by the province of Manitoba to provide child and family services have done little to establish helping networks within the Métis community. First, their location is often distant from the people served and they usually provide only itinerant social work service delivered on a crisis basis. Second, preventive services such as parenting courses and teen treatment groups are seldom offered. Third, the intervention of these agencies is culturally alien and few workers speak the languages common to the Métis population. Thus the service offered (as with the youth justice system) is little more than physical removal of the child from the home community.

In a study of child and family services commissioned by the MMF, Ryant (1988) reported that although agencies were aware of the fact that services should reflect the cultural and linguistic heritage of the client there was an evident lack of priority given to this. The number of Aboriginal workers on staff—if any—is minimal in most of the mandated agencies, and "....the apparent lack of priority for Native awareness could imply a lack of cultural sensitivity when dealing with Métis families. This affects the effectiveness of service and could mean that more Métis children end up in care than necessary." He went on to note that if there were more focus on preventive and supportive services which are culturally appropriate there could be a significant reduction in the number of Métis children in care.

Ryant (1988) also found that there were many impediments (mostly financial) to alternate care being provided to Métis children within the Métis community. He recommended the following measures to rectify the situation:

1. A greater use of special needs foster care rates thus allowing more Métis families to provide foster care.

2. Implementation of Section 73 of the Child and Family Services Act, which deals with subsidized adoption. The use of subsidized adoption would assist Métis families who wish to adopt but cannot do so without financial assistance.

3. Section 5(1)(f) of the Social Allowances Act states that financial assistance may be made available to a child whose parents "are unable to contribute to his maintenance and who is wholly dependent on another person for his basic necessities." Too often, the income security workers ignore the fact that the child can be given the needs test for eligibility and they test the care-providers instead. Because the foster family is not in dire straits, aid to which the child would be entitled in his or her own right is withheld. A different implementation of 5(1)(f) would permit more Métis children to be cared for by relatives or neighbours.

4. Another impediment to many Métis homes being accepted for foster care may involve the standards set for approval of provincial foster homes. Physical requirements of space, availability of running water and material resources may not reflect the life circumstances of many Métis families and communities. Often, those who design these standards are not familiar with cultural and traditional values of Native groups. Standards may be both inappropriate and extremely difficult for many Métis homes to reach.

Under these policies and this method of service delivery it is estimated that, from the 1960s to the early 1980s, about 3,000 Aboriginal children were removed from their homes in Manitoba and exported out of the province for adoption. In most cases they were placed with urban non-Native families. "The Indian and Métis children were submerged in another culture, and their Native identity soon disappeared. They became a lost generation" (York, 1989:206). At the beginning of the 1980s from 40% to

60% of all children removed from their families in western Canada were Indian or Métis. For Canada as a whole, five Native children were removed from their families for every non-Native child placed. York states that in 1981 about 55% of Manitoba's adopted Aboriginal children were sent out of province while the rate for Caucasian children placed out of province was only 7%.

Indian and Métis communities had virtually no control over the children who were seized from their homes. Until 1976 there was not a single native-controlled child welfare agency in Manitoba. Decisions about the future of native children were made by white social workers and urban-based bureaucrats (York, 1989:207).

In 1981, the MMF acted on the available public information regarding the numbers of Métis children being exported to the United States and to other provinces to non-Native families. It had been learned that many of these children had experienced post-adoption breakdowns that were having a disastrous effect upon them. Others had become the victims of physical and sexual abuse. Therefore, the MMF lobbied successfully for the Government of Manitoba to institute a moratorium on out-of-province adoptions and out-of-province placements for "treatment". The MMF developed a rural and urban strategy for implementation to ensure increased Métis involvement in the child and family service jurisdiction.

In March of 1982 the government of Manitoba agreed to impose a moratorium on out-of-province placements of Aboriginal children. The province also established a Review Committee on Indian and Métis Adoptions and Placements headed by Associate Chief Family Court Judge Edwin Kimelman. After reviewing the file of every Native child who had been adopted by an out-of-province family in 1981, Judge Kimelman stated in the committee's 1984 File Review Report: "Having now completed the review of the files...the Chairman now states unequivocally that cultural genocide has been taking place in a systematic, routine manner" (Kimelman, 1984:51).

The statistics given by Judge Kimelman were even worse than the Métis people had suspected through anecdotal reports.

The Review Committee noted that 53% of the children placed outside of Manitoba were sent to the United States and 86% of the children placed out-of-province were of Native ancestry. Meanwhile, at the end of 1981, the departmental statistical bulletin indicated that there were 145 adoption homes in Manitoba which had been approved but were not in use and there were 1,377 adoption applications which were awaiting study for approval. Was it any wonder then that Aboriginal groups felt there was a racial bias in operation?

TABLE 3: STATISTICS OF MANITOBA CHILDREN PLACED OUT OF PROVINCE IN 1981

	Number Placed	% of Total
Registered Indians	52	48%
Indian (other)	4	4%
Métis	37	34%
Non-Native	15	14%
Totals	**108**	**100%**

Source: Kimelman, 1984:23

Judge Kimelman was of the opinion that the political and administrative acquiescence to these practices had served to delay the development of Aboriginal resources and specialized services to Aboriginal people. "Rather than providing the resources on reserves to build economic security and providing the services to support responsible parenting, society found it easier and cheaper to remove the children from their homes and apparently fill the market demand for children in Eastern Canada and the United States."(Ibid.)

He also noted that under the guise of providing children with a family of their own, children were not only separated from their parents, but were also separated from their siblings. The study also revealed that for the majority of older children who became wards, the chances of adoption were remote, and the reality for most of them was to be placed in a series of foster homes and institutions with the " ....real possibility of spending some of their adult years as residents of the province's correctional facilities." (Ibid.)

In 1982, the MMF established a Board committee, which was to be responsible for the operation of the Métis Child and Family Support Program. The MMF also submitted a position paper to the provincial government calling for local control over child and family services for Métis people.

The MMF immediately established local community-based Métis child and family service committees. The committees assumed responsibility for:

a) developing community awareness of needs of children;

b) assessing community needs and currently available resources;

c) developing resources and participating in training;

d) conjoint planning with social workers from mandated agencies, in order to reach decisions on child and family services issues respecting the community;

e) strengthening Métis families in the community;

f) reviewing and recommending changes to relevant legislated standards, policies and practices to more properly reflect the needs of Métis children, families and communities.

The MMF readily identified the following difficulties involved in the implementation phase of this specific mandate:

a) lack of an agreed-upon definition of Métis people;

b) lack of access to existing child and family services files;

c) provincial regulations regarding foster home standards and payment rates, which excluded potential Métis foster homes;

d) lack of knowledge of referral procedures within the mandated agencies;

e) lack of MMF resources to respond to the volume of referrals;

f) referrals so late in the process that effective plans could not be formulated in the time available.

The MMF began support service delivery under the terms of a negotiated bilateral agreement with the department of Community Services and Corrections. This funding enabled the MMF to employ a provincial coordinator to develop a model for local control of support services. The MMF contracted two additional family support worker positions and at the request of the Director of Child and Family Services, established pilot projects in the Dauphin and Thompson regions.

In 1984, the MMF signed the first memorandum of agreement commonly referred to as Policy Directive 18. A subsequent agreement was signed in 1985 regarding the MMF's role in the notification of the placement of Métis children outside of Métis homes.

Policy Directive 18

This directive to mandated child and family service agencies (those who are empowered to take guardianship), was issued by the Child and Family Support Directorate in 1984. The directive outlines the proper procedures to be used in notifying, reporting and placing Aboriginal children away from their natural parents.

The intent of this directive was to elicit the fullest possible participation of Aboriginal agencies. It is based on the principle that the best interests of the child are served when the child's cultural and linguistic heritage and life-style are taken into consideration.

Under Directive 18, when an agency becomes involved in the protection of a registered Indian child, it must inform the appropriate Aboriginal agency of all details of the case for purposes of identifying placement resources.

When the agency is in contact with an Aboriginal child who is not a registered Indian, it may ask if the family wishes to declare, and if so, to sign a self-declaration form. The mandated agency is then obliged to notify designated persons within the Aboriginal organizations which have entered into a legal agreement with the Director of Child Welfare. However, this does not hold for voluntary surrender of guardianship, and MMF is only notified in cases where the family has declared itself Métis.

Since 1987, the MMF has been funded with approximately $140,000 annually for these activities, whereas Indian agencies have been granted some $8 million yearly to deal with Indian child care matters. This financial limitation, and the fact that referral frequently occurs too late in the process to permit the MMF to be involved appropriately, has given the mandated agencies an image of the MMF as having a relatively minor role.

Since it is not clear how Métis citizens are being identified (workers frequently are not aware of self-declaration procedures), and because there are difficulties with the self-declaration practices themselves, referrals from mandated agencies to the MMF have been few or non-existent.

For example, over the last two years, there have only been forty-one referrals to the MMF regarding Métis children and families throughout the province of Manitoba (Moar, 1989). Incredibly, some agencies have not made even one referral.

Over the two-year time period the following referrals were received:

TABLE 4: REFERRALS TO MMF

Manitoba Community Services Regional Services		Private Mandated Child & Family Service Agencies	
Eastman	0	C&FS Central Manitoba	0
Interlake	0	C&FS Western Manitoba	14
Norman	2	C&FS Eastern Manitoba	3
Parklands	5	C&FS Winnipeg West	2
Thompson	2	C&FS Northeast Wpg.	2
		C&FS Winnipeg South	0
		C&FS Northwest Wpg.	11
		C&FS Central Wpg.	0
Total	**9**	**Total**	**32**

The mandated agencies have not moved with alacrity on this standard. It is obvious that Policy Directive 18 (and its replacement, known as Standard 421) are not meeting their intended purpose. It is estimated that of the 3,803 children in the care of mandated child and family service (C&FS) agencies, 1,027 are Métis children (27%), 1,235 are Indian children (32.5%), and 1,540 are of other ethnic backgrounds (40.5%) (Longclaws, 1989). Given the large disparity between the number of Métis children brought into care and the actual number of cases that are referred to the MMF, one has to doubt whether the government has any commitment to implement its own policy and standards.

An MMF survey of members (University of Manitoba Research Ltd., 1988) found that child and family services were a key concern for 90% of those surveyed. Eighty-three percent stated that they would like to see child welfare services provided by a Métis organization. Over 7% of the respondents indicated that they have a child under the age of eighteen placed away from home. Ten percent of the families indicated they were raising a child who was not one of their own. This is convincing evidence that the Métis community is carrying the bulk of the burden for child and family services without payment and out of its own resources through custom adoptions and placements with relatives. These matters are not being referred to the "official" agencies. Thus, Métis people are not receiving their fair share of government resources.

There are a number of reasons for reluctance to approach the mainstream system, one of which is indicated in a survey showing that 71% of Winnipeg Métis respondents feel that child welfare does not give enough consideration to Métis culture (University of Manitoba Research, 1988).

Another reason is the previously cited finding that potential Métis foster homes are often turned down because of a lack of material resources. Since this has become widely known, potential applicants are now reluctant to come forward.

In a study commissioned by the MMF (Ryant, 1988) it was revealed that:

a) Even with Directive 18, Native children are still being placed in non-Native foster homes because agencies, using existing resources, have not been able to develop a sufficient supply of Native foster homes.

b) There is an inappropriate concern with material standards in approving potential foster homes in the Indian and Métis communities.

c) There is unwillingness (or inability) on the part of agencies to authorize special foster rates where these would clearly be appropriate for Native placement.

d) There have been cases where the child caring agency has not made use of a placement resource which was referred by the designated group.

e) Oftentimes, notification of a Native child in care comes too late in the process for the designated resources to locate a culturally appropriate placement.

The deplorable situation described above has been made worse by changes to Directive 18. A section which clearly identified procedures with regard to non-status Indian and Métis families was removed. The current standard, Native Child Placement, Section 421 (Manitoba Community Services, 1984: 1-7) in the Child and Family Services Program Standards Manual, effectively buries the reference to Métis children.

It is the current assessment of MMF child and family services staff (Moar, 1989) that:

a) The majority of child and family services social workers in Manitoba are poorly informed or uninformed regarding Directive 18 and Program Standard 421. It seems the only persons who have a working knowledge of these are Native social workers and field staff.

b) People are asked to declare as Métis only if the workers "think they are Métis".

c) It was only with much badgering that MMF began receiving referrals.

d) When the MMF forwards names of Métis families wishing to foster or adopt, many are placed on waiting lists and many are never contacted for home assessment.

e) The MMF has not been able to lobby for more referrals due to lack of staff and budget.

f) The 1982 moratorium has resulted in fewer Métis placements outside the province, but has not reduced the number of Métis children placed outside the Métis community.

g) The MMF was effectively left out of negotiations on the development of Standard 421, and did not receive a satisfactory reply to its submitted negotiating document.

h) As the proportion of Métis children removed from their homes under the Child Welfare Act so closely approximates the proportion removed from their homes under the Young Offenders Act, there is strong evidence to support the MMF thesis that Métis people are subjected to a high degree of social control while social development needs have gone unmet.

Although the thrust of the Kimelman report, *No Quiet Place* (Kimelman, 1985), and the intent of subsequent child and family services revisions to placement and adoption standards, were to ensure that Indian and Métis children were either placed or adopted into culturally appropriate homes, our research reveals that there are still significant numbers of Aboriginal children being adopted into non-Native homes, a practice which Judge Kimelman had earlier denounced as "cultural genocide" (1984:51).

In the period between January, 1988 and October, 1989, 29.2% of registered Indian adoptees went into non-Aboriginal homes and 55.8% of Métis adoptees went into non-Aboriginal homes. Furthermore, 62% of all the Aboriginal children placed by way of adoption during this time period were Métis.[5]

TABLE 5: MANITOBA ADOPTIVE PLACEMENTS
January 1988 to October 1989

Registered Indians Adopted	24	
Placements		
1. Registered Indian Homes	15	(62.5%)
2. Other Native Homes	2	(8.3%)
3. Non-Native Homes	7	(29.2%)
Non-Status Indians Adopted	2	
Placements		
1. Non-Native Homes	2	(100.%)
Métis Adopted	43	
Placements		
1. Métis Homes	19	(44.2%)
2. Non-Native Homes	24	(55.8%)
Total Non-Native Placements	33	(47.8%)

Clem Chartier has argued that under the Canadian Charter of Rights and Freedoms (Part I of the Constitution Act, 1982), the practice of adoption of Métis children into non-Métis homes violates what should be a recognized group right in addition to the child's right to remain in the group "....based on the section 7 security of the person provision (of the Charter) particularly as it applies to cultural heritage. In the absence of this right, and in the face of the continuing removal of Métis children from the Métis community, Canada could be viewed by the international community as committing ethnocide, which is basically a form of cultural genocide" (1988:55).

An additional issue is the repatriation of Métis children who were adopted by families outside of Canada. The complex set of issues is outlined by Audreen Hourie (MMF Education Coordinator) in a 1989 submission to the Aboriginal Justice Inquiry.

> Public records may not indicate actual figures on numbers of Aboriginal children who are lost to their families but it is believed by the Aboriginal community to be many. These children are now attempting to return to their province of birth and the barriers they face are numerous. Many have reached the age of majority (eighteen years) and require established citizenship to receive service in the province of Manitoba.

> The province of Manitoba as represented by the Department of Community Services claims little or no responsibility to repatriate adults who were in their care or custody as children. Citizenship papers and birth certificates were confiscated on apprehension, new names given and a new identity forced upon the children....

> There were many cases during the Aboriginal Justice Inquiry of grievance relating to specific cases that would reflect abduction as opposed to apprehension, for example, one very young Métis boy crossing the USA border in a van filled with children, being taught their new names in preparation for border crossing.

> Too many times, Aboriginal people have attempted in vain to raise questions about missing children. One small survey in the Métis community of Camperville and surrounding area indicated that approximately fifty children were missing, no known whereabouts. Members of remote communities attending a meeting in Thompson where the subject arose "Where are the missing children?" led one very quiet mother to say, "They took my boy a long time ago, he would be fourteen years old now, they said they would send me a picture, they never did" (Hourie, 1989).

Conclusions

It is our assessment that there are a number of factors which account for the high number of Métis adoptions in comparison to the number of children at risk and these same factors account for the fact that over one-half of these adopted Métis children go into non-Native homes.

1. The Métis do not have an agency of their own mandated to provide adoption services.

2. The MMF Child and Family Service is not funded to provide province-wide preventive services.

3. Referrals to MMF Child and Family Services come infrequently or too late in the process to make a difference. Although adoptions account for only a small proportion of the Métis children removed from their families, over the last two years MMF received only 41 referrals under Standard 421, while provincial government figures show that there were at least 43 Métis children placed for adoption alone.

4. Section 54 of the Child and Family Services Act requires that the Provincial Director perform a regular review of all children in placement. We believe these reviews to be cursory 'paper checks' and in no case has MMF Child and Famiy Service ever been consulted.

These studies and material lead to the obvious conclusion that Métis children and families have not been served well by traditional child and family service agencies. In fact the consensus of Métis people is that they have received inadequate and inappropriate services. The feeling of the Métis community as a whole (at least as expressed by their elected officials on the Board of Directors of the MMF) is that this disparity in service is racially motivated. The MMF applied for recognition and funding of a child and family services agency that would lead to a full mandate to deliver these services to Métis people. They have received no positive response to date.

NOTES

1. The Canadian Journal of Native Studies IX, 1 (1989: 33-35). Copyright 1990, Canadian Journal of Native Studies. Reprinted by permission.
2. The opinions expressed herein are those of the authors and do not necessarily represent those of their employers.
3. J. M. v. R., Manitoba Court of Appeal, October 2, 1986 (unreported).

4. A. L. v. R., Manitoba Court of Appeal, October 3, 1986 (unreported).

5. These figures and those contained in Table 5 were obtained through interviews with departmental officials of Child and Family Services.

THE STRUGGLE FOR METIS RECOGNITION: EDUCATION AND SURVIVAL

Audreen Hourie

The history of the struggle of the Métis towards self-determination in education is not easily understood unless one considers the cultural concept of caring and sharing that is so deeply ingrained in the Métis community. All too often the Métis suffer gross injustices at the hands of others, now as they did so often in the past, yet this cultural trait survives as vibrantly as do the Métis people who continue the struggle.

Canada, as we know it today, has an education policy that is deeply entrenched in land, taxation and citizenship. This policy is foreign and alien to the Métis concept of caring and sharing.

EDUCATION AND THE METIS

In the context of Canadian education policy, the consequences of the Métis resistance in 1870 were far reaching in their effects. Deprived of their land through militant action by the early non-Aboriginal governments and land hungry speculators of Canada, the Métis were left defenseless and unable to maintain a lasting share in the new order, including anything close to their fair share of the extensive government services that developed. This pattern still exists today, in 1990, and will continue until such time as justice prevails, when the Métis are recognized and a just land settlement is concluded.

The treatment of the Métis people by the Canadian Government since 1870 can best be measured by the present condition of Métis people generally and young Métis people in particular. The Manitoba Métis Federation Inc. Socio-economic Survey (1988) captures a realistic picture of the oppressive conditions which the Métis people of Manitoba endure:

- 54% of the respondents indicated that their total family income was under $20,000;
- 60% of all respondents indicated that for some period in the last two years they had been unemployed;
- 80% of Métis respondents had no high school diploma;
- only 6% of respondents were 65 years of age or over.

It is clearly youth who suffer most from the economic annihilation inflicted upon the Métis by Canada:

- 60% of household members surveyed were under twenty years of age, whereas in Manitoba as a whole, 30% of household members are under twenty years of age;
- 2/3 of respondents aged from eighteen to twenty-four were out of school; of those youth not in school full time, only 22% were employed full time. Almost 2/3 of those between the ages of eighteen and twenty-four were not employed at all;
- of those youth between the ages of eighteen and twenty-four, only 2% are in, or have completed university. One might expect them to be the most highly-educated of all Métis people, but while they are generally better off educationally than most respondents, they fall dramatically behind the Manitoba population as a whole in post-secondary training.
- although 36% of youth aged eighteen to twenty-four have completed Grade XII, relatively few have the academic skills required to proceed directly into post-secondary training.

It can be said that the strength of any nation depends upon how well it serves its young people and how well they are educated. Canada has done a great injustice to Métis youth in this regard.

THE LONGBODY CREEK METIS

The dependence of Canadians upon land and property rights for economic well-being, and how this affects the education system, can best be seen through a specific example, the move of a group of Métis people from an Indian reserve to a new community.

On April 24, 1986, the Métis living on the Bloodvein Indian Reserve were notified by the Chief and Council that they had to vacate their homes and leave the Reserve within six months. The reasons given were twofold: first, that the Band had not been given any additional land (presumably by the Province) to compensate them for the land occupied by the Métis on the Reserve, and second, that all of the land on the Reserve was needed for the exclusive use of the "Treaty People".

Métis history is filled with examples of the Bloodvein situation. Land alienation, poverty and exodus from home lands is not new to the Métis people.

As early as the 1870s a small group of Métis were pre-empted from their land along what is now known as the Boyne River in Manitoba. As Sealey and Lussier have pointed out (1975:97-98), the Métis occupied the area which was rich in game and wild fowl, had good water, fuel, and timber in abundance, and was a sugaring spot on a main route to buffalo hunting areas. In 1871, while the Métis inhabitants were away on a buffalo hunt, a party of non-Aboriginal immigrants moved in from Ontario, settled on the land, and claimed it as their own. Following threats of violence and the intervention of the Lieutenant-Governor, the land was confirmed as the property of the settlers, not the Métis.

Again, by the time both treaties and the government concept of Métis status were well in place in the 1880s, the federal government effectively encouraged Aboriginal people to select either one or the other, considering both Indian status and "Half-breed" status, as it was then called, to be virtually interchangeable. By 1901, however, the bureaucratic gate of rigidity dropped, and individuals could no longer exchange one Aboriginal status for another. By 1942, the rigidity had increased even further when the government decided arbitrarily to remove some 663 people from Alberta treaty lists on the grounds that they were really Métis who had entered treaty in the previous thirty years. In that period the Aboriginal people of northern Alberta had been denied the right to accept any Aboriginal status other than that of Indian. Thus the attempt to retroactively deny them Indian and by extension, Métis-status, while at the same time expelling them from those reserves where they lived with relatives, was doubly injurious. The outcry in the House of Commons led to a Royal Commission, but in classic non-Aboriginal fashion it considered more matters of government policy and British and Canadian law than it did of Aboriginal rights. Only eighty-nine of the 663 people were re-admitted to full Indian status, while forty were re-admitted "conditionally". The remaining 534 Métis became—officially—non-Aboriginal persons! It is easy to call the above cases historical accidents, but the lesson is clear. To the successive Imperial, Dominion and Federal governments of Canada, Aboriginal people can and have been used as pawns, to be shuffled about any which way in the hope that they will simply disappear. Land, of course, that most valued of all non-Aboriginal chattels, provided both the focus and the means for this depersonalization, whether in 1871 in Manitoba, in 1942 in Alberta, or in 1986 in Manitoba.

In this most recent case, approximately 117 Métis lived on the Bloodvein Reserve when the Chief and Council acted. They would be left homeless when the expulsion order took effect in October of 1986. All of the Métis were related to Band members on the Reserve. The matter of their precarious tenancy on the Reserve had been raised by the Métis three years prior to the notice of expulsion. The Métis organized a community resettlement committee and asked the Manitoba Métis Federation Inc. (MMF) for assistance in getting a resettlement land grant. At the heart of their plan was a request to the province of Manitoba for a land base consisting of three sections of land to the east of the Reserve, on the banks of Longbody Creek.

The Bloodvein Indian Reserve is located on the east shore of Lake Winnipeg, about 400 km (250 miles) northeast of Winnipeg. There is no access other than by winter road and by air. The Indian population is approximately 500, in addition to the 23 Métis families.

The Métis occupied nine Band-owned houses, which had been designated as condemned, houses which ranged in size from 600 to 800 square feet. Approximately thirteen people lived in each house. Almost 60% of the Métis were under eighteen years of age. Twenty-six Métis children attended the Indian school, controlled and operated by the Band, which received a grant from the province for each Métis child in attendance.

Most of the Métis families were unemployed. They were not permitted to vote in the affairs of the community, nor were they allowed to start businesses on the Reserve. The Métis were totally dependent upon the Band Council for housing, education and health services.

This was the situation on the Reserve when the MMF took on the challenge of assisting the Bloodvein Métis in the spring of 1986.

By June a series of community meetings had taken place. On June 7, 1986, thirty-three people attended a meeting at Bloodvein to put the process of relocation into motion. The MMF, the Provincial Minister responsible for Northern and Native Affairs, Elijah Harper, and various officials from Canada Mortgage and Housing Corporation, Manitoba Housing and Renewal Corporation, Manitoba Northern and Native Affairs, the MMF Housing Branch and the MMF Education Branch were there to discuss land, housing, education and community infrastructure in the proposed new Métis community of Longbody Creek.

Although the Bloodvein Métis had the support of the only cabinet minister present at the meeting (Elijah Harper), the following statement was made by the staff representative from Manitoba Northern Affairs clearly indicating the overwhelming stress which non-Aboriginal people place upon land:

> Number 1, you're starting with your land situation with your community. You have to have a waste disposal system of some fashion or environment won't approve it. It has to go through thirty-seven departments, and number 1, is you have to get the land first, so you

have a point to start...Now, you might end up with twenty-five lots for your whole community development. In that, each one of these people are going to apply for permits....There may be permit fees for that....

It is ironic that the Métis land base had disappeared in the 19th century due to the often fraudulent action of non-Aboriginal persons and in the 1980s in part due to the insistence of non-Aboriginal governments upon significant land discrimination between Indians and Métis, combined with the refusal of the non-Aboriginal government to recognize the land entitlement of the Bloodvein Indians. Now the Longbody Creek Métis were being asked to jump through thirty-seven hoops of a non-Aboriginal bureaucratic land regime in order to have a place to live. The Métis families, including twenty-six children attending school, would have to be relocated before the winter freeze-up. In assessing the housing situation, it had previously been decided by the MMF that five units from a Canada Mortgage & Housing Corporation Demonstration Program would be made available to the Bloodvein Métis to meet part of their relocation crisis.

Education, as a provincial responsibility, was to be negotiated by the MMF with the Manitoba Minister of Education regarding a new school at Longbody Creek for the Métis children.

Political and racial tension on the Bloodvein Indian Reserve, stemming from a variety of factors, had caused a drop in enrollment at that school from over two hundred to fifty, twenty-six of these being the Métis children who were being evicted.

The racial tension was in part caused by non-Aboriginal persons on the Reserve as opposed to being simply a Métis/Indian conflict. The only Métis teacher at the Bloodvein school was terminated, leaving a largely non-Aboriginal teaching staff and a non-Aboriginal principal. Many families kept their children out of school rather than have them suffer the developing racial tension, apparent especially within the school.

The political tension on the Reserve was caused in part by federal legislation, Bill C-31, and the Department of Indian and Northern Affairs. The former was a series of amendments to the Indian Act which came into effect in June of 1985. It allowed many people who had been deprived of Indian status through various discriminatory gender and ancestry provisions in the Indian Act to regain their Indian status. With that status came the absolute right of those who became Band members to reside on their reserves, to participate in community decision-making, and to receive both housing and education services.

The latter, a giant bureaucracy made up almost entirely of non-Aboriginal persons, had the authority to deny those critical housing and education services to any non-Indians, including the Métis, by controlling the funding available to Indian Bands. This, of course, exacerbated the tension on the Reserve, increasing the fear that the Chief and Council would not be able to provide adequate services for Bill C-31 returnees let alone for the Métis kinfolk of Band members.

These political issues were unfamiliar to provincial Ministers of Education who legally have sole jurisdiction over education. The provinces, however, have no jurisdiction on Indian reserves: it was this legal roadblock which had such a negative impact upon the Métis families who had lived on the Bloodvein Reserve for fifty years.

Against great odds, and with little support from either the provincial or the federal government, the Métis families agreed to a peaceful exodus from the Reserve by October 1986, as requested by the Bloodvein Band Chief and Council. With little more than a borrowed boat and the help of the MMF, the Métis began their relocation from Bloodvein Indian Reserve to Longbody Creek, a distance of five miles up the Bloodvein River.

Plans for housing and a school at Longbody Creek were of immediate concern. Under the conditions of the Canada Mortgage & Housing Corporation's Demonstration Program, the Métis would build their homes using sweat equity towards ownership. The MMF and the now 'Longbody Creek' Métis arranged meetings with the Manitoba Minister of Education and the Public Schools Finance Board for approval of a new school. In the meantime, negotiations with the Chief of the Bloodvein Band provided the Métis children with the use of the Church chapel as a temporary school until the relocation could be completed.

Initially, there was no access to Longbody Creek other than by air, so the MMF arranged with the Department of National Defence in Ottawa and Edmonton to do a community assistance airlift of two mobile trailers using a helicopter. Stalling by the province caused disruption of this plan and the trailers intended for a temporary school were taken in by other means.

By the fall of 1986 families were housed at Longbody Creek. The five demonstration homes, built by the Métis people, housed thirty-four adults and children. Emergency housing was an issue for Métis families still on the Reserve, and there were requests from Métis families living farther north, who were in the same predicament, to come to Longbody Creek. An emergency request was made for more trailers until permanent housing could be constructed.

Three sections of land were reserved by the Department of Northern Affairs for the development of the new Métis community of Longbody Creek. The trailers for the school and teacherage were in place, and other buildings including a shed and a pumphouse were erected. Hydro and telephone services were installed and basic fire equipment was made available.

Subdivision plans were accepted by the Department of Northern Affairs for a total of forty-two residential lots measuring 150' x 200'. The land was cleared, and the locations of a garbage dump and access roads were approved.

It became apparent that the MMF and the Longbody Creek Métis were capable of accomplishing what others considered would take a miracle. The Province of Manitoba became more co-operative in the face of this Métis determination to succeed, as did the Canada Mortgage & Housing Corporation. At last the new Métis community of Longbody Creek became a reality through this determination, co-operation, and the hard work of the people themselves.

The residents of Longbody Creek are an ambitious and enterprising people who wish to carve out a community that will be self-sufficient, a community of which they can be proud. There is still a need for more housing, however. With a portable mill, the Longbody Creek Métis could use the standing timber on their three sections of land to cut and construct homes utilizing rough sawn lumber.

Future plans for Longbody Creek include a recreation and cultural centre and a town hall. Tourism is also being considered as a form of economic development, as the Bloodvein River is considered a Heritage River. Fish and wildlife are abundant. The harvesting of wild rice along the Bloodvein River, Longbody Creek, Beaver Creek and on adjacent lakes is also an untapped resource for the community.

One of the major achievements of building the new community of Longbody Creek is the social well-being of the people. The community is, for all intents and purposes, isolated. They need help to accomplish what they set out to do and they will need assistance to continue with future plans. The school is continuing to operate and the enrollment is stable. As more housing becomes available, other families will be able to relocate to the community. Longbody Creek could be a proving ground for those in similar situations. Just as the Métis of the Red River moved west to the Saskatchewan River to establish their own successful township of St. Laurent, amidst the prejudice and discrimination which dogged them following the resistance of 1869-70, so the Longbody Creek Métis have successfully established a new Métis community in their drive to become self-sufficient.

EDUCATION, LANGUAGE, AND SURVIVAL

Education has many faces beyond that which can be seen in the academic culture of Canadian society. In the Métis community, education is the key to survival as a people. Historically, the Métis were dependent upon oral and visual processes of learning as the languages of the Métis were not written languages. The forced learning of both English and French in the Canadian school system has drastically changed this learning process and is a basic root of conflict for those Métis people who resist and do not adapt.

There are many examples of this resistance by the Métis, as can be seen in the community of St. Laurent on the eastern shore of Lake Manitoba. A variety of forms of discrimination, including ridicule and the refusal to permit the use of the Michif language in the school, have not extinguished the Michif language in St. Laurent. The language, and the significant cultural value set of the Métis which the language communicates, remain intact.

The importance of oral history to the Métis can be seen through the study of the Michif languages, for the real story of the Métis is recorded in large part through oral history.

The concept that the Métis were an inferior people is seen in the attitude held by recent immigrants to St. Laurent towards the Michif languages. This attitude of ignorant superiority is related by Lavallee (1990:8-9) when he speaks of the community's recollections of initial language contact:

> Some elders attribute the disappearance of the Saulteaux language among the Métis to the presence of the priests and nuns at St. Laurent and to the arrival of the Breton families from Britanny, France, in or around 1907. They introduced the Canadian French language in the community which in a short time became the status or prestige language. Thus, the missionaries and the Bretons were responsible for establishing a hierarchy of languages: Canadian French, Michif French and Saulteaux.

> To the missionaries and the Bretons, the Canadian French language was considered a superior language. To speak 'proper' Canadian French was to be superior to those who did not speak it. In their eyes, Michif French, as a language, did not have a status in its own right. As a non-standard form of the language, it was considered a bastardized language, a corruption of 'proper' language usage, and evidence of incapacity to learn on the part of the speaker. Teachers apparently targeted Michif French immediately as an impediment to assimilation.

The Métis people of St. Laurent are an example of the resiliency of the Métis in general to survive and to rise above repression. Lavallee illustrates this further (Ibid:13-14):

> Among the Métis students who attended high school in St. Laurent, only a few speak the Canadian French language. Most of them have retained and still speak their Michif language. Thus, students who obtained a high school education at St. Laurent did not, in the

process, give up their language. They preferred their own language, as a symbol of their identity, to a higher education.

The origins of the Michif languages are not known. Three distinct Michif languages exist today and are spoken in various Métis communities throughout Manitoba. Michif French, Michif Cree and Michif Saulteaux are recognized as the languages of the Métis and are identified as such for language development purposes.

To promote the learning of the Michif languages, and thus Métis cultural values, the MMF held a Language Conference in Winnipeg in June of 1985. Métis people from Manitoba, Saskatchewan, Alberta and North Dakota met to share information and to make plans towards language and cultural development.

Although the Michif languages have gained the interest of linguists around the world, the MMF has not been able to obtain support from either the provincial or federal governments for cultural development. Indeed, Michif is taught at the university level only in the United States, and is effectively denied recognition as a language in Canada.

EDUCATION FOR THE METIS OF THE FUTURE

Since it started in 1967, the Manitoba Métis Federation Inc. has endeavoured to bring recognition and justice to the cause of the Métis people of Manitoba.

The failure of both Canada and Manitoba to recognize Louis Riel as a Father of Confederation, and the fact that Manitoba was a Métis province when it joined Canada in 1870, have been sources of conflict between the two societies for several generations.

Meanwhile, the Manitoba Métis Federation Inc. quietly continues the work set out by the Métis people.

In December of 1985, the MMF appointed a working group to study the feasibility of establishing an institute which would serve as a vehicle to deal with the educational concerns and aspirations of the Métis people of Manitoba. The government of the province of Manitoba agreed to participate, and the Minister of Education appointed members to a joint working group. In January of 1987, agreement was reached regarding the purpose of the institute, and its goals and objectives. Recommendations were made for further developmental work, including advocacy, research, infrastructure, a literary resource centre, publishing and eventually educational program development. It was also agreed that the institute should be established immediately and be known as the Louis Riel Institute.

Although it is expected that in time there will be a fully functioning Louis Riel Institute as a secondary, post-secondary and resource educational facility, the current concern of the MMF is the promotion of the cause of the educational needs of the Métis people of Manitoba. This battle is only just beginning for, since 1986, the development of the Institute has gone through two provincial administrations and four Ministers of Education. Successful negotiations and the eventual physical establishment of the Louis Riel Institute will depend upon the strength of the Métis people to endure, and the hope that Canada and Manitoba will some day honour their agreements with the Métis.

Education is a critical element in the growth, maintenance and transmission of culture. By the middle of the 19th century significant numbers of Métis were being educated in the schools of the Red River Colony, Southern Ontario, Quebec, and Scotland. By 1870, when Manitoba became a province, there were many highly educated Métis leaders, not least of whom was Louis Riel.

The majority of the people of Manitoba were Métis in 1870, and that majority, through the Provisional Government of Louis Riel, insisted upon constitutional safeguards to preserve elements of Métis culture, including linguistic and education rights. Over the ensuing decades, and especially during the period between 1870 and 1890, many of these safeguards were legislated away as the population balance changed. Many Métis moved west to the Northwest Territories, while many immigrants arrived from southern Ontario bringing with them a great deal of racist baggage. Although at least some of the repressive and discriminatory legislation was later struck down, it had a dramatic and cumulative devaluation effect upon the Métis. Indeed the education figures cited at the start of this chapter simply indicate the extent of this devaluation.

Even more than the loss of language and education rights, the Métis of the 1870s and 1880s suffered dreadfully from a self-serving non-Aboriginal land regime which effectively deprived them of a land base. The combination of the loss of the pre-1870 subsistence bases of hunting and commerce, the removal of the educational and linguistic guarantees of 1870, and the fraudulent disappearance of the post -1870 promised land base resulted in appalling poverty. The devaluation which developed over the next century, and its results, are amply illustrated in the preceding chapters on the correctional system and child care. The problems in those areas also reflect the loss of Métis educational opportunities and the consequent contemporary failure to recognize the Métis ability for self-determination. In an attempt to persuade the federal and provincial governments to acknowledge the pressing needs of the Métis people to that recognition, and to obtain the restoration of their just opportunities, Manitoba Métis Federation

Inc., acting on behalf of the Métis of Manitoba, sued both the Canada and the Manitoba governments to have twenty-six statutes passed over the years declared ultra vires. The effect of such a declaration would be to force those non-Aboriginal governments, and the bureaucracies which interpret and carry out their policies, to recognize and negotiate with the Métis as a people once again. The likely electrifying result of that upon the Métis, both individually and collectively, would do more to ensure the survival of a strong people than any government action in the last 120 years. Such a conclusion would be strong testimony to the cultural integrity and survivability of the Métis since the early 19th century.

The final outcome of the legal action taken against the governments of Canada and Manitoba by the Métis people of Manitoba may relieve part of the injustice that the Métis have had to endure. Both the federal and provincial governments sought to prevent the suit from continuing, and used every legal means at their disposal to stop it. However, a unanimous ruling by the Supreme Court of Canada in March of 1990 "....saw no reason why the action should not proceed to trial". As a result, the MMF will now proceed with its suit in the Court of Queen's Bench in Manitoba. In the course of this litigation Canadian history will be put on trial in the highest Courts of Manitoba and Canada.

NOTES

1. Manitoba Métis Federation Inc., File: Re-settlement of Bloodvein Métis to Longbody Creek, (1986-87).

2. Manitoba Métis Federation Inc., Michif Languages Conferences Report, Winnipeg, MB (1985).

3. Supreme Court of Canada: Yvon Dumont, et al v. Attorney-General of Canada—Appeal Proceedings, (March 2, 1990).

4. Manitoba Métis Federation Inc., The Louis Riel Institute and Manitoba Métis Federation Inc. Education Policy, (November 10, 1986).

Part Three

Into the Twenty-first Century

INTRODUCTION

David N. Chartrand

Part One of this volume clearly indicates that Métis cultural distinctiveness and our common political consciousness developed long before the establishment of the Canadian federation. The Métis are one of the founding peoples of Confederation, but have been denied their rightful place in the constitutional scheme. The Métis people ante-date the Canadian state. The union with Canada which came later was based upon a bargain that Canada and Manitoba reneged on after 1870. The failure of both Canada and Manitoba to recognize Louis Riel as a Father of Confederation, and the fact that Manitoba was a Métis province when it joined Canada in 1870, have been sources of conflict between the two societies for several generations.

Our ancestors were the children of the unions between North American Aboriginal mothers and European fathers. They developed into a separate people with the necessary group consciousness to promote their cause collectively. A Métis was not a French-Canadian, nor Canadian, nor a Scot. Neither was he an Indian. Accordingly, we sometimes waged war against our maternal relatives, as we did against our paternal kin. We also forged treaties and declared a Bill of Rights which marked our identity as a "New Nation." We did not choose to assimilate, but fought to maintain both our dual heritage and our status as Métis. As a historic national minority, we have the right to remain separate and distinct from both the French and English versions of Canadian society and to develop along lines dictated by our own cultural aspirations.

Section 31 of the Manitoba Act sets out special recognition, in the constitution of Canada, of the distinct and corporate character of the Métis people. The failure of the governments to perform the obligations implied and understood in Section 31 is well-documented. Because of that failure, the obligations of the government to provide a land base for the continued survival of the Métis people are outstanding, and are currently before the Manitoba Court of Queen's Bench. We are continuing to strive for the entrenchment of justiciable rights that are not subject to unilateral amendment by the province.

The rights of the Métis are not limited by the terms of the constitutional provisions of Canada. Some are supraconstitutional in nature. We claim all the human rights recognized by domestic and international law. It is within the context of Article 27 of the United Nations Covenant on Civil and Political Rights that we demand recognition of our collective rights to the instruments of self-determination, enjoyment of culture and use of language. The languages of the Métis have been eroded by the educational systems of the province; the practices of cultural genocide are still felt by the uprooted Métis children who are placed outside of our culture by the province's child and welfare system, and we are disproportionately affected by a justice system which serves only to compound these problems. Such practices, as well as the continued refusal of Canada and Manitoba to remedy their effects, are incompatible with the values declared in the Canadian Bill of Rights.

Some of these collective rights are now entrenched in the constitution of Canada, including the Aboriginal rights of the Métis recognized in section 35 of the Constitution Act of 1982 and section 31 of the Manitoba Act of 1870. However, the historical and legal rights of the Métis people to manage their own institutions and economies on their own lands must be recognized and reinforced in constitutional terms. If these rights are to be defined in such a way as to accommodate the existing constitutional framework, it will be necessary to reach agreement respecting institutional and other arrangements to rectify the historical inequalities which have placed the Mßéßtis in a disadvantaged position.

The Manitoba Métis Federation Inc., as the recognized representative body of the Métis of Manitoba, is currently engaged in tripartite negotiations with the governments of Canada and Manitoba on the question of self-determination. These discussions involve detailed examination of the following areas:

1. The type and nature of Métis institutions required to enable a constituent body to govern itself;

2. The type and nature of the mechanisms which would empower such institutions to act;

3. The scope and extent of the jurisdictional powers that would be provided to such institutions; and

4. The source, quantity and nature of the financial resources that would enable these institutions to operate.

The assumptions which guide this tripartite process include the following perceived needs as long-term goals:

1. that Métis people exercise, through their own governmental institutions, management and control over matters directly affecting them;

2. that Métis people participate in the design and delivery of services and programs directed towards their particular needs and circumstances;

3. that Métis culture and heritage be protected and enhanced;

4. that Métis economic development be promoted.

There are three distinct avenues which have the potential to enhance Métis participation in the public decision-making apparatus. One focusses on increasing representation within existing institutions, while a second leads to the establishment of new institutions which would in themselves provide the capacity to self-govern. A third avenue involves the recognition of Métis government supported by federal transfer and equalization payments, and concomitant provincial support. The Métis, while a significant minority within the overall population, are few in number, and are therefore not likely to exercise control in any of the existing governing institutions. In order to create a majority situation, we must establish institutions which are limited to Métis membership. These institutions must provide mechanisms to ensure legitimate representation. As there is no land base reserved exclusively for Métis people (although this claim is pending before the courts), we envision non-land based representative institutions with membership being exclusive to the Métis people. In Manitoba, as an interim short-term measure, we have been negotiating to achieve a degree of control over child care, education and justice even without wholesale changes to the system. We believe that in the interim this will effect positive changes simply because our people relate more easily to their own than to outsiders and because control of delivery by people living in contemporary Métis culture, inherently creates cultural appropriateness. More importantly though, through the tripartite process we are trying to negotiate the sectoral transfer of authority. This transfer of authority is a means of ensuring that issues relating to Métis people will be resolved by Métis people. Part Three of this book includes our proposals to the Aboriginal Justice Inquiry. However, even if the government decided to allow Métis people significant remain. The 70-80% unemployment rate we face in most communities, the high rate of removal of our children by the child welfare system and attendant cultural genocide continue, as do the poor housing conditions in which we are forced to reside either by location or because of our race. The biassed and untrue history we are taught as children will continue to exist.

MANITOBA METIS FEDERATION JUSTICE COMMITTEE PRESENTATION TO THE ABORIGINAL JUSTICE INQUIRY

Ron H. Richard
David Chartrand
Denise Thomas

INTRODUCTION

The plight of Métis and other Aboriginal people in the criminal justice system has been well documented over the last three decades with thousands of pages of recommendations forthcoming from various boards and commissions studying these social issues.[1]

The study group on prevention at the Federal/Provincial Conference on Native Peoples and the Criminal Justice System (1975) noted that for too long, Natives have been gathered to discuss proposals at endless conferences resulting in defining and re-defining the issues. This did not translate into change because"....no commitments are ever extracted from the myriad of government officials, or those extracted are so general as to amount to a virtual mandate for inaction" (Ibid.: 17).

It is the assessment of the Manitoba Métis Federation that both the federal and provincial governments have a disproportionate amount of their resources tied up in institutional services at the expense of community -based services. These services are located mainly in large population centres, so that the system affects Métis people in terms of displacement, in terms of lack of access to programs and services, and in terms of the dislocation of jobs, people and economic benefits. Métis adults and youths are incarcerated at rates which go beyond random factors or which can be explained by high crime rates.

This is borne out in the submission of the Attorney-General of Manitoba to the Aboriginal Justice Inquiry which noted (1989:29):

Commonly raised issues with respect to the detention and custody of northern youth in southern facilities are as follows:

- reduced access to legal counsel
- longer detention periods
- high escort costs
- less likely access to bail
- greater proportion of northern youth sentenced to custody
- northern youth do not have the same access to families and communities
- high cost of travel for temporary absences
- trauma of entering a strange correctional facility in an unfamiliar city
- lack of native workers
- more difficult for northern probation officers to prepare court reports when youth are held in southern facilities.

Of a total provincial correctional budget of $39.4 million in the 1987-1988 fiscal year, about $20 million were spent on adult corrections (the bulk of which were jail and remand centre costs), leaving $18.8 million for community and youth corrections. Of this money, $11.2 million were spent on the large youth institutions (Manitoba Youth Centre and Agassiz Centre for Youth), and only $0.7 million were spent in communities on open custody (the majority of this in Winnipeg, Brandon and Thompson). This left somewhat less than 19% of the budget to attack corrections problems within the community.

In 1983, the Manitoba Métis Rights Assembly, in preparation for the Constitutional Conference on the Rights of Aboriginal People, took a strong position on Justice issues:

In the past, the Métis had no jails or lawyers; community pressure kept people in line and elders imposed the penalties on offenders. Today, many Métis people are not aware of their legal rights. There are few Métis lawyers and no Native judges (sic). Legal aid should be improved and more counselling should be made available to explain the legal system. We need more Métis Family Court Workers and community designates to act in an advisory capacity.

Métis people should be in the Legislative Assembly and have a say on all levels of the law. Local Justice Committees and Magistrates should be created to maintain law and order at the community level. Métis people should be educated to be lawyers and Judges (1983:28).

It is interesting, but sad, to note that the high numbers of Indians and Métis in the jails is a rather recent phenomenon. The rising proportion is observed only after World War II. The best data from the prairies on incarceration rates comes from Skinner et al (1981:76-77).

Numbers Of Indian & Metis Male Admissions To Jail
In Saskatchewan 1920-1943

	NUMBER	%
Indian	235	2.7%
Métis	269	3.0%
Total Indian/Métis	504	5.7%
All admissions	8823	100.0%

Current rates of admission show a tenfold increase, and reflect the disastrous effects of the Depression, coupled with the erosion of hunting, fishing and trapping (both commercial and subsistence), along with the constant degradation of the environment, and inadequate and counter-productive government resource regulation. The Commission is referred to Pelletier (1977), Sawchuk (1978), Tough (1984), and Waldram (1988) for reviews and analyses of the economic strangulation of the Métis through land surveys, illegal expropriations, eastern competition, and the importation of regulations or sheer neglect. The Métis industries and occupations affected were diverse, including fishing, forestry, farming, prairie transportation, trapping, seneca root and frog picking, maple sugar production, vinegar production, the production of lime and limestone, wild rice farming and salt mining. This resulted in gross dislocations of people. As a consequence, the rural to urban migration of the 1970s and 1980s parallels the displacement and dispersal of the Métis across Canada which occurred in the 1800s.

In 1981, John Hylton of the Prairie Justice Research Consortium, pointed out that:

Since governments do not acknowledge any special commitment to Canada's non-status Indians and Métis, it is more difficult to locate statistical data relating to their social and economic conditions. However, there is good reason to believe that their conditions are substantially different from those of Treaty Indians who have left the reserve. Indeed, it may be argued that non-status Indians and Métis do not have access programs available to status Indians (1981).

The process of colonization and under-development have created situations where Aboriginal people live on the margins of social, political and economic viability. This is borne out by the observed high rates of unemployment, suicide, alcohol abuse and illness among Aboriginal people (Hylton, 1981; Conroy, 1988). Aboriginal people are trying to maintain organization in their communities in the face of high dislocation rates, family violence, sexual abuse and the breakdown of gender roles and customary social relations. This is the context which provides impetus to the high rates of involvement of Aboriginal youth in both the youth justice and child welfare systems (La Prairie, 1988).

The Manitoba Métis Federation Justice Committee members were appalled that the Attorney-General's report to the Inquiry makes no attempt to analyze the status of Aboriginal persons within the justice system. Having done no analysis, it follows that no substantive actions or initiatives are suggested. One would hope that they would at least be embarrassed to present the outcome figures they have produced (failure rates as high as 65%).

This seems to us to be a logical consequence of program planning that takes place without significant involvement or consultation with major Aboriginal groups, other than the documented low-level line staff work that takes place.

In our experience, voluntary cooperation and coordination of effort will not accomplish the desired outcome. A coordinated and empowering effort is necessary with significant portions of the provincial and federal mandate to be turned over to Aboriginal political, correctional and social service delivery organizations.

As Havemann (1983) has pointed out, Aboriginal groups prefer autonomy within the justice system, whereas the government prefers to co-opt indigenous individuals and organizations to assist in the delivery of the imposed programs, policies and laws of the colonizer. This process is only one step removed from the old programs of pacification through subjugation and assimilation.

The Attorney-General's submission reveals no significant budget allocation or strategy for research on the effectiveness of programs. Giving research funds to Aboriginal groups would not only hold the Department of Justice accountable for delivering effective services, it would assist in determining the relative efficiency of various programs for Aboriginal offenders.

POLICING

Policing issues, like most problems with which the Manitoba Métis Federation will deal, have no clearcut solutions. And, again as with most problems, the issues are the same, but the solutions, as we see them, must be defined along geographic lines.

Simply put, the police have, by their own admission, a problem in the Aboriginal community. They are neither trusted nor wanted, and the job they have to do is made more difficult because of this.

Native people feel victimized by the legal process in Manitoba. This is not limited just to the criminal justice system, but it is most evident there. Because the first contact Native people have with the system is as a victim, a witness, or an accused, the police should be able to promote the best interests of that system to Native people, but their first impressions are rarely positive impressions. As noted, Native people are represented disproportionately in the criminal justice system. That statement bears amplification. Native people are over-represented as victims, witnesses and accused persons; they are under-represented as court or police officers, lawyers or social workers, or defenders in the system. It is interesting to note that the Winnipeg City Police, on the last figures seen by us, advise that only ten Native people are officers, of the 1,119 member total (.9%). Similarly, Brandon has one officer out of 66 or (1.5%), and the RCMP have 60 Aboriginal officers out of 950 or (6.3%), of which 30 are 3 (B) constables, that is, specially trained Native constables for work in Native communities. How many of these are in senior or supervisory positions has not been published, but we know of none. The total complement of the three principal Manitoba police forces is 2,135 officers, of which 3.8% are Aboriginal.

Similarly, the civilian staff is almost universally non-Native. It is instructive, for instance, that a Métis woman with legal experience, accounting background and eight years as a typist had her application for employment with the RCMP rejected, because it was delivered "....too late in the day...." even though the published deadline did not include a time. Prejudice to other candidates could not have been a factor as the process had not been started. Is this what the RCMP means when it says that "....it makes positive efforts to recruit Native people"?

It is the common opinion of Native persons who have left the police structure that there remains an almost indelible double standard. In most cases, officers are completely supported by their superiors (too much so in many cases). Native officers often feel that the same is not true for them, especially 3 (B) constables, who by their very designation and restrictions, are placed separate and apart.

From this scenario, we then draw a typical involvement. The officers involved are almost always non-Native. In the case of RCMP officers, they are usually from another part of the country, often having had little contact with Native people. Sadly, they are in most cases soon indoctrinated into the stereotypes that foster prejudice. They have at most a three-day course in cross-cultural awareness. This course begins with a strongly-worded statement authorized by the commissioner that any evidence of racism or discrimination could be grounds for dismissal, goes on for two days providing blanket generalizations, and concludes with an assessment/test that is multiple choice, to determine if any racism exists. Not surprisingly, these tests demonstrate, to the standards set by the RCMP, that little or no racism exists in these officers. Training such as this is obviously of little practical benefit or use.

As far as we are able to ascertain, no appropriate cross-cultural training is available to Winnipeg City or Brandon City police officers. We then have a system where uninformed, dogmatic (even prejudiced) outsiders attempt to police people, and there is great surprise that the police are not trusted. It may rather be surprising that the police are trusted at all.

A second problem is that current policing is not cost effective. In many communities (such as Barrows, Duck Bay, Pelican Rapids, Matheson Island), there are no resident police (except perhaps community constables, of which we will speak shortly). The result is that, for every incident, police have to drive sometimes up to 100 kilometers. In many of these cases, there are daily (often more than one) treks to the community. The cost in person-hours, gas, and automobiles is staggering. In some communities, we understand police fly in. This creates an unreasonable expense; but consider the costs of lack of respect, increased difficulty of policing and lack of a preventive/deterrent effect. When taken together with "hard" cost, who could reasonably agree to such policing?

Thirdly, time and time again we have heard from community leaders of persons arrested without explanation to the community, without determination of where the accused will be taken, and without arrangement to return persons later released.

A particularly insidious tool in rural and northern Manitoba is the Intoxicated Persons Detention Act. Under the Act, as the commissioners are aware, all that needs to happen is that an officer determines that an individual is intoxicated to the extent that he poses a threat to himself or to others. When the nearest "holding facility" is 20, 40, or 60 miles away, and no provision for return is made, the result is clearly punitive. There is no independent assessment made of the officer's judgement. Those judgements are, in the opinion of many, often made on bad faith and without reasonable justification.

We have already mentioned the problems of centralized policing in rural and northern communities. The effect of outsiders such as the police, their lack of information, the necessarily long response times, and their general lack of training, knowledge, empathy or understanding of Aboriginal people, values or languages, leads to significant loss of respect for police. These traits and behaviours, when exhibited by police officers, are of critical importance to us as Métis people. Again, as has been noted in other presentations, Native crime is business-as-usual for many non-Native people. We cannot overstate these problems.

In summary, we believe all major police forces in the province systematically discriminate against Aboriginal people. We believe that these forces deliberately leave Aboriginal people out of the decision-making process. We believe that many officers are racists, and that most other officers harbour these racist individuals and, despite rhetoric to the contrary, we do not believe claims that this will change in the foreseeable future.[2]

Most important is the issue of control over a land base. Inherent in that control is policing. To that extent, this inquiry cannot help but comment upon the issue redundant of self-determination. We anticipate people pointing to the issue of community constables. These "popcorn" policemen, or RCMP spies, as they often become considered in the communities, are ineffective, and often increase the problems they are intended to solve. Even a cursory view of the material demonstrates the disparity between community constables and RCMP officers.

First, community constables have little real authority. What authority they do have is continually undermined by the requirement to report more serious matters to the RCMP.

Second, community constables receive little training and are not allowed to carry weapons.

More important, the financial supports are vastly different. The average cost of an RCMP constable in Manitoba exceeds $56,000 (Attorney-General submission to Inquiry, 1989). This figure includes staffing required for federally-related work in Winnipeg but does not include training or other preplacement costs, and is therefore lower than the actual cost. Some estimates have placed the cost of one RCMP officer at more than $70,000 annually. Compare this to the $28,000 for the total cost of community constables program (Attorney General submission to Inquiry, 1989). One can even note that the cost per mandated officer for the Dakota Ojibway Tribal Council police was $29,950 per officer (calculated from Attorney-General's submission to the Inquiry, 1989) even though "....the force has a mandate for 25 officers, but due to recruiting difficulties and attrition the full complement has not been filled."

In short, when the total cost of fielding an officer, including salary, in the community constable program represents approximately 65% of the salary of an RCMP officer, based upon a salary quoted by the RCMP of $43,263 per annum, and 73% of the $41,106 salary of a City of Winnipeg constable, (telephone survey September, 1989), can the program expect to be recognized or effective? We think the answer is obvious. We also point out that, although the efforts for Dakota Ojibwa Tribal Council are inadequate, they are vastly superior to the community constable program for Métis people. This we suggest is symptomatic of the whole justice system: Aboriginal police officers are under-trained, have no developed support system, are underpaid and do not have adequate equipment or authority. Given those problems, inevitable negative comment can only be a comment upon the system, not the individuals. We further assert that to tear the loyalties of a Native community constable between Non-Native police officers and the Native people with whom he lives is unfair. These problems need to be addressed before we can assess these people adequately.

LAW ENFORCEMENT REVIEW

The Law Enforcement Review Agency (LERA) is, in the Aboriginal community, a synonym for police cover-up. It is incredible, but here is a mechanism liked by no one. The police, quite rightly, claim that it takes too long to address a complainant's concern. Police argue that all complaints are handled by hearing, without dismissal of frivolous complaints thereby making the process inequitous. We, to an extent, concur.

It seems to us that LERA, in order to be effective, must have the following changes:

1. There must be an investigative unit that prepares a report, gathers evidence and makes speedy determinations as to which cases have some probability of a finding of fault. Such investigators should not be retired officers who are sent to investigate the actions of their former colleagues.

2. The complainants need access to counsel for those cases which do proceed to full hearing and police officers should be compellable witnesses.

3. There should be greater emphasis on mediation and resolution before hearing.

4. The constitution of the board should be reviewed to ensure that all parties are satisfied with the possible panels.

5. LERA should have some effective authority. In particular, it should have authority to ensure dismissal or suspension, to ensure fairness in the institution of criminal or civil proceedings, and to order the payment of charges and costs.

Not one of the foregoing is new. From the first Métis leaders, control of local functions, such as policing, was an important concern. These concerns were renewed in the constitutional process leading up to the patriation of the constitution in 1982.

In that year, in a series called Métis Anoutch, Métis people asked for certain self-determinative rights. One of these was control of policing functions within our land base. At that time, it was also recognized that access to power was necessary for other Métis people. Only through the foregoing suggestions can this crucial aspect of criminal justice be truly responsible to this body of citizens.

ADVOCACY

Legal Aid

Since the onset of Legal Aid in Manitoba, few offenders have lacked the opportunity for representation at trial. The Osborne case, however, points to a stark difference between Aboriginal people and non-Native people. Generally, Aboriginal people have not understood the process well enough to know when to retain counsel. In remote areas, too, Legal Aid may even be a hollow right. For instance, a person arrested in Norway House cannot, without making a long distance telephone call, retain counsel. If the accused does not happen to have a telephone, calling is not possible unless the person has enough credit to bill such a call or the self-confidence to call collect. That is not an easy thing to do, especially if one does not know any lawyers and it is 2:00 A.M.

Also, the Legal Aid process creates a "sausage" effect. For the private bar, obviously the more sausages processed, the higher the profit. Few members of the Law Society have ever argued that a higher profit is not welcome. In a recent Legal Aid evaluation, the cost per case of matters received showed the private bar as more expensive than staff lawyers. This happened in all cases, and in some, was double the staff lawyer rate.

The role of Legal Aid, and other agencies, needs to be re-defined and expanded. In a recent Legal Aid evaluation, services such as public interest law, duty counsel, drop-in advice and Outreach were still identified as "discretionary services." As set out in the evaluation report of Legal Aid

Manitoba by the Social Planning Council of Winnipeg (Sloan, 1987:37), the process should include (or does include):

1. the development and delivery of community legal service (preventative law);

2. aiding and representing groups and organizations within its community in matters relating to "poverty law" (e.g. consumer protection, environmental protection, housing, welfare and related social rights);

3. "institutional service" (juvenile court duty counsel, family court duty counsel system); services to senior citizens through the Age and Opportunity Bureau Programme; Mental Health Institutions; services in association with social agencies; for example, the Family Bureau; and services to remote communities including Aboriginal people;

4. giving information and advice to people in the community, both within the community office itself and in Outreach programs, in association with a whole variety of community organizations;

5. the carrying by the staff of manageable caseloads, which will include advice, assistance and representation in both civil and criminal matters.

Since the establishment of Legal Aid, next to nothing has been spent in advertising the above services. Legal Aid clearly has not done its job in letting people know its mandate. Again from the Legal Aid evaluation, we note that only 48% of the respondents knew the role of Legal Aid. It is a perception amongst the people we represent that lawyers of Legal Aid do not work as hard for their clients. Nearly one-third of those questioned in the Legal Aid survey felt that way. While it may not be true in every case, the system needs to assess why the feeling exists.

Finally, of those clients dealing with Legal Aid, only 18% had incomes over $5,000, which leads us back to the socio-economic problems underlying the way people perceive the system. It seems clear not only that the people using Legal Aid are poorer than the average person, but also that they are in fact the poorest of the poor.

Unfortunately, neither the board of Legal Aid Manitoba nor the investigators thought it significant to separate clients in terms of Aboriginal/non-Aboriginal status.

We do not agree with the Legal Aid Manitoba evaluation in terms of accessibility. To that question, rural clients supposedly said that their lawyer's office was conveniently located. That is simply not borne out by what we hear from the Métis community. Unless Métis people represent most of the 12% of respondents who were dissatisfied with access to legal services, the evaluation is not reflected in the concerns expressed. Most Métis people accept that lawyers will, for economic reasons, locate in larger centres. How, though, can it be convenient or effective to have duty counsel fly in with the judge, the prosecutor and the probation officers, stay for one day and leave? Time constraints alone make accessibility unlikely in such a case. It is instructive to note that the Native Probation Caucus stated that Aboriginal accused usually do not know who their lawyer is, do not have time to discuss their case in detail, are not aware of their options, and sometimes plead guilty out of frustration (1989:10-11).

We note that over 82% of the Legal Aid client group earns less than $5,000 annually per family unit. When, if ever, is travel to a lawyer then convenient?

Clients for Legal Aid do not often retain counsel early enough. In fact, the Legal Aid evaluation noted that applications were received by duty counsel prior to the client's first appearance in only 27% of the cases, and at the first appearance in 20% of the cases; thus 53% of the applications were received after the first appearance. One important question was not asked, however: how many people retain counsel before being charged, or immediately following arrest? From experienced criminal counsel, and our observations in the courts, we think it likely that few Aboriginal people avail themselves of counsel at any early opportunity. In short, while access to counsel has improved, improvement can yet be made.

The availability of Legal Aid services depends greatly upon the presence or absence of a local office. Communities with Legal Aid offices had a utilization rate of 14.22 clients served by a lawyer paid by Legal Aid per 1,000 population, whereas the comparable utilization rate for areas without an office averaged 9.49 per1000 population. The locations served by circuit court where duty counsel services are provided are an exception to this trend.

In studying Legal Aid accessibility, the Social Planning Council found that offence rate within a defined service area was not related to criminal Legal Aid certificate utilization rates. They felt that this surprising finding was indicative of unmet need.

The Social Planning Council notes that in residual areas, those without Legal Aid offices, where many persons speak a Native language as their mother tongue (35% in northern residential areas), special problems are created for Legal Aid services, as well as the other demographic factors affecting policy and planning concerns:

Native people are among the poorest of LAM's (Legal Aid Manitoba's) clients, and, to a considerable extent, are the Manitobans who live farthest from LAM's service delivery network. Average native income (1980) was $8,600, two-thirds of the non-native average of $13,000, and native people in rural areas had particularly low incomes.

Seven out of ten natives were under 30 years of age, compared with the national average of five out of ten. A significantly larger proportion of the native population is in this younger age group, because native people do not live as long as other Canadians, and because they tend to have more children (Sloan 1987:134).

It is our analysis that Legal Aid access for Indian and Métis people in centres without Legal Aid offices would be even worse were it not for the fact that those persons not granted judicial interim release are usually transported to custody in larger centres where they do have access to legal aid duty counsel.

Court Communicators

A second portion of the advocacy process within the Justice System involves ensuring that accused persons understand the issues of their cases. The Legal Aid evaluation found significant numbers of people who did not feel properly informed about their cases. Indeed, where clients felt they had lost their cases, 29% did not feel informed at all.

It is, of course, the role of the court communicator to explain possible outcomes to clients and to represent the interests of the clients to the lawyers.

Both the Sinclair (1977) and the Lajeunesse (1987) reviews of the Court Communicator Program pointed to serious problems in the system. Whether the issue is training, numbers of communicators, client knowledge of the program or control and information flow, it seems apparent that successive governments have failed to address these views and recommendations for improvement.

What the Lajeunesse study may have demonstrated is that there is not sufficient time in 1989 to do all of the things named in the earlier review, given current staffing levels.

It is our opinion that the role of the court communicator needs to be expanded. Indeed, making court communicators full partners in the process should be made a priority. From various studies, the best of which was conducted in Saskatchewan just prior to the government terminating its program, it can be demonstrated that where the court communicator role is expanded to include an advocacy function (on behalf of the client to the lawyer), and information dissemination roles between lawyer and client, client and family, family and lawyer, the returns to society can be staggering. The basis of these savings ranged from lesser sentences (because more facts were known) to a greater client satisfaction. In the Saskatchewan example, the cost-saving amounted literally to millions of dollars per year.

It is significant that many respondents in the Lajeunesse study in Manitoba, claimed not even to have known of the Court Communicator Program. Although in some cases this seemed to be unlikely, again the client reference is in itself a point of concern, and has been substantiated in other submissions to the Inquiry. The Native Probation Caucus (1989), for example, cited a recent survey at Portage Correctional Institution for Women which found that of sixty-five Aboriginal women, only five knew about the Court Communicator Program, had used it, or had found the program useful.

Of significance also is that of the twenty-six recommendations for court communicators in the Sinclair report only those which decreased or limited their involvement have been implemented. We agree with that report which stated:

> It is recommended that each communicator be fully informed as to the hazards of seeking and obtaining information relating to the particulars of the offence(s) with which the accused is charged.

> There is no legal privity between Court Communicator and accused. If communicators become involved in investigating particular offences and seeking information pertaining thereto, it is entirely possible that a communicator may be called upon as a witness on behalf of either the defence or the Crown. Such a possibility should be avoided at all costs.

But the solution, it seems, may be to extend the solicitor's privilege if the court communicator can be said to be an agent on behalf of the defence.

It is clear to us that the number of court communicators, paralegals or other community-based information providers needs to be increased. It seems to us that the role of paralegals for Native people within Legal Aid can better be handled by expansion of the role of the Court Communicator.

MMF research led to the same analysis as the 1987 Lajeunesse Report:

> There is no official contact between the management of the program and key actors in the system, to explain and clarify the purpose and mandate of the program and discuss suggested improvements.

The program lacks visibility and promotion with criminal justice professionals, and with Aboriginal communities.

Manitoba is the only province where Native court worker services are delivered and controlled by a non-Native agency. Devolution in child welfare services, in our view, has not started to occur.

The federal-provincial cost-sharing agreement for court communicators requires an advisory council of representatives from Native organizations for Native policy input. Rather feeble attempts have been made on this, but no council has been in existence for a number of years.

Other problems with the program can be noted:

- Over the years, formal training for court communicators has been lacking.
- In 1987, four permanent court communicator positions were unfilled.
- There is confusion as to the communicator's responsibilities for interpretation; little use is made of the budget and referral system to obtain professional interpreters.
- Probation officers were very critical of the Court Communicator Program. They felt the liaison role with probation, outlined in the Manual for Court Communicators, was not being carried out (with a few notable exceptions). In the north, probation officers often carry the court communicator function, as well as their other duties (Native Probation Caucus, 1989).
- There are needs for stronger links between court communicators and the communities they serve. Court communicators (particularly those on circuit courts) are perceived as having too strong an inherent link to the Attorney-General's department and Crown prosecutors.
- Remand staff reported that the court communicators had no systematic way of contacting potential clients and the system was not visible.

All Aboriginal groups contacted were critical of the operation of the program and the lack of input from Native groups.

The Manitoba Association of Friendship Centres (MAC) in 1986 proposed that they become the carrier agencies for this service. They were the original providers of the service from the mid-1960s to 1971. Friendship Centres are carrier agencies in the Yukon, Saskatchewan and Ontario.

In fact, overtures made by the Manitoba Friendship Centres have not been well-received by the Chief Court Communicator. In a workshop sponsored by MAC in 1987, he categorically stated that the program should not be situated in a Native organization, because private agencies are not recognized in court, and for reasons of autonomy. (One need not guess at the amazement of those present, many of whom were involved with mandated—private—Aboriginal child and family service agencies!)

When questioned on the demise of the Court Communicator Advisory Committee (a requirement of the agreement with the federal government), the Chief Court Communicator had this to say:

> In the past, some members on the committee did not attend scheduled meetings and those that did, didn't know anything about the Justice system or how to implement programs, and therefore, made it an ineffective committee (MAC, 1987:9).

The Manitoba Métis Federation would have hoped that the Chief Court Communicator would view training of his own advisory committee as being at least a minimal part of his job given that his own program brochure states:

> The main objective of the Program is to assist all Native people of Manitoba who are involved with the criminal justice system to better understand the procedures, their rights, privileges and responsibilities.

The former Chief Judge of the Provincial Court, while denying that the Program was controlled by the Provincial Court, nonetheless took it upon himself to respond to the Lajeunesse Report and recommendations (letter to Lyle Thompson, Director, Research & Planning, Department of Attorney-General, April 8, 1987). He also gathered all the responses of the court communicator staff, which he attached to the letter.

A few excerpts from his response should suffice to explain why the Manitoba Métis Federation feels there is little will to improve the Program, and little understanding within the highest levels of the court of what the issues are.

On the whole report:

> I can find little in the report deserving of merit....There is a pre-occupation with having the program administered by an independent Native agency....

> The author of the review appears critical of the fact that the program operates below budget, and that we have not increased the number of Court Communicators, even though there is no discernible requirement for an increase in staff....

Having said this, he then states that the Lajeunesse recommendation number 1 (Consultation process with Native groups) "....has no merit and cannot be implemented; For reasons...above including economics". This statement was made in spite of the fact that the Program was coming in under budget. He does concede:

There is no question that the Advisory Board needs to be re-established.

While agreeing that the vacant court communicator positions could have been of use in youth court and in fact, this was being done as an adjunct, amazingly, he states:

The fact of the delivery of this service was concealed from the (Federal) Department of Justice, because they could immediately reduce their portion of the grant....

So much for forthright federal-provincial negotiations for needed services. He also seems to have been unaware of cost-sharing provisions resulting from the implementation of the Young Offenders Act.

Manitoba has shown less commitment than other provinces to funding court communicator services. Manitoba's per capita funding is only 38.5% of the British Columbia level (the best funded), and 71.4% of the expenditures per Native person in Ontario (the second lowest level). Ontario provides 11 Native youth court workers in contrast to the single position in Manitoba. The evaluation of the Ontario Native Courtwork Program (Ontario Ministry of the Attorney-General et al, 1989:60) gives the following financial comparisons:

**AVERAGE 1984-85 TOTAL EXPENDITURE
PER NATIVE PERSON IN THE POPULATION**

Manitoba	$2.20
Ontario	$3.08
Alberta	$4.38
Northwest Territories	$4.38
British Columbia	$5.72

In Manitoba in 1986-87, the per capita expenditures actually dropped to $1.33 (60% of budget), because the budget was underspent by $172,900 due to unfilled positions.

The Ontario study notes that the provision of services to Native victims and witnesses is a difficult role for Native Courtworkers as most of their time is allocated to offender services. In Manitoba this issue is not being addressed and there are no Aboriginal staff attached to the victim-witness assistance program.

The Trial System in Manitoba

A recurring theme of this paper is that non-Aboriginal people keep making decisions about and for Aboriginal people. We are not going to regurgitate a long series of anecdotes or statistics. Other submissions have demonstrated the higher than average Aboriginal involvement and incarceration rates, the high rates of Aboriginal care, the low involvement of Aboriginal people in the Administration of the Justice system, and particularly, in positions of authority. Because you are judges, we ask you to evaluate our assertions. We ask you to rely on our best evidence, your own eyes and experience. We now wish to present problems with several elements of the judicial system leading to trial.

Search, Seizure and Arrest on Warrant

We note that in the document prepared by the Attorney-General's Department of Manitoba (1987), as a draft for a "northern" Justice proposal, the idea is put forward that several secretaries of the (RCMP) have "signing authority only". This pattern, we note, is repeated throughout the province. The purpose of having a judge or magistrate sign a warrant is to provide independent verification of the evidence upon which the application is based, so that the rights of individuals are protected. The same, of course, is true of informants. What the Attorney-General's Department has proposed is that the essence of judicial review and safeguard be omitted.

Bail

Experience has shown that, where judicial interim release is opposed by the police, magistrates are extremely reluctant to release accused persons. While recognizing the need for protection of society it is imperative that the relationship between the police and the magistrate should be distanced, just as it would be inappropriate for an independent arbitrator to be susceptible to pressure from an accused person, it is improper for the police to exercise too great an influence on the judicial process.

Magistrates

Why should non-Aboriginal RCMP officers approve magistrates in Aboriginal communities, and why should the selection of magistrates not be in the hands of local community councils or Manitoba Métis Federation locals? This, more than anything else, is evidence of systemic discrimination against Aboriginal people.

Communication

Local communities complain about the lack of consultation and the lack of information about people removed from the community and the difficulty they have contacting a detained accused person once the police have begun an investigation (Manitoba Métis Federation Internal Report; Métis Anoutch; Manitoba Métis Rights Assembly, 1983).

For both northern and southern communities, Manitoba Métis Federation locals should select appropriate community justice committees. The role of these committees should be to review all cases arising in the area involving Métis persons, to receive and disseminate information to families and persons from the community removed (whether through criminal justice or child agencies), and to monitor the actions of those agencies. Additionally, these committees could relieve the pressure on court communicators and probation officers, and provide the leadership in community involvement for parole review and supervision.

In the courts, we see several problems. These are:

- lack of interpreters;
- poor location and timing of courts;
- poor location of preliminary hearings;
- inadequate jury selection;
- inconsistent representation, and;
- lack of Aboriginal court officers.

Fundamental are the insensitivity and lack of understanding in the Department of Justice generally, as evidenced by the presentation of that Department to this Inquiry. Much of this section will juxtapose our views against those of the Department. The sign of a healthy system is low defensiveness. In reading that submission, it is hard not to note the almost incredible litany of fallacy, part-truth, self-deception and apology. If taken at its face value, the report would have us conclude that two successive attorneys-general were ludicrously lacking in information about their own Department. The only other interpretation is, as some Aboriginal sceptics have alleged, that the purposes of the Inquiry are purely public relations and political manipulation. If the submission of the Department of Justice is totally accurate, then there clearly is no need for the Aboriginal Justice Inquiry as every problem is currently being addressed. This is not borne out by any other credible presentation. Only time and the actions of the Minister of Justice will demonstrate which of these possibilities is true.

Interpreters

The report of the Department of Justice (to the Inquiry) is fundamentally in error with regard to interpreters. First, it assumes in its opening sentences, that Aboriginal people are simply a "different culture". To lump Aboriginal people into multicultural mosaic is to fail to recognize the special place which Aboriginal people occupy in our society.

Second, it assumes, as do courts generally, that an Aboriginal accused will understand the proceedings simply because he or she has a fundamental grasp of English and does not ask for an interpreter. In fact, Native people in Manitoba have a substantial first language retention rate. This is true of many Métis people whose first language is Cree or Saulteaux. The Courts should take more time (as should defence counsel) to determine the level of understanding of an accused for the proceedings. We note that both the Law Society of Manitoba and the Legal Aid evaluations have stated that the vast majority of client problems relate to poor communication between lawyer and client.

While it may well be true, as the Attorney-General's submission notes, that the "....demand for the services of interpreters in our courts has usually been minimal" (Ibid.:15), the need is indeed very great. The problem is twofold: the ethnocentric assumption by non-Aboriginal language-speaking lawyers, judges and court personnel that Aboriginal people who appear to speak English must comprehend the language reasonably well, and the lack of adequate communication between accused persons and lawyers (itself a function of that assumption and of the need for interpreters).

We must also comment on the well-defined, easily accessible model presented in that flawed paper. It would be an adequate system, if improved by some test of understanding; if it bore any semblance to reality. In a recent telephone survey of Friendship Centres in Manitoba, all those contacted could recite instances when emergent first requests for interpreters were made by court officials. Appraisal would have noted that no request for interpreters is made until the morning of trial. Note also that the Lajeunesse Report on Native Court Communicators felt it important enough to note the dangerous dual role that court communicators have been asked to fulfill (Lajeunesse, pgs. 24, 45). This, of course, was a restatement of the Sinclair Report recommendation (1977:119). In the face of their own reports, it is incredible that the Department of the Attorney-General would continue to present such unadulterated fallacies.

In short, the department of the Attorney-General does not, it seems, care one iota about the understanding Aboriginal people have of its proceedings. This is confirmed by many other officials, such as sheriff's officers and probation officers who have often reported accused persons who "....did not seem to understand either the findings, the reasons for same, nor the disposition." We also find it insulting that the department should suggest that it "....has produced a Native Court Interpreters Manual...designed for use by...non-Native interpreters, with simple phonetic pronunciations in Cree and Saulteaux dialects." Can one imagine the uproar (pre-Forest, of course) of using a non-French-speaking interpreter, armed with a Coles Notes of French, interpreting for French-speaking defendants? The prospect of a unilingual Japanese person translating for a unilingual Spanish speaker to an all English jury may not, in such logic, be too remote.

Child welfare, welfare appeals, all other board and tribunals (including driving licence suspension hearings) and Small Claims Court are all defined as "civil litigation" by the Attorney-General thus many of the criminal court services designed to assist Aboriginal people are not available. In matters of guardianship, refusal of welfare, removal of necessary driving privileges and other administrative tribunals, the justice system does not concern itself with the right of Aboriginal people to understand what is happening.

Jury Selection

The fact that the Attorney-General has not ever seen fit to determine the level of Aboriginal participation in the jury process may be statement enough as to apparent lack of concern.

A recently hired counsel for the MMF recalls three of the jury trials which he conducted. Each involved an Aboriginal accused. In each of those cases, the Crown Attorney chose to stand down every prospective Aboriginal juror. In the example used by the Attorney-General for the northern district, why should only sixty Aboriginal people of two hundred and fifty have been selected? This represents only 24% of the panel, yet Aboriginal people constitute 50% of the districts population. A statistical anomaly this great on random sampling would occur less than 1% of the time according to the laws of probability.

Besides the open joking of police officers and lawyers reported to us by Métis and other observers, the example of juries is the most blatant example of institutional racism in the justice system.

The selection of juries is a problem that is inherent to a system where sublimated prejudice is allowed to exist. In the hiring of staff, being Aboriginal ensures that the person will work predominantly with Aboriginal people. While these half measures are better than nothing, they are, simply put, racist and not good enough. Would it not be better if Aboriginal staff persons were seen to be as competent as their colleagues to deal with all people, and not just as staff who have a racial specialty?

The situation is the same with juries. The Aboriginal population of Manitoba is somewhere between 10% and 20%. Surely, on average, across the province and in each judicial district (centre), the percentage of Aboriginal people on a panel should approximate the total population. In order to accomplish that, a full review of the system is necessary to determine why there is consistent Aboriginal under-representation.

As well, we must end the right of a Crown Attorney simply to stand aside Aboriginal people. In such cases the crown attorney should explain decisions which have the effect of limiting jury participation. The underlying theme for this selection is, of course, racism. The theory, advanced by such Crown Attorneys, is that Aboriginal people will be more sympathetic to Aboriginal accused, and, therefore, less likely to convict. It is an overtly racist stereotype to believe that Aboriginal persons are any more tolerant of criminal behaviour than the general population. In short, the Department's position is preposterous.

Judges — Make-up of Court Officials

There are three factors presenting problems with judicial process which require discussion. These are:
1. the low numbers of Aboriginal people employed in the Criminal justice system;
2. the recruitment and training of court officers;
3. prejudice and the "unwritten rule".

(1) Aboriginal People Within the System:

In the Dauphin Judicial District, we have the statistics on the following page from an MMF 1989 telephone survey.

The Native population of the region is approximately 25% of the total population. The involvement rate for Native people is estimated to exceed 50%, however.

It is worth noting that successive authors of papers on aspects of Aboriginal/non-Aboriginal relations have described the system as "colonial".

We also note, that although no formal study of the statistics has been made for all judicial districts of the province, reports indicate a similar pattern elsewhere.

Turning to the submission to the inquiry by the Department of Justice, undergraduate university students in Manitoba are taught to use statistics properly, and are also taught the potential use of statistics to mislead. The lawyers of the Department of Justice must have learned their lessons well, for in a classic example, the Department claimed with pride that 20

Aboriginal people worked at the Youth Centre. What their presentation failed to disclose was that all but two of these were part time only and some of these part time worked as few as eight hours per week.

CATEGORY	TOTAL	NATIVE
Judges	3	0
FT Court Clerks	9	0
Court Reporters	3	0
Probation Officers	4	1
Correctional Officers	36	4
Sheriff's Oficers	5	0
Lawyers	26	1
Paralegals	1	1
Child Care Workers	35	3
Social Assistance Workers	18	0
Native Court Communicators	1	1
TOTAL	**141**	**11**

(2) Recruitment and Training

The recruitment and training received by court officials gives us concern. There is a general lack of adequate cross-cultural training throughout the system, but we will focus upon the Judiciary. We address these concerns of recruitment and training specifically in terms of Aboriginal people.

Judges are recruited by an entirely political process. We understand that lawyers' groups are upset by this, as are Aboriginal people. Lawyers have lobbied for, and received, the right to comment upon and to suggest names for potential judges. It would seem appropriate that Aboriginal people should have these same rights, especially in areas where a high proportion of Aboriginal people are likely to be involved as accused persons.

There appears to be no set criteria to appointments other than political service. This is not to say that judges of outstanding merit have not been appointed, but if political service is the criterion rather than scholarship and legal performance, meritless appointments are inevitable. We suggest that a system is judged by the majority, not the few. We suggest that in a system which truly showed concern for the interests of Aboriginal people, a judge who said "....If you took away all the evidence of drunken Indians I've heard, you wouldn't have very much left...." would be chastised, not promoted. We suggest, further, that criteria — such as publication, type of previous legal practice, balance in types of representation, jurisprudential views, record of community involvement, record of respecting Aboriginal (and minority) rights, reputation in a variety of communities, and knowledge of a broad range of law — are essential qualities of a balanced, reasonable judge. Additionally, selection criteria should reflect a need to balance the various socio-economic groups in society.

We also ask that you consider recommending training for judges. Although, after at least five years and usually much longer, being away from academia and writing may leave a lawyer well-versed in the practicalities of law, it will not ensure an understanding of all areas of law or of current trends in law. To ameliorate this, some justice systems provide for separate and specific training for judges upon appointment.

We could present a listing of stories of ill-prepared, careless or just plain foolish judges. None of them would add to this presentation, and it is not our intention to embarrass any sitting or retired members of the Bench. We ask you to use your own knowledge to see the real root of our concern. We assert that the problem is a fundamental lack of training. The pedagogy of "watch me for a while and learn" is entirely discredited as a learning technique by all serious authors. In short, intensive training for a period of at least six months is usually justified.

We must add that there appears to be little or no training concerning Aboriginal people or Aboriginal values. This, of course, should be an absolute requirement for the training of judges, many of whom, especially at the Provincial Judges Court level, will see a majority of Aboriginal accused in their dockets and many Aboriginal victims. We contend further that the make-up of the Bench in Manitoba is neither reflective of, nor appropriate to, racial, ethnic and gender levels here. It is clear that privileged, non-Native males are over-represented. It is obvious that such a composition does not encourage a wide range of judicial perspective.

(3) Prejudice and the "unwritten rule"

The "unwritten rule" can be described as the belief in any case where the credibility of a police officer is juxtaposed against the credibility of a civilian, that it is the police officer who should be believed. The courts propagate this fallacy with "reasoning" such as "what reason would a police officer have to lie?" They do this by pretending that they do not know the importance which police officers and police forces attach to convictions. They do it by refusing to believe that police witnesses compare notes and stories, or refusing to recognize the psychological phenomenon of people talking themselves into believing their own story.

People involved with the system have reported to us that his "rule" and its operation are commonplace. Certainly there is a belief in the Métis community that the rule operates. One author has even described and documented this rule (Dershowtz, 1982). In short, the rule is both pervasive and destructive; it completely erodes faith in the system. The attempts of police officers to lie, misrepresent the facts, exaggerate, stonewall and hide behind such phases as " I don't remember" in this Inquiry are the outgrowth of that "unwritten rule".

This is, of course, legitimized by the unequivocal tendency of non-Aboriginal judges to openly and contemptuously deride the testimony of Aboriginal people on the grounds that they must be prejudiced. If those who judge us hold such ludicrous racist attitudes, can the non-Aboriginal police be expected to do otherwise?

LEGISLATIVE HISTORY

The Hudson Bay Company was given control of the area now covered by Manitoba boundaries without the acquiescence agreement of Aboriginal people. Nonetheless, the British Parliament monitored the land grant and the relationship between the Métis and the Indian. On March 2, 1857, evidence was given to the Select Committee of the British House of Commons on the Hudson's Bay Company:[2]

1747.   Mr. Grogen: What privilges or rights do the Native Indians possess strictly applicable to themselves?—They are perfectly at liberty to do what they please; we never restrain Indians.

1748.   Is there any difference between their position and that of the halfbreeds?—None at all. They hunt and fish, and live as they please. They look to us for their supplies, and we study their comfort and convenience as much as possible; we assist each other.

1749.   Lord Stanley: You exercise no authority whatever over the Indian tribes?—None at all.

1750.   If any tribe were pleased now to live as the tribes did live before the country was opened up to Europeans; that is to say, not using any article of European manufacture or trade, it would be in their power to do so?—Perfectly so; we exercise no control over them.

1751.   Mr. Bell: Do you mean that, possessing the right of soil over the whole of Rupert's Land, you do not consider that you possess any jurisdiction over the inhabitants of that soil:

— No, I am not aware we do. We exercise none, whatever right we possess under our charter.

1752.   Then is it the case that you do not consider that the Indians are under your jurisdiction when any crimes are committed by the Indians upon the whites?—They are under our jurisdiction when crimes are committed upon the whites, but not when committed upon each other; we do not meddle with their wars.

1753.   What law do you consider in force in the case of the Indians committing any crime upon the whites; do you consider that the clause in your licence to trade, by which you are bound to transport criminals to Canada for trial, refers to the Indians, or solely to the whites?—To the whites, we conceive.

1754.   Mr. Morgan: Are the Native Indians permitted to barter skins inter see from one tribe to another?—Yes.

1755.   There is no restriction at all in that respect?—None at all.

1756.   Is there any restriction with regard to the half-breeds in that respect?—None as regard dealings among themselves.

The fact that Métis people had Aboriginal rights was not recognized again after the eighteen eighties), until the Constitution Act of 1982. The significance, of course, being that the rights of the Métis to carry on traditional avocations of hunting, fishing, trapping and gathering were substantially abridged by the successive governments of Canada and Manitoba. The further significance being that, because of treaties, and the British North America Act and interpretations given by successive governments, there has been created a separation of the rights óf Aboriginal peoples. Both of these need an appropriate redress.

Of general concern to Aboriginal people is the fact that the courts have consistently ruled the agreements made with Indians or on behalf of "Indians" nonetheless are subject to unilateral, arbitrary amendment by the federal government. The above examples include:

Frances v The Queen (1956) S.C.R. 6/8 in which the Court held that where an agreement made with the United States that Indians were not required to pay duty, and the Customs Act was silent as to this exemption, duties were still payable.

and

Sikyea v The Queen (1964) S.C.R. 642; R.V. George (1966) S.C.R. 267 where, despite treaty assuring the contrary, Indians were made subject to the Migratory Birds Convention Act.

In the minds of the lawmakers and the Hudson Bay Company prior to Confederation the Aboriginal right of the Métis was assured. The fact of this right was once again confirmed 1982 [Constitution Act section 35(2)]. This issue, amongst others, is currently before the courts and is in the Supreme Court of Canada on procedural issues (Dumont et al v. A/G (Canada) and A/G (Manitoba)). Judicial authority for this position can be found in the judgement of O'Sullivan, J. (dissenting), and is not rejected by the majority.

Provincial government meekly agree that the Métis are not Indians for the purpose of Section 91 (24) of the B.N.A. Act. They do so because the federal governments say so. Yet, the federal governments maintained until 1939 the same about the Inuit. In Re Eskimos (1939) S.C.R. 104, the Supreme Court held that it is important to note that the framers of the B.N.A. Act contemplated the issue of Inuit (and by implication Métis). This was confirmed by Duff, C. J. C.:

> The British North America Act is a statute dealing with British North America and, in determining the meaning of the words "Indians" in the statute, we have to consider the meaning of that term as applied to the inhabitants of British North America. In 1867 more than half of the Indian population of British North America were within the boundaries of Rupert's Land and the North-Western Territory; and of the Eskimo population nearly ninety percent were within the boundaries. It is, therefore, important to consult the reliable sources of information as to the use of the term "Indian" in relation to the Eskimo in those territories. Fortunately, there is evidence of the most authoritative character furnished by the Hudson's Bay Company itself (p 106).

He then continued;

> A committee of the House of Commons in 1856 and 1857 investigated the affairs of the Company. Among the matters which naturally engaged the attention of the Committee was the Company's relations with and conduct towards the Aborigines; and for the information of the Committee a census was prepared and produced before it by the officers of the Company showing the Indian populations under its rule throughout the whole of the North American continent.

The rationale for this is clear. Duff, C. J. C. determined that

....the officials of the Hudson's Bay Company which, in 1867, as already observed, exercised powers of government and administration over this great tract; (Ibid.:109).

The essential point the federal government makes is that Métis were never "under the protection" of the Crown. But Duff, C. J. C. again says that this is nonsense.

Then it is said they were never "connected" with the British Crown or "under the protection" of the Crown. I find some difficulty in affirming that the Eskimo and other Indians ruled by the Hudson's Bay Company, were never under the protection of the Crown, and in understanding how, especially in view of the Proclamations cited" (Ibid.:115).

Clearly, if the Hudson's Bay Company accepted responsibility for the Métis at least to the same level as to the Indian and regarded each as "Aboriginal" then they were, in fact, "under the protection" of the Crown because the Hudson's Bay Company was a creation of and therefore in effect (under international law) an agent of and responsible to the British Crown. What other interpretation can make sense of the committee debate cited earlier.

In a separate opinion, Cannon, J. went further to say:

This, I think, disposes of the very able argument on behalf of the Dominion that the word "Indians" in the British North America Act must be taken in a restricted sense. The Upper and Lower Houses of Upper and Lower Canada petitioners to the Queen, understood that the English word "Indians" was equivalent to or equated the French word "Sauvages" and included all the present and future Aborigines native subjects of the proposed Confederation of British North America, which at the time was intended to include Newfoundland.

By use of the words "present and future Aborigines Native subjects", there is ample support for the suggestion that the 1982 Constitution Act, by including Métis as an Aboriginal people, must also include them as "Indians". We suggest no other interpretation is appropriate.

From this, theorists have drawn the conclusion that while the federal government has legislative authority over other Aboriginal peoples, they have chosen not to act accordingly in matters where it was not in their interest to do so.

The province of Manitoba has legislative authority over natural resources. If the province chooses to correct this historic wrong perpetrated upon Métis people, if it has the will finally to correct this error it can be done. It can also be done if responsibility is forced upon them as was the case in *Forest V. R.* respecting the enactment of statutes in English only.

The example of natural resources rights can be added to separate Indian child caring agencies, separate control of education, greater power of freedom with respect to the paroles and releases and greater autonomy for justice committees. None of these have been afforded the Métis. These functions are subsumed respectively within education, child care, provincial corrections, and the administration of justice, all provincial responsibilities.

A further piece needs to be written about the continuing drain of natural resources from aboriginal control. With the exception of one agreement (Sherridon), there is no Aboriginal impact upon the decision-making process. As other parts of our presentation make clear, the problems of Aboriginal people in Manitoba cannot be so compartmentalized that neat categories of "child welfare problem", "criminal justice problem", and so on can be made easily.

The problems are, in fact, more fundamental. As the social and economic base of Aboriginal peoples were either destroyed (fishing and trapping), or stolen (the current Manitoba Métis Federation land claim regarding scrip is an example), it became more and more convenient to blame the victim. It is not uncommon to hear non Aboriginal peoples say, "If Native people want to go back to their old ways, let them, but cut off all of our help to them, otherwise they should be just the same as the rest of us".

The lack of logic and sensitivity, of this argument is truly astounding. It is understood by all that the traditional ways of living are no longer totally possible. That does not, we assert, end the centuries long socio-cultural ties with these traditional ways. Most importantly, the "argument" cited above fails to recognize a now fundamental tenet of Canadian law. If you have a duty of care, breach that duty and cause damage, then you are liable to correct the damage. We suggest that society has a duty to protect each of its members and has clearly caused damage to Aboriginal people generally and Métis people in particular. Far from government recognizing the need to correct the damage it continues to inflict damage.

The interests of Aboriginal people in management of resources is well-documented. The setting of rules and their enforcement are left almost entirely to non-Aboriginal people. There are almost no Aboriginal conservation or parks officers, and there are none at any meaningful senior level. Studies, reports, and expressed concerns of Aboriginal people fall entirely on deaf ears.

A case in point involves the new Swan-Pelican Forest Management Area. This area borders nine communities, of which seven use it as a primary border area. The nine are Pelican Rapids, Shoal River Indian

Reserve, the Rural Municipality (RM) of Minitonas, the Local Government District (LGD) of Mountain, Birch River Indian Reserve, Briggs Spur, Camperville, Pine Creek Indian Reserve and Duck Bay.

Department of Natural Resources officials asked the Aboriginal communities if they agreed with development of small areas near their communities. The small communities were concerned about maintaining traditional hunting, fishing, trapping and gathering places. These, they were assured, would be protected.

At a public meeting involving the nine communities, after a series of questions, the representatives of the RM of Minitonas and the LGD of Mountain left after it was apparent that none of their rights would be affected. The Aboriginal communities argued that their traditional lands should be renewed, that this area had been banked on for some time by them for economic development, and that this was a perfect opportunity for the provincial government to begin the self-determination process. The communities were assured by (then) Minister of Natural Resources, Leonard Harapiak, that further meetings would take place, and that no decision would be made without consultation. Three subsequent letters written by the Swan-Pelican Aboriginal Management Committee requesting consultation went unacknowledged by this minister, and finally the communities learned by a happen stance reading of the Manitoba Gazette that the Forest Management Area had been created by fiat.

While this anecdote does not reflect directly upon the administration of justice, it is instructive in that:

1. no senior officials were Aboriginal people;

2. Aboriginal views were entirely ignored;

3. the effect will be to create, to label a new class of Native offender under Manitoba law;

4. it provides among the clearest recent evidence that government in Manitoba is not concerned enough to address Aboriginal issues.

This sound of injustice rings familiar in our ears when we hear the words department of justice and court officials, lawyers, off-reserve child caring agencies, probation departments, corrections and police officers!

NOTES

1.   This chapter is an edited version of the portions of the MMF presentation that were not included in Part Two of this book. David N. Gray and Lawrence J. Barkwell provided the research for this section.

2.   PAM, Report HBC, House of Commons, England, August 1857:91-98.

3.   As it turns out this point was quite well taken. Since this report was presented to the Aboriginal Justice Inquiry further examples of discriminatory treatment of Metis and Indians have come to our attention. The 1989 Annual Report of the Manitoba Human Rights Commission documents a common type of complaint regarding police behaviour.

> The complainant, an aboriginal woman, was arrested and taken into custody by two male police officers of a Police Department in Manitoba. During her detainment, she was physically assaulted by the officers. At one point, when they searched her person, she objected to being searched by male officers. One officer poured water on her head and crotch area in the course of which a racially derogatory remark was made. The officers examined her various pieces of identification and they questioned the complainant about the fact that they bore different surnames. She explained that she had had one name change when she remarried a few months earlier and that the other surname was her birth name. One officer remarked "What's the matter? Can't hold on to a man?" The officers also questioned the complainant as to her occupation. When she advised them that she was an Economic Development Officer, they made derogatory as to her occupation and that of aboriginal peoples. During her detention, the complainant asked permission to phone a lawyer on several occasions. When she was finally permitted to make a phone call, she called one individual. As she was describing to this person how she was physically assaulted and how water had been poured on her, one of the officers told her that her time was up and ordered her to get off the phone. (Human Rights Commission, 1989:25)

The Human Rights Commission investigation revealed that:

> Medical reports based on an examination of the complainant on the same day confirmed injuries sustained to various parts of her body. The complainant's account to medical staff were consistent with her allegations of physical assault by the police

officers. A witness confirmed that he recieved a phone call from the complainant during the period she was in custody at which time she told him that the police officers physically assaulted her and poured water on her. This witness also confirmed that this phone conversation ended abruptly when the complainant told him that she was being ordered to get off the phone. (Ibid.:25)

The Human Rights Commission decided that:

There was clearly a discrepancy between the complainant's account of the incidents concerning her arrest and subsequent detainment, and the version of the police officers themselves. However, on the totality of the evidence on all facts in dispute and the credibility of all witnesses, the Commission concluded that an ajudicator could find in the complainants favour. As a result, conciliation was attempted.

Although the police department was not prepared to admit to a contravention of the Human Rights Act, they did acknowledge the complainants detention did contain procedural irregularities.

On that basis, the department was prepared to resolve the complaint. In addition to a monetary payment of $1,500 to the complainant, the department provided a letter of apology. It also agreed to issue a police notice to its members that discriminitory treatment, including verbal or physical harassment based upon the group factors set out in the Human Rights Code is unacceptable conduct and that, where evidence establishes that such conduct has taken place, serious disciplanary consequences shall occur. The respondent police department also agreed to reassess its present cross-cultural training program for entry level police officers as well as the cross-cultural training presently done on an in-service basis for all its members. (Ibid.:25)

RECOMMENDATIONS

Ron H. Richard
David N. Chartrand
Denise Thomas

We think it necessary to divide our recomendations into three distinct categories. We have not had time in the development of this paper to address various problems such as the Mental Health Act, rights to education or problems within the justice system, as given reference in the Manitoba Ombudsman's reports to the legislature. We have not addressed the structure or details of a proposed Metis justice system. The Manitoba Métis Federation (MMF) intends to address fully all such issues at a subsequent time given further resources.

The first group, Section A contains recommendations respecting the self determination of Métis people. The second, Section B, contains recommendations for short term transfer of specific programs to Aboriginal control. The third group, Section C, deals with systemic changes necessary for the remaining "parts" of the system.

These recommendations are advanced with the understanding that they are neither exhaustive or exclusive of the position the MMF is developing. These should be seen as the minimum standard the MMF expects and not as limits on its position. The process, which has come to be known as "tripartite" should now include references to the judicial system.

SECTION A

1. It is necessary that the respective governments recognize the necessity of self-determination and of judicial control of Aboriginal peoples for Aboriginal peoples. It is equally imperative that the governments of both Canada and Manitoba negotiate *in good faith* with Aboriginal peoples to transfer necessary power and authority for this.

To this end, we adopt the recommendations, *inter alia,* of the Canadian Bar Association, and specifically:

a) that there be established alternative, parallel Aboriginal justice systems;

b) that Aboriginal communities have the opportunity to divert cases out of the existing justice system;

c) that Aboriginal communities and organizations be encouraged and supported (both administratively and financially) in the establishment of separate correctional and after-care facilities;

d) that appropriate programming be established to provide for the treatment, training and reintegration of Aboriginal offenders, with the appropriate planning with the offender and the community for such reintegration;

e) that provision for appropriate spiritual, religious and traditional activities be made for Aboriginal offenders.

To implement this would entail, as is noted on page 86 of the Canadian Bar Association report:

> Two broad approaches are needed to respond to the unique situation of native offenders. The first and the most far-reaching would involve the enactment of legislation to enable native people to assume control of correctional processes that affect them. This enabling legislation would transfer to native groups a significant degree of jurisdiction for providing correctional services. The locus of services would rest with such groups as Indian Bands, Tribal Councils, Inuit or Métis communities or Aboriginal correctional organizations. The legislation would also include provisions to negotiate specific administrative and financial details of the transfer of jurisdictions. After successful completion of the negotiations, the native groups would be mandated to provide a range of services, through the establishment of correctional institutions, parole and after-care facilities or other culturally-appropriate services in their communities.

2. That all natural resources be transferred through an appropriate agreement to an agency represented equally by Métis, Indian and provincial government officials with full authority to manage, control, improve and allocate the benefits therefrom.

3. That the provincial government allocate an appropriate land base for Métis people. The court of jurisdiction for offences on such land would be the courts created under Recommendation 1(a).

4. Specifically we recommend the establishment of a self-contained, separate, parallel Métis justice system with appropriate funding and authority. While enabling legislation is pursued through the tripartite process, the following steps should be undertaken in consultation with the Manitoba Métis Federation:

SECTION B

1. a) That the expenditure base for correctional facilities be restricted and the expenditure base for community programming and alternatives to incarceration, including Aboriginal traditional, non-adversarial, and adult diversion programs be correspondingly increased.

    b) That full and meaningful disclosure of the expenditure be provided to assure compliance with Recommendation 1(a) above.

    c) That the Department of Justice clearly states goals for reduction of recidivism amongst Aboriginal offenders, and to account for any failure to achieve those results.

2. That the provincial government, together with the Manitoba Métis Federation and appropriate Indian organizations, begin negotiations with the federal government to correct the problems with federal Corrections and the criminal law identified herein and in other submissions to the Inquiry.

3. That the Province of Manitoba immediately mandate a Métis child and family services agency to be called Michif Child and Family Services as proposed to the Minister of Family Services.

4. That in areas under the authority of the Department of Northern Affairs, the number, authority and responsibility of community constables be increased, with all the necessary improvements as to wages, training and equipment.

5. That the existing community constable program operating under the Department of Northern Affairs be transferred to the Manitoba Métis Federation Inc.

6. That a permanently staffed, toll-free Legal Aid telephone line be established and be accessible from all points in Manitoba with the number prominently displayed in all police stations. We feel that the availability of this service should be made known to all suspects and accused as a matter of policy. This line would be staffed by lawyers or trained paralegals and would provide quick, easy-to-understand advice and begin the involvement of an advocate.

7. That immediate funding be provided to the Manitoba Métis Federation Inc. to establish its own advocacy services to act in matters of criminal justice, family law and public interest law.

8. a) That control of the court communicator program be *portaged* to an appropriate Aboriginal carrier agency.

   b) That the remaining outstanding recommendations of the Sinclair and Lajeunesse Reports be implemented by such an Aboriginal carrier agency.

9. a) That there be more and better trained court communicators, with increased responsibility for informing clients and for follow-up of cases to ensure satisfaction and understanding. They should also act as a client reference for issues, such as police conduct.

   b) That court communicators assist those clients who are unhappy with the legal services provided in the resolution of their complaints.

10. That court communicators act as investigators and reference people for defence counsel to reduce the cost of preparation and thereby the Legal Aid payout, and to provide:

    a) greater, and more reliable, information for defence counsel.

    b) better information flow to clients and their families, thus assuring better understanding of the process and issues, including the competence or commitment of counsel.

11. That interpreters be provided for Aboriginal persons appearing in civil, as well as criminal, matters and particularly in family court actions with respect to guardianship of their children.

12. That the Province undertake the establishment and support of Métis Justice Committees in each Manitoba Métis Federation local, which will:

a) review the apprehensions and interventions under the Child Welfare Act; and

b) monitor the conduct of agencies; and

c) provide an information flow between the system and the community; and

d) assist in the development and operation of diversion, prevention, after-care programs; and,

e) provide appropriate reporting and supervision for parole releases.

13. That the system of appointment of Métis magistrates, particularly in remote communities, be changed to allow nomination by the community council or the Manitoba Métis Federation local.

14. That the Province of Manitoba and the City of Winnipeg conjointly fund an MMF-based, Métis/Police Community Relations Officer position, and that the province and the RCMP conjointly fund a similar rural position without restricting any similar, necessary positions for Indian people.

15. That the province fund Aboriginal groups to establish an Aboriginal victim-witness assistance program. Particularly, the Criminal Injuries Compensation Program should be advertised, and victims should be assisted in making claims to the Criminal Injuries Compensation Board.

16. That the Chief Judge of the Manitoba courts enter into immediate negotiations with the MMF and other Aboriginal groups with a view to setting up a cross-cultural training program for judges and magistrates. This would be subsequently delivered by Aboriginal organizations.

17. That appropriate sections be added to the Criminal Law curriculum at the Law School of the University of Manitoba based upon the training package proposed for judges and magistrates.

SECTION C

1. That all non-Aboriginal people involved in the justice system and programs arising therefrom, take mandatory sensitivity training to enable them to understand the cultural background and needs of Métis and other Aboriginal offenders.

This training curriculum should be prepared and delivered by the Manitoba Métis Federation and other appropriate Aboriginal organizations.

2. That the Province of Manitoba be required to adhere to the standards for institutions and community supervision outlined in the Canadian Criminal Justice Association Standards manuals.

3. That institutional housing of open custody offenders cease, and that Aboriginal families be recruited and trained to operate open custody homes for Aboriginal youth.

4. That the provisions of Section 30(1-6) of the Young Offenders Act (Review Board), be implemented in Manitoba. This review board would provide opportunity for input from the community. If the board has sufficient representation from the Aboriginal communities and Aboriginal organizations, it could monitor custody sentences, facilitate reintegration into the community, and ameliorate what appears to be discriminatory over-use of this sanction for Aboriginal youth.

This review board should have appropriate regionalized membership in order to be credible and effective.

We advocate that in adult corrections (for people from provincial sentences), there be established a provincial parole board under the provisions of the Manitoba Corrections Act, Part IV, Sec. 47(1).

Amendment would have to be made to the Corrections Act to allow for a larger and more regionalized Board.

5. That the federal Institute for Women in Kingston be closed or alternately, that all Manitoba women, and particularly Aboriginal women prisoners, be repatriated to Manitoba via the federal/provincial arrangements already in existence.

6. a) That the long delayed review and amendment of the Manitoba Corrections Act should be expeditiously completed with full public input and mandatory input from Aboriginal organizations.

   b) That, while it is recognized that fine options and community service orders are a generally successful alternative, more study must be done on the reported problem of lower success rates for Aboriginal women.

7. That the National Parole Board cease the practice of using police officers to carry out community assessments for the purpose of parole consideration, and contract this work out to appropriate Aboriginal groups.

8.   That there be an immediate study of "gating" practices (by the National Parole Board) as they pertain to Aboriginal "detainees" in the prairie region. Why Aboriginal people are disproportionately affected should be determined through (amongst others) representations from Manitoba Metis Federation and other Aboriginal groups.

9.   a) That the province enter into negotiations with the federal government, or enact provincial legislation, making it a criminal or quasi-criminal offence for ANY person in a position of authority knowingly to discriminate or commit any discriminatory act or make any racist comment or statements.

   b) Similarly, it should be an offence to acquiesce in, or fail to report any such act or comment.

10.   That in parts of Manitoba not served by community constables, police be required to recruit and maintain numbers of Aboriginal officers in proportion to the Aboriginal people in the population, and thereafter to provide for promotion to increase the influence of such officers.

11.   That the province amend the legislation governing the Law Enforcement Review Agency to provide a process as delineated in the policing section.

12.   That Counsel be available for all Law Enforcement Review Agency and other like cases, to ensure that client interests are observed.

13.   That there be an increase in the number of legal aid providers (even on an itinerant basis) to expand the outreach and other roles and mandates of Legal Aid Manitoba.

14.   That circuit courts be better organized with either permanent court communicators (or paralegals) in each community and arrival by all defence counsel to meet with clients, witnesses, and others before court dates.

15.   That where sufficient numbers of youth court cases exist, night courts be instituted so that working poor are able to attend court with their children.

16.   That attempts be made by advocates in ensuring contact with clients and perhaps including being available outside of offices.

17.   That the Manitoba Department of Justice adhere to the "United Nations Draft Rules for the Protection of Juveniles Deprived of Their Liberties".

18. That courts insist on a report by court communicators or a lawyer appearing on behalf of an accused, assuring that the accused person is fully familiar with English (or French), and is competent to understand all proceedings against him or her.

19. That recruitment of Aboriginal people for openings in all courts and related agencies be made a priority until levels of appointment approximate population trends.

20. That the Native Alcholism Council/Children's Home sniffing project proposal for solvent abusers, the Ma-Mawi-Chi-Itata Centre program for domestic violence, and all like prevention/diversion programs secure immediate financial assistance and the active support of the Department of Justice.

21. That the Ikwewak Project and other like projects for Aboriginal women offenders receive immediate financial assistance and the active support of the Department of Justice.

CONCLUSIONS

It has been the recurring theme of this submission that non-Aboriginal people keep making decisions about and for Aboriginal people. The Manitoba Métis Federation research and analysis of the impact of the justice system on the Métis is ultimately a study of the social control of Aboriginal people within the contemporary state.

The irony is that to discover indigenous people with any type of formal legal autonomy in North America, one has to look at the USA. There, Indian Tribal courts and codes of law exist, while in Canada they do not. Indeed, little or no customary law has been incorporated into Canadian law, let alone has it survived in a coherent form. In this respect, the pacification of the Canadian Indian has been even more complete than that of the Australian Aboriginal people. The federal government in Australia has, for some years, referred the task of examining and retrieving Aboriginal customary law to its Law Reform Commission (Havemann, 1983: 3).

Even a cursory overview of Métis history in Manitoba reveals that natural resource development and other capitalist ventures have fueled the exploitative relationship between Canada and the Métis Nation. This set of uneven exchanges has resulted in the damaging under-development that the indigenous people now experience, whether they be rural residents or urban migrants. The unfair application of the law has also degraded this relationship.

There is a growing body of national and provincial knowledge that suggests a deep problem does exist in our justice system...Findings from reviews of literature and direct research by associates of Prairie Justice Research suggest that discrimination against indigenous people operates at every stage of involvement in the criminal justice system (Harding, 1989).

These same forces have shaped the "corrections industry" where non-Aboriginal job creation is pursued at the expense of justice for indigenous people, its ostensible reason for existence. The image of regular airlifts of highly-paid white professionals into isolated communities to dispense justice, followed by the subsequent airlift out of Aboriginal offenders to fill large urban institutions, is an image that the MMF finds distasteful. No one has yet argued that this practise is done because it prevents crime or rehabilitates people; they argue that irt exists as a practice for economic reasons. But there is clearly one class of people who benefit from these economics and another group that is harshly penalized—each for the sake of the economics.

The MMF would argue, as have others, that semi-autonomous justice services delivered and controlled by Aboriginal groups are only appropriate when indigenous people can also participate in making rules which are to be enforced, and, when an aboriginal agency also has an advocacy role. MMF research has revealed that the integregation of indigenous people into the imposed social control system has been a painfully slow process simply co-opting Aboriginal people into an alien value system which has produced mostly negative results.

Racial stereotyping is only reinforced by the observed double standard with respect to lower pay, lower qualifications, and the lesser support structures and inadequate budgets, which are the hallmarks of the affirmative action type of programs implemented to date. Examples which come to mind are those of the Native Clan Organization and Dakota Ojibway policing contracts, the RCMP Special Constable Program, the Provincial Court Communicator Program and the integration of probation and correction services.

More importantly, the causes (of the ever-growing rate of indigenous people in jail) are also found in the marginal position of indigenous people in the economy, and the roots of this are in the colonization of British North America.

Until the process of under-development in Canada are squarely faced, and it is financially admitted that the criminal justice system cannot treat socio-economically rooted "crime" (as is the vicious circle of poverty, crime, rebellion, and repression) will continue.

It is the solution of these underlying problems, not further criminalization of social issues that the public policy process in Canada should be emphasizing (Harding, 1989).

The racism that the MMF has observed in the justice system resides in the individuals and their lack of respect, sensitivity and awareness of Aboriginal peoples. This racism is perpetuated and exacerbated, if not created, by the dehumanizing and depersonalized institution of the dominant society police, court and correctional responsibilities.

There is no observed plan on the part of individuals or any conspiracy in the system to be racist, but we can also fairly state that:

- there is no effective plan *not* to be racist;
- there is no comprehensive plan to be culturally sensitive;
- there are no significant affirmative action results; and
- there is no plan to overcome the structural racism that disallows Métis people meaningful participation in a system which, by all measures, has a disproportionately negative impact on Métis youths and young adults, and is particularly harsh in the treatment of Métis women.

The annual reports of the government which we reviewed are replete with numbers—numbers of people processed and numbers of dollars spent. It is a system managing numbers, not social problems; there has been an almost complete abrogation of this responsibility by government agencies.

By labelling a problem as too complex, or related to what they wish to perceive as non-justice issues—poverty, alcoholism, low education, lack of jobs—the justice system cradles and nurtures a philosophy of despair. It becomes apparent that this system of so-called justice cannot and will not be held responsible for either the improvement of offenders or the deteriorating situation. Furthermore, by not relating their programs to measures of effectiveness, they avoid responsibility for failure, they avoid questions as to relevancy and feed the syndrome of blaming the victim.

This situation cannot be allowed to continue in a civilized society. As Dr. Keith Jobson, Faculty of Law, University of Victoria, pointed out as early as 1977:

The availability of a tax supported prosecution and court branch of the industry must not be allowed to continue as a magnet to draw to it cases that should properly be dealt with by alternative sanctioning systems.

To this end, prosecutorial and police services should be reviewed to ensure that relatively non-serious cases are not put forward for entry into the crime industry or unnecessarily processed into the penal sector. Restraint, economy, and justice demand this at the front gate of the industry.

It is our assessment that there are clearly a number of factors which interact to produce the over-representation of Métis people as offenders (and especially as offenders with high re-involvement rates). These same factors interact to make Métis people more susceptible to victimization.

1. There has been an historical repression of Métis custom (traditional), social structures and support systems.

2. The Metis have little discretionary time or money available to respond as a community to the problems of the crime.

3. Official responses to the problems documented above are usually framed in terms of social control rather than social development.

4. Aboriginal people as a visible minority have been denigrated and their history has been conveyed in a distorted way. In youths this leads to self-derogation, feelings of helplessness and alienation.

5. The intended child welfare remedies have not worked for Metis children.

6. Official justice system interventions have been culturally alien or irrelevant and poorly understood by the Métis community.

7. Participation in lawmaking and the administration of the laws has been effectively denied the Métis.

8. The official justice system has acted in ways which engender disrespect and cynicism within the Métis community.

9. In many instances correctional and other related services have been denied or not made available to the Métis.

When a people are weakened by these factors which we view as additive as well as interactive, the symptoms as above, of which crime is but one factor, are inevitably found to be in ascendancy.

It is obvious from the foregoing that the only reasonable, appropriate long-term solution is to transfer authority in all matters of justice, corrections and child and family services to Aboriginal people and Aboriginal-directed agencies where the advancement of their specific interests is at stake. It is only through this transfer that the vast economic windfall created by the "consumers" of the justice system can be eradicated and redirected toward amelioration of the factors identified by the MMF. *We, therefore, urge the* **commission of inquiry to recommend, and the respective** *governments to take the necessary actions and enact the necessary laws to ensure compliance with the fundamental principle that issues affecting Aboriginal people predominantly should be controlled by Aboriginal people predominantly.*

We recognize, of course, that this will not be accomplished in the short- to medium-term. Both the federal and provincial governments have vested interests to protect. Within the structure we have developed, and on behalf of Métis people, we propose the initiation and development of negotiated settlements of the trasnfer of control through the tripartite process that has been so successful in other areas. In suggesting this process, we do not in any way abrogate our position, nor do we propose that by entering into such discussions the respective governments in any way prejudice their positions. We do propose, however, that entry into such negotiations must be genuine, for the purpose of resolving these issues, not prolonging them.

In the short term, and in addition to the other systemic changes herein recommended, we propose the transfer of specific programs to the Manitoba Métis Federation on behalf of Métis people in Manitoba. The Manitoba Métis Federation would propose bilateral negotiations with the Province of Manitoba in this regard concerning the particular service areas outlined in the recommendation section. We believe that transfers could be effected without any substantial new monies and could be accomplished by transfers from existing budgets on a per capita formula. (Current per capita costs for all provincial justice services in Manitoba are currently in the vicinity of $120 per year.)

As we have said earlier, there are two recurring themes of this presentation. First, that the history of the "justice" system in Manitoba reflects the ongoing reality of Aboriginal people as premium payers and non-Aboriginal people as general beneficiaries. This is most evident in the fact that white people perpetually make the decisions that directly effect the Aboriginal people.

Perhaps more importantly, however, the Commissioners and the government will not be judged on how long it takes. You will not be judged on how "pretty" the report is, nor necessarily upon what words are spoken or recommendations given. Like all players on the stage of history, you will be judged upon actions and results. The only satisfactory action, the only proper result is the transfer of appropriate responsibility. Without this, we will consider the exercise a failure. We have long known that the system, and some people within it, were biased against us. Some of the presentations at these hearings confirm this belief. What we now expect is the correction of that iniquity.

SOME IMPLICATIONS OF THE CURRENT METIS CASE

Samuel W. Corrigan

In one sense all history, like the common law of Canada, is revisionist. Historians as well as judges seek to interpret a particular set of circumstances, documented in various ways, in light of contemporary thought. Although the particular "facts"—the "files" or documents—of a situation may remain the same, the interpretations of their balance and their significance are likely to vary with the social and intellectual philosophy of their interpretor, especially in light of persuasive but hitherto unstated arguments.

The Métis of Manitoba appeared sporadically in the history books of Canada and the west in the middle third of this century (Stanley, 1936; Giraud, 1945; Morton, 1957), but did not become the subject of intense external scrutiny until the 1970s. Then, as research into Métis land rights began to demonstrate some glaring inequities of process, a spate of writers emerged either to set the record down in detail or to set the record straight (Sealey and Lussier, 1975; Sprague, 1980; 1988; Friesen 1984;). This was complemented by many new collections of Métis research (Petersen and Brown, 1985; Lussier, 1983). Most recently, such agencies as the federal Department of Justice have funded research on Métis land rights, in the face of the Manitoba Métis Federation suit in the Court of Queen's Bench (Flanagan, 1991).

All of these works are revisionist to some degree, either because they offer new interpretations of old facts, or because they examine old material for the first time and place it in the context of previous research. Several salient and long noted points have remained unscathed through these new volumes of old history however. Virtually all have acknowledged the concept of a Métis culture and society (or possibly societies) in the west prior to 1870. This idea, simple though it might seem, is of critical importance for any discussion of current or future Métis rights. It is acknowledged that the

Métis, frequently referred to as the Red River Métis, were relatively numerous (over 2500 in 1839, 6000 by 1857, and 9800 in 1871), a very significant proportion of the population of Red River (65% in 1839, 84% in 1857, and 86% in 1871), organized at several levels and clearly conscious of being Métis. They had, by 1870, a history as a people spanning several generations, a history replete with heroes and folklore, with a tradition of standing up for their interests as a community against the putative "owner" of their territory, the Hudson's Bay Company.

Another point which has survived the latest histories is the role of the Métis in the fur trade, notably in the buffalo fur trade. More details have been added to the specifics of the Métis in trade relationships with the Hudson Bay Company and as traders themselves. As well, more information has been published documenting the Métis role as traders and carters, and in the agricultural life of the Red River community.

A further point, generally long recognized, of the Métis as an organized people, has been strengthened by the publication of additional information (as in this volume) on the legal nature of Métis society, specifically in terms of the buffalo hunt, but also in terms of inter-governmental negotiation.

There is no dispute then in this lengthy list of recently published works that the Métis of the west in 1870 formed an identifiable and viable culture and society, played a significant economic role in the developing Red River colony, and were both organized in activities and legalistic in their approach to the maintenance of orderly social relations.

Where disputes have arisen in very recent decades the concern has often been over two major issues. The first is over the root causes of the migration, dispersion and loss of land base of the Red River Métis following 1870. The second is over the possible continuing viability of Métis society and culture. Both of these are certainly factors in the current legal proceedings between the federal government and the Manitoba Métis Federation, and both need to be examined to some extent. But first it is useful to outline the suit now in progress.

DUMONT ET AL. v ATTORNEY GENERAL OF CANADA AND ATTORNEY GENERAL OF MANITOBA

In 1985, Yvon Dumont, acting as President of the Manitoba Métis Federation and 17 others, all members of the Manitoba Métis Federation, and the Native Council of Canada representing Métis nationally, sued on behalf of all Métis of present day Manitoba to correct what is viewed as a major inequity of law over the past 120 years.

It is necessary here to recap some of the features of that turbulent period in 1869 and 1870 leading to the creation of Manitoba as a province within Canada on an equal footing with Ontario, Quebec, New Brunswick and Nova Scotia, the four original provinces of the 1867 Dominion of Canada.

It had been proposed that the Dominion of Canada purchase the rights of the Hudson's Bay Company to what is now western and northern Canada. The territory would be incorporated into the Dominion, and administered as a territory, essentially as a colony, by the federal government in much the same way as the Yukon Territory and the Northwest Territories were to become effectively colonies of Ottawa for most of this century. Self-determination, or community decision-making, would exist only at the whim of politicians in Ottawa elected by and from the four original provinces only. Any rights which either individuals or groups might possess would be, in effect, allowances from those eastern politicians and bureaucrats, gifts which could be either bestowed or taken away at the whim of people from other parts of the country, as it were. Thus they would not be "rights" in any real sense, but simple political dictates by outsiders which could change as easily as those outside politicians could be changed by the electorates in their eastern communites.

During much of the 19th century the area of settlement around the confluence of the Red and Assiniboine Rivers had a form of local government called the Council of Assiniboia, with a Governor and a Council, both however appointed by the landowner, the Hudson's Bay Company. The Governor of the Red River Settlement and the Council of the District of Assiniboia effectively controlled life in the colony, in part through the actions of a judge called a Recorder. The Métis did regularly object to the periodic heavy-handed rule of the Company through this Governor and Council, and did occasionally achieve victories which had the effect of curtailing some of the worst abuses of the Company. For example the Company claimed a total monopoly over the trading of furs in its territory, a fact which restricted many Métis from selling their pelts to the highest bidder. In one famous trial, in 1849, Guillaume Sayer was charged with illegal trade. Métis living in the area acting under the leadership of Louis Riel, Sr., surrounded the scene of the trial in an angry mood. Although Sayer was found guilty, the jury recommended that he not be punished. The Recorder agreed, and the effective monopoly power of the Hudson's Bay Company was broken (Stubbs, 1967:26-30).

Obviously then there is a lengthy history of Métis organization and representation in the early years of this territory. Moreover, there is a history of organized Métis objecting successfully to externally-imposed restrictions upon their freedom. It should have been obvious—but apparently was not obvious—that the overwhelming majority of the population of the Red River Settlement would protest any inclusion in the Dominion of Canada, in the role of a colony, a role which to the Métis meant merely the exchange of British and eastern Canadian overlords for Ontario and Quebec overlords.

The Métis protested in the form of the famous Riel Rebellion. The Métis seized Hudson's Bay Company property and control of the Red River Settlement. A Provisional Government was declared on November 23, 1869 to replace the Council of Assiniboia. It is of not inconsiderable importance that this Council represented all Métis of the community, both speakers of Michif and speakers of English. The Canadian government of Sir John A. MacDonald sent negotiators out from the east. In January, a Convention was established to draft demands. These included effective provincial status and self-determination. The former must be considered critical, for in theory Canada is a construct of provinces equal to each other in powers and equal to the federal government with which the provinces divide all governmental powers. In March and April, representatives of the Provisional Government negotiated in Ottawa. Most of their demands were met, and *The Manitoba Act,* which was to become the constitution of the new province, was introduced in Parliament. It contained, as well as the creation of the Province of Manitoba, a section which specifically recognized the rights of Métis to land and to education in a culturally appropriate manner.

The Province of Manitoba came into being on July 15, 1870, as a small part of the territories transferred by the Hudson's Bay Company to Canada. *The Manitoba Act* which created the Province included particular provisions for the Métis majority. Sections 31, 32 and 33 read:

> Section 31: And whereas, it is expedient, towards the extinguishment of the Indian Title to the lands in the Province, to appropriate a portion of such ungranted lands, to the extent of one million four hundred thousand acres thereof, for the benefit of the families of the half-breed residents, it is hereby enacted, that, under regulations to be from time to time made by the Governor General in Council, the Lieutenant-Governor shall select such lots or tracts in such parts of the Province as he may deem expedient, to the extent aforesaid, and divide the same among the children of the half-breed heads of families residing in the Province at the time of the said transfer to Canada, and the same shall be granted to the said children respectively, in such mode and on such conditions as to settlement and otherwise, as the Governor General in Council may from time to time determine.

> Section 32: For the quieting of titles, and assuring to the settlers in the Province the peaceable possession of the lands now held by them, it is enacted as follows:

(1) All grants of land in freehold made by the Hudson's Bay Company up to the eighth day of March, in the year 1869, shall, if required by the owner, be confirmed by grant from the Crown.

(2) All grants of estates less than freehold in land made by the Hudsons's Bay Company up to the eighth day of March aforesaid, shall, if required by the owner, be converted into an estate in freehold by grant from the Crown.

(3) All titles by occupancy with the sanction and under the license and authority of the Huson's Bay Company up to the eighth day of March aforesaid, of land in that part of the Province in which the Indian Title has been extinguished, shall, if required by the owner, be converted into an estate in freehold by grant from the Crown.

(4) All persons in peaceable possession of tracts of land at the time of the transfer to Canada, in those parts of the Province in which the Indian Title has not been extinguished, shall have the right of pre-emption of the same, on such terms and conditions as may be determined by the Governor of Council.

(5) The Lieutentant-Governor is hereby authorized, under regulations to be made from time to time by the Governor General in Council, to make all such provisions for acertaining and adjusing on fair and equitable terms, the rights of Common, and rights of cutting Hay held and enjoyed by the settlers in the Province, and for the commutation of the same by grants of land from the Crown.

Section 33. The Governor General in Council shall from time to time settle and appoint the mode and form of Grants of Land from the Crown, and any Order in Council for that purpose when published in the *Canada Gazette,* shall have the same force and effect as if it were a position of this Act.

The Manitoba Act was legislation of the federal government. A year later, in 1871, the British Parliament validated the Act as part of *The Canadian Constitution Act, 1871.* As part of the Canadian constitution it is subject to the normal amending formula of *The Constitution Act,* 1982. Section 6 of *The Constitution Act, 1871* reads:

Except as provided by the third section of this Act, it shall not be competent for the Parliament of Canada to alter the provisions of the last mentioned Act of the said Parliament, in so far as it relates to the Province of Manitoba, or of any other Act hereafter establishing new Provinces in the said Dominion, subject always to the right of the Legislature of the Province of Manitoba to alter from time to time the provisions of any law respecting the qualification of electors and members of the Legislative Assembly, and to make laws respecting elections in the said Province.

The meaning of *The Constitution Act, 1871,* would seem to be clear. The federal government can admit territories or parts of territories—such as the Red River Settlement—into Canada as full provinces, but once that is done, then the federal government can do only two things to change legislation of that province. One is to change the boundaries of a province, but only with the consent of the province, and laws which relate to that boundary change. A second is to change laws relating to electors, elections and the legislative assembly, again only with the consent of the province.

The Manitoba Métis Federation contends the following:

1) After extensive negotiations between the Provisional Government of Mantioba and the Dominion (federal) Government of Canada, held both at Red River and in Ottawa, the Manitoba Act was deliberately drafted to include Section 31 and the grant of 1,400,000 acres (approximately 20%) of the new province "for the benefit of the families of the half-breed residents" to be divided "among the children of the half-breed heads of families residing in the Province."

2) Métis adults, who were of course the overwhelming majority of the population along the two main rivers of the Red River Settlement, were assured their land through Section 32 of *The Manitoba Act* which recognized existing land grants.

3) The English language is simple, and the use of simple construction in English yields clarity. Because Métis adults already possessed land, and because Métis children did not, and given the expectation that many non-Aboriginal eastern Canadians would soon come to Manitoba, the Provisional Government sought to maintain land for their children in the face of the expected immigration. Thus the simple wording of Section 31 was both deliberate and determined, following extensive negotiation by such intellectual luminaries as Donald A. Smith and Abbé Richot, and with the agreement of Sir John A. MacDonald, a skilled Father of Confederation. That simple wording—"to appropriate a portion of such ungranted lands"— is clear: a bloc of land totalling 1,400,000 acres was to be set aside as expansion land as it were, so that the children of Métis who were already landholders (and the children of those who might not be at the time) would be assured of land in the new

Province of Manitoba, no matter how many immigrants came from the other provinces.

4) This straight forward construction was especially critical given the refusal of the federal government to give the new Province of Manitoba control over its natural resources, including land. Thus Section 31 of the Manitoba Act represented a trade-off. The federal government got the land and the authority to parcel it out to new arrivals in the province, while, in return, the Métis majority was assured of a bloc of land for their own title and use.

5) Section 33 of the Manitoba Act was intended to allow the federal government to pass regulations to give effect to the creation of the bloc—"portion"—of land, the 20% of the new Province of Manitoba which was to given to the Métis "children of the half-breed heads of families". It was also intended to allow for the distribution of federally-owned land—in the remaining 80% of the province—to the expected flood of non-Aboriginal immigrants. It was *not* intended to allow non-Aboriginal persons to decide later that they did not like the carefully negotiated concept and then effectively destroy it.

6) By a year later, with railway plans under way and Indian title surrender in preparation, and a considerable demand for land by new non-Aboriginal arrivals (including troops sent out in 1870), the federal government sought to change the grant of a bloc ("portion") of land, to individual small land grants drawn by lottery and scattered throughout the province. They did this by passing a series of laws and Orders in Council (cabinet orders) which in effect deprived the Métis of that bloc of land now referred to in court documents as a "Métis reserve."

7) All told, some 26 federal and provincial laws and Orders in Council violated Section 6 of *The Constitution Act, 1871,* the foundation of Manitoba's constitution. By doing so, they were *ultra vires,* that is, beyond the authority of either government to do, and are thus null and void.

THE METIS AND THE LAND

Some explanation is necessary for a few points here over which there is sharp disagreement among scholars.

Conventional wisdom, replicated over many decades, would have it that those who negotiated extensively both for the Provisional Government and for the government of the Dominion of Canada, and those who drafted the actual legislation for the Parliament of Canada, and the federal government, including Sir John A. MacDonald, Sir Georges-Etienne Cartier and the Cabinet, and the Members of Parliament, and, a year later, the entire British government, including the constitutional experts who drafted their legislation, and their Prime Minister and his Cabinet and the Members of Parliament in both the British House of Commons and the House of Lords, made a simple little mistake. What an assumption! The claim now is that nobody spotted this little error until long after the deal was done! It would seem more likely that those who complained about the wording of Section 31, and who sought changes over several years beginning in 1871, did so because of a particular non-Aboriginal perspective on land holding, one which considered land to be a commodity for the market, not a homeland for settlement and residence. Thus their insistence that all Métis must receive land, but that the land be scattered among that of non-Aboriginal land—holders, and their development of complex regulations for the then individual small holdings makes sense in the context of the non-Aboriginal view of land. These regulations must also be seen in light of the significant non-Aboriginal immigration and the not inconsiderable dispersion of the Métis from Manitoba which had the effect of seriously damaging the viability of the Métis community. Much of the dispersion came about through the attraction of land and opportunity further west and the negative behaviour of the immigrants towards those Métis who remained.

This dispersion would have been much less likely to occur if the land had been granted, as promised, as "a portion" (or bloc) to the children of the Métis, and if it had it been granted promptly as had been expected.

It cannot be stressed enough that this suit asks the Court of Queen's Bench of Manitoba to affirm the supremacy of the Canadian constitution, and especially *The Manitoba Act,* often described as the Manitoba constitution, over the actions of the federal parliament and provincial legislature. Whatever the decision of this court, it will be appealed to the Manitoba Court of Appeal and thence to the Supreme Court of Canada. Should the Manitoba Métis Federation be successful in their suit, then the practical effect will be to uphold *The Manitoba Act* and in particular Section 31 of the Act. This supremacy will in turn support a second suit, in the Federal Court of Canada, claiming a breach of trust by the government of Canada. The claim here is that the federal government, by not living up to the provisions of *The Manitoba Act,* caused the Métis of Manitoba to suffer the loss of both land and opportunity. The claim can be extended, of course, to speak of the significant contemporary devaluation of the Métis people noted in earlier chapters of this volume. There is some feeling that much of this stems ultimately from policies which effectively deprived large numbers of Métis the opportunity of developing an economically viable community in a province which had initially a Métis majority and guarantees of religion and language. The thesis is that all three of these provisions, religion, language and land rights, were quickly discarded once the Province of Manitoba was formally established. The Métis now seek redress in the form of new opportunities to develop their communities as both economically viable and socially stable, to overcome the dreadful effects of that long history of devaluation.

Recent research has dealt with aspects of the land question. Both Ens (1990) and Flanagan (1991) have posited, on the basis of archival research of land holdings, titles and sales, that a significant number of Métis voluntarily sold their land in the period following 1870. Although both carefully note the twin pressures of economic opportunity elsewhere, notably in what are now Saskatchewan and Alberta, and the increasing non-Aboriginal immigration to Manitoba, with the subsequent extensive discrimination and bitterness by many of the new arrivals against the Métis, they found that many Métis landholders benefitted economically from the sale of their land. The general conclusion is that far from being involuntary dispossessed, many Métis took concious advantage of sellers' markets and sold their land willingly in a rational free market atmosphere. That might well be the case, but it misses the point: the constitutional agreement between the Provisional Government, representing the overwhelming majority of the residents of the Red River Settlement, and the Dominion of Canada, was sorely breached. The average person must ask in wonder, why do non-Aboriginal people and governments make agreements, and then draft and enact constitutions, only to break them? Given the extended efforts in Red River in 1869-70 by the Aboriginal majority to reach a consensus and then to enter an agreement through an open and democratic process, what can one think of non-Aboriginal governments and individuals who consistently tinker with the agreement after the fact—over an extended period of time— in a manner which has the net result of benefiting themselves, without even paying lip-service to the processes of negotiation and open democratic decision-making with all parties? This litigation then is about *The Manitoba Act* and the validity of constitutions, but it is also about process, especially the processes of negotiation, decision-making and change.

THE SURVIVAL OF THE METIS

One of the issues raised in the Court of Queen's Bench was the question of who can represent the Manitoba Métis of 1870. The federal government maintained that all of the beneficiaries of *The Manitoba Act* —that is the "children of the half-breed heads of families"—were deceased. Thus the law was no longer valid anyway. Further they argued that neither the Manitoba Métis Federation nor the Native Council of Canada nor the individual applicants could represent those deceased beneficiaries of *The Manitoba Act*. The Court of Queen's Bench dismissed this line of reasoning in 1987, holding that, if the facts alleged (the violation of the constitution and the failure to create a "Métis Reserve") were proven, then the individuals and the two groups suing for that declaration would in fact also be suffering a current violation of their rights.

The Manitoba Court of Appeal overturned this decision in 1988, with four members of the court ruling that the rights involved "were individual rights and did not create a community interest for the Métis peoples" and one member asserting that "the Métis have certain rights" and asking "Who is in a better position to enforce such rights than the current plaintiffs"?[1]

It is obvious that the legitimacy of any organization representing the Métis will be called into question when the matter finally proceeds to trial, so it is worth noting the basis for the Manitoba Métis Federation pursuit of this case.

Métis organization in Canada obviously predates the creation of Mantioba as a Province of Canada. The Provisional Government was clearly representative of the Métis, who were in turn the overwhelming majority of the population, and in fact included non-Aboriginal settlers as well. There is little argument for the legitimacy of the Métis of 1870.

Métis organization in Manitoba certainly continued past 1870. As early as 1909 a group of Métis, including men who had served with Louis Riel in 1870, formed a historical committee which in turn became a sub-group of a reformed l'Union Nationale Métisse Saint-Joseph de Manitoba, a group originally formed in 1887. Their task was to record Métis history, especially the events of 1869-71. The parent organization continues to exist. Moreover, as Lussier has noted, it was distinct from other francophone organizations, to the point of major friction among them (1982: xix-xxi). Sawchuk has noted that the St.Laurent local of the Manitoba Métis Federation was originally a branch of L'Union Nationale Métisse Saint-Joseph de Manitoba, and was able to join the Manitoba Métis Federation without losing its ties to the old cultural organization (1978:51).

Obviously Métis organization continued until the formation of the Manitoba Métis Federation in 1967. At the same time a strong sense of identity as Métis survived in dozens of Métis communities across the province. This was reinforced by the use of Michif, the language of the Métis, as opposed simply to French. Métis people themselves were, over many generations, both conscious of and adamant about the difference between the two languages and the two lifestyles, even if governments interpreted the Manitoba constitutional language requirement as French rather than the Michif intended by the Provisional Government of 1870 (Crawford, 1983; Lavallee, 1990).

A significant proportion of the current Métis of Manitoba are descendents of the Métis of 1870, that is of those who were entitled to share in the portion of land allotted to the "children of the half-breed heads of families", and all of the individuals whose names appear on the statement of claim for the lawsuit are descendents of those children. It can only be noted that if any people have an entitlement based upon the The Manitoba Act it is the people represented by the contemporary Manitoba Métis Federation.

FEDERAL vs PROVINCIAL AUTHORITY

A further implication of the current litigation relates to the issue of federal versus provincial legislative authority. The Constitution Act, 1867 (formerly called The British North America Act) contains a provision dividing the power to legislate in particular areas between the federal government and the provincial governments. Section 91(24) gives the federal government exclusive authority to enact legislation in matters concerning "Indians, and lands reserved for the Indians." Of concern in this case—as well as a continuing concern over many decades across the country—is the meaning of the term "Indian" as it is used here. Does it mean status Indians covered by the Indian Act only, or does it mean all Aboriginal people? In 1939 the Supreme Court of Canada held that Inuit people are Indians within the meaning of that constitutional provision, but there has never been a full test of whether or not Métis are covered by that term for constitutional purposes. Without reviewing the details of the claim, it is worth noting that a subsidiary argument of the suit would seek a declaration that at least the Métis of Manitoba are included in that phrase, so that only the federal government would have legislative competence for the Métis. For over a hundred years now the Canadian government has denied any special responsibility towards the Métis, in spite of agreeing to include significant provisions in Manitoba's constitution relating to the Métis. This avoidance of responsibility by what is arguably the economically strongest government of the country has allowed significant social and economic neglect by government to continue, along with the devaluation and its results which have already been noted. It is possible that the Supreme Court of Canada will hold that Métis are included in that provision, and that there is thus a significant federal responsibility towards the Métis.

CONCLUSION

I noted initially that both history and the law are always revisionist in some sense, at least in terms of contemporary perception if nothing else. With significant changes in the Canadian constitution in 1982 leading to a much greater judicial awareness of Aboriginal rights, governments, courts and historians alike are being forced into a much more searching examination both of documentary facts and the possible interpretations of those facts. Guidelines for weighing the rights of individuals and groups are being refined with great care, and court deliberations increasingly seek to balance the strict letter of the law with the liberty and privileges of being Canadian. More and more, as significant questions of the relationships between Aboriginal and non-Aboriginal people and governments are called into question, the courts are asked to address matters of process and procedure, of fairness and intent. Those elements are the real players in the lawsuits now underway. It is striking that there appear to be such differences of attitude between Métis and government over the simple—on the surface—question of the negotiation, enactment and implementation of a constitution for Manitoba. Whatever the courts finally decide, we will end up with judicial notice of the process leading to that development of 1870, sometime later in this century.

NOTES

1.   Manitoba Métis Federation Inc. V. Attorney General of Canada. [1988] 3 C.N.L.R. 39.

THE METIS: A BIBLIOGRAPHY OF HISTORIC AND CONTEMPORARY ISSUES

Joe Sawchuk

This bibliography is intended to give the interested reader an idea of some of the classic scholarly writings on the Métis, along with a sampling of some of the more recent issues and concerns. It does not claim to be an exhaustive study. A more extensive bibliography (although limited to the time frame of 1980-1986) can be found in Madill (1987).

There has been an explosion in Métis scholarship over the last decade; to the extent the Métis have become a mini academic industry in their own right. While recent work is becoming increasingly diverse and sophisticated, it is still possible to isolate some general themes and approaches. Some of the more readily identifiable main streams in Métis scholarly literature are historical treatments, Métis identity and nationalism, both in past and contemporary times; constitutional issues; and the issue of Métis rights. Unfortunately, the main theme of this volume, Métis legal development, is badly under represented in the literature, to the extent of being almost non-existent.

THE METIS IN HISTORY

Not surprisingly, the bulk of writing on Métis history concerns early developments of Métis society and subsequent conflicts with the Canadian government over claims to nationhood and land rights. The best review of the development of the mainstream historical interpretations of the Métis vis-a-vis Canada can be found in the "Historiographical Introduction" to Sprague (1988). He traces this establishment historical interpretation through Stanley (1936), Morton (1937, 1956, 1957, 1964), Giraud (originally published in 1945, translated into English 1986), Creighton (1955), and finally to Flanagan (1979).

The first major treatment, by Stanley, is interesting in that it places much of the blame for the two armed resistance movements on the Canadian government, particularly on "ministerial incompetence, parliamentary indifference, and administrative delay" (p. 294). That interpretation fell by the wayside once Giraud's interpretation of the Métis as inferior mixed bloods, incapable of looking after their own interests, took hold. This affected Morton's interpretations, so that he saw the Métis as incurable nomads incapable of accepting agriculture. This became the generally accepted interpretation; that the great migration westward after the first Riel resistance was due to pressures from white immigrants from the East, and the depletion of the buffalo herds. Then, Creighton's totally unsympathetic interpretation of the Métis' demands as blackmail, and the machinations of "a single half-breed megalomaniac" (1955:415) seemingly capped the mainstream historian's interpretations of the causes of the two resistance movements as outside the Canadian government's responsibility, but they were reinforced later by Flanagan (1979) who specifically attacked Stanley's original interpretation that the Métis had legitimate grievances.

One of the problems with all these historians, whether they were sympathetic to the Métis cause or not, was their basic misunderstanding of the nature of Métis society, and their ethnocentric attitudes. This led to many problems in understanding the relationship of the Métis to the dominant society, the nature of their economic and social organization, and their reaction to the Manitoba Act and the various scrip programs as they were administered by the central government.

Most historians never stopped to consider the nature of Métis society; instead they made various subjective and biased comments on the "nature" of that society, of which Stanley's characterization of the Métis as "indolent, thoughtless and improvident, unrestrained in their desires, restless, clannish and vain" (1936:8) unfortunately is typical. There are many other examples, such as Giraud's characterization of the "inherent weaknesses of their nature" (1986:374) and so on. Thus the personality of the Métis themselves, the consequences of their lifestyles on agriculture in the Red River Settlement, their participation in the first and second Riel Insurrections, along with the literature devoted to the personality of Louis Riel represented until recently the sum total of historical writings on the Métis.

The most common characteristic attributed to the historical Métis population was that of a small scale and primitive society oriented to the past. George Woodcock referrred to Riel as the "defender of the past" (1975:8), W.L. Morton referred to the Métis as the "anti-representatives of... Westerners" (1937:169), while Stanley said "they did not want to be civilized, they only wanted to survive" (1936:12-13).

Another common theme was to equate the struggle of the Métis with the French-English conflict. Thus Morton characterized Manitoba as a province of "peculiarly French Creation," and virtually equates the Métis with the French when he states that the Red River Settlement was "about half-and-half French and English," and explains how "the balance of numbers shifted against the French" as more and more people came from the East to the Northwest (1964:51-55). What he means here is Métis, not French; the two terms are not, and never were synonymous.

RECENT TRENDS IN HISTORICAL INTERPRETATION

Fortunately, interesting and new interpretations are being offered by Métis historians or by historians supported by the Métis. Much of this stems from land claims research conducted by various provincial and national Métis political organizations, such as the Manitoba Métis Federation on the provincial level and Native Council of Canada on the national level. Examples of these include the two annual reports of the Métis Association of Alberta land claims department (1989, 1990) and Sawchuk, Sawchuk and Ferguson (1981).

One of the more provocative interpretations to come out of this recent research into Métis land claims can be seen in the work of D.N. Sprague, whose original work was supported by the Manitoba Métis Federation. Sprague has documented in detail government duplicity in the way Métis lands under the Manitoba Act passed from Métis hands into those of non-Aboriginal settlers (1980a, 1980b, 1988). The main thrust of Sprague's thesis is that Prime Minister MacDonald and the Canadian government deliberately attempted to dispossess the Métis of their lands by structuring scrip and land grant regulations in such a way as to encourage fraud, misappropriation and forced sales. Recently Sprague has been challenged by Ens (1988), who suggests that Métis immigration from Red River was closely tied to changes in political economy from the 1830s to 1870, changes which saw many Métis abandon agriculture and sell their land, as new economic opportunities offered themselves. As well, Flanagan, based upon research funded by the Federal Department of Justice, examines the market for childrens' allotments, and heads' of families scrip. He concludes that rather than being dispossessed or defrauded, the Métis sold their land and scrip because money was more useful to them than land was at the moment (1991).

McLean and Schulman (1983), and McLean (1985) offer a different interpretation of the Métis uprising of 1885, asserting that the entire rebellion was the result of a conspiracy between Sir John A. MacDonald and certain of his agents, such as Lawrence Clarke, a Chief Factor of the Hudson's Bay

Company, in order to facilitate subsidization of the Canadian Pacific Railway Company. While the work suffers from the same difficulties that attend all conspiracy theories (easy to postulate; difficult to prove) at least the ethnocentric characterization of the Métis as irresponsible primitives has been excised. Some of this work was supported by the Gabriel Dumont Institute and the Association of Métis and Non-Status Indians of Saskatchewan. McLean attempts to answer some of his critics plus give a general history of the Métis in *Home From the Hill* (1987), also from the Gabriel Dumont Institute. Other useful investigations of Métis land issues has been done by Gerhard Ens (1983) Diane Payment (1983, 1990) and Nicole St-Onge (1985).

A good general-interest introduction to the history of the Métis is provided by Purich (1988). He sheds the ethnocentric bias of Stanley et al, while maintaining a sympathetic portrayal of the birth of the Métis nation, their early struggles, the Manitoba and North West rebellions. He goes further than most historians in considering events *after* the North West Rebellion, covering the history of Alberta's Métis Settlements, the Métis' political activities of the 1970s, 1980s and 1990s, including their contributions to the Constitutional accord.

Another important treatment of the Indian and Métis political development in the 1930's and 1940's can be seen in Dobbin's *One and a Half Men* (1981) a biographical study of two of the founders of the Métis movement in both Alberta and Saskatchewan: Malcolm Norris and Jim Brady.

METIS IDENTITY AND NATIONALISM

The processes of "being and becoming Métis" has become an important theme in scholarly writing on the Métis. An especially important impetus to this current interest in the development of Métis identity and nationalism came with the conference on the Métis at the Newberry Library Center for the History of the American Indian in 1981. Many of the papers at this conference were collected in Peterson and Brown (1985). The collection looks at several distinctive Métis communities that had previously been ignored in the literature, including groups in the United States.

There has been a lot of work on the complexities of Métis origins in the West. Examples would include Foster (1978, 1985, 1986) and his treatment of the rise of English halfbreed populations in Red River. Olive P. Dickason isolates some of the particular circumstances which resulted in the rise of a "New Nation" in the Northwest, contrasting these to other areas in Canada that saw the rise of mixed ancestry populations, but saw no parallel development of nationalist feelings (1985). Jacqueline Peterson has examined the roots of Métis populations around the Great Lakes (1978). There have also been some works on historic Canadian Métis populations outside the Northwest, such as David McNab's work on Métis participation in Treaty-making in Ontario (1985) and John S. Long's work on Treaty 9 negotiations(1985).

METIS IDENTITY

The difficulty in defining who are and who are not Métis either for historic populations or contemporary ones can cause problems for researchers. Jarvenpa and Brumbach (1985) attempted to evaluate the relationship of occupational status, ethnicity and ecology for three "Métis Cree" in the late 1890s and early 1900s by using Hudson Bay Archival material, but the difficulties of making such ethnic identifications consistently and convincingly probably limit the applicability of their approach.

There has been some interest in the problems of contemporary Métis identity, and the role that modern political organizations, the Canadian Constitution, Bill C-31 and issues like self-government have played in the development of contemporary identity patterns. An early effort was Sawchuk's *Métis of Manitoba* (1978) which examined the effects of the political unions of Métis and Non-status Indians that were common in the 1960s and 1970s. James Waldram (1986) has further commented on the effects of legislated Indian status on Native communities in northern Manitoba and Saskatchewan.

Kienitz has attempted to explicate the meaning "Métis nationalism" has achieved over the years, and the importance of a land base to Métis nationalism (1988). Patrick Douaud has also attempted to clarify the "evolution" of Métis identity (1983). That the question "Who are the Métis?" can still be asked is evidenced by a recent article by Boisevert and Turnbull (1985) which attempts to assess the impact of the Constitution on Métis identity, and the problems of who should and who should not be able to identify as Métis. They point out that the Canadian census reports that 98,260 individuals self-identify as "Métis," but as these self-proclaimed Métis seem to be found in every part of Canada, the concept conflicts with definitions posited by the Métis National Council and other Métis organizations, which limit the Métis to western Canadian, and particular historic, populations.

Sawchuk (1985) has suggested that Constitutional recognition of Métis, with the concomitant failure to mention Non-status Indians in the Constitution, plus the effects of Bill C-31, would exacerbate political relations between the Métis and Non-status Indians in several provinces, and would likely result in the dissolution of several joint Métis and Non-status organizations. The recent split of the Association of Métis and Non-status Indians of Saskatchewan in 1989 has proven him at least partly right.

THE METIS AND ABORIGINAL RIGHTS

As the Métis have been recognized along with Indian and Inuit as distinct Aboriginal peoples in Canada's Constitution, one would expect that much ink would have been spilled over what these Aboriginal rights are and what they mean for the Métis. Not as much has been written on the subject as one would think. But two opposing views can be seen here: Thomas Flanagan has suggested that there are no clear cut historical or legal reasons for recognizing Aboriginal rights of the Métis (1985, 1990), while Clem Chartier has argued that the Aboriginal rights of the Métis stem from the same source as those of Indians (1985).

REFERENCES

Boisvert, David and Keith Turnbull
1985   Who are the Métis? *Studies in Political Economy* 18:107-47.

Chartier, Clem
1985   Aboriginal Rights and Land issues: The Métis Perspective, pp. 54-61, in Menno Boldt and J. Anthony Long (Editors): *The Quest for Justice: Aboriginal Peoples and Aboriginal Rights.* Toronto: University of Toronto Press.

Creighton, D.G
1955   *John A. Macdonald: The Old Chieftain.* Toronto: Macmillan.

Dickason, Olive P.
1985   From "One Nation" in the Northeast to "New Nation" in the Northwest; A Look at the Emergence of the Métis, pp. 19-36, in Jacqueline Peterson and Jennifer S.H. Brown (Editors): *The New Peoples: Being and Becoming Métis in North America.* Winnipeg: University of Manitoba Press.

Dobbin, Murray
1981   *The One-and-a-Half Men: The Story of Jim Brady and Malcolm Norris, Métis Patriots of the 20th Century.* Vancouver: New Star Books. Reprinted 1987, Regina: Gabriel Dumont Press.

Douaud, Patrick C.
1983   Canadian Métis Identity: a Pattern of Evolution. *Anthropos* 78:71-88.

Ens, Gerhard
1983   Métis Lands in Manitoba 1870-1887. *Manitoba History* 5:2-11.

1988   Dispossession or Adaptation? Migration and Persistence of the Red River Métis, 1835-1890, pp. 120-144, in *Canadian Historical Association Historical Papers,* Windsor 1988.

Flanagan, Thomas
1979   *Riel and the Rebellion: 1885 Reconsidered.* Saskatoon: Western Producer Prairie Books.

1985   Métis Aboriginal Rights: Some Historical and Contemporary Problems, pp, 230-245, in Menno Boldt and J. Anthony Long (Editors): *The Quest for Justice: Aboriginal Peoples and Aboriginal Rights.* Toronto: University of Toronto Press.

1990　The History of Métis Aboriginal Rights: Politics, Principle and Policy. *Canadian Journal of Law and Society* 5:71-94.

1991　The Market for Métis Lands in Manitoba: an Exploratory Study. *Prairie Forum* 16: 1-20.

Foster, John E.
1978　The Métis: The People and the Term. *Prairie Forum* 3:79-90.

1985　Some Questions and Perspectives on the Problems of Métis Roots, pp.73-91, in Jacqueline Peterson and Jennifer S. Brown (Editors): *The New Peoples: Being and Becoming Métis in North America*. Winnipeg: University of Manitoba Press.

1986　The Plains Métis, pp 375-403, in Bruce Morrison and R.C. Wilson(Editors): *Native Peoples: The Canadian Experience*. Toronto: McClelland and Stewart.

Giraud, Marcel
1945　*Le métis canadien: son role dans l'histoire des provinces de l'Ouest. Paris: Institute d'ethnolgie*. Translated by George Woodcock as: The Métis in the Canadian West, 2 vols. Edmonton: University of Alberta Press, 1986.

Jarvenpa, Robert and Hetty Jo Brumbach
1985　Occupational Status, Ethnicity, and Ecology: Métis Cree Adaptations in a Canadian Trading Frontier. *Human Ecology* 13(3):309-329.

Keinitz, A.
1988　Métis "Nationalism" and the concept of a Métis Land Base in Canada's Prairie Provinces. *Canadian Review of Studies in Nationalism* XV,1-2:11-18.

Long, John S.
1985　Treaty No. 9 and Fur Trade Company Families: Northeastern Ontario's Halfbreeds, Indians, Petitioners, and Métis, pp. 137-162, in Jacqueline Peterson and Jennifer S.H. Brown (Editors): *The New Peoples: Being and Becoming Métis in North America*. Winnipeg: University of Manitoba Press.

Madill, Dennis F.K
1987　Riel, Red River, and Beyond: New Developments in Métis History, pp. 49-78, in Colin G. Galloway (Editor): *New Directions in American Indian History*. Norman: University of Oklahoma Press.

McLean, Don
1985   *1885: Métis Rebellion or Government Conspiracy?* Winnipeg: Pemmican Publishers

1987   *Home From the Hill: A History of the Métis in Western Canada.* Regina: Gabriel Dumont Institute.

McLean, Don and Schulman, M.
1983   Lawrence Clarke: Architect of Revolt. *Canadian Journal of Native Studies* 3:57-68.

McNab, David
1985   Métis Participation in the Treaty-Making process in Ontario: A Reconnaissance. *Native Studies Review* 1:57-79.

Métis Association of Alberta
1978   *Origins of the Alberta Métis: Land Claims Research Project 1978-79.* Edmonton: Métis Association of Alberta.

1979   *The Métis and the Land in Alberta: Land Claims Research Project 1979-80.* Edmonton: Métis Association of Alberta.

Morton, W.L.
1937   The Red River Parish, pp. 89-105, in R.C. Lodge (Editor): *Manitoba Essays.* Toronto: Macmillan.

1950   The Canadian Métis. *The Beaver* September, 1950

1956   Alexander Begg's Red River Journal and other Papers relative to the Red River Resistance of 1869-1870. Toronto: Champlain Society.

1957   *Manitoba: A History.* Toronto: University of Toronto Press.

1964   Manitoba's Historic Role. *Papers Read Before the Historical and Scientific Society of Manitoba* 3(19):50-57.

Payment, Diane
1983   *Batoche 1870-1910.* St. Boniface: Les Editions du Blé.

1990   *The Free People—Otipemisiwak: Batoche, Saskatchewan 1870 - 1930.* Ottawa: National Historic Parks and Sites, Parks Service (Environment Canada).

Peterson, Jacqueline, and Jennifer S.H. Brown (Editors)
1985   *The New Peoples: Being and Becoming Métis in North America.* Winnipeg: University of Manitoba Press.

Peterson, Jaqueline
  1978   Prelude to Red River: a Social Portrait of the Great Lakes Métis. *Ethnohistory* 25:41-67.

Purich, Donald
  1988   *The Métis.* Toronto: James Lorimer & Co.

Sawchuk, Joe
  1978   *The Métis of Manitoba: Reformulation of an ethnic Identity.* Toronto: PMA Associates.

  1985   The Métis, Non-Status Indians and the New Aboriginality: Government Influence on Native Political Alliances and Identity. *Canadian Ethnic Studies* 17:135-46.

Sawchuk, Joe, Patricia Sawchuk, and Theresa Ferguson
  1981   *Métis Land Rights in Alberta: A Political History.* Edmonton: Métis association of Alberta.

Sprague, D.N.
  1980a   The Manitoba Land Question, 1870-1882. *Journal of Canadian Studies* 15:74-84

  1980b   Government Lawlessness in the Administration of Manitoba Land Claims 1870-1887. *Manitoba Law Journal* 10:415-441.

  1988   *Canada and the Métis, 1869-1885.* Waterloo: Wilfrid Laurier University Press.

St-Onge, Nicole
  1985   The Dissolution of a Métis Community: Pointe a Grouette, 1860-1885. *Studies in Political Economy* 18:149-172.

Stanley, George F.C.
  1936   *The Birth of Western Canada: A History of the Riel Rebellions.* London: Longmans Green and Company. Reprinted 1960, Toronto: University of Toronto Press.

Waldram, James B.
  1986   The "Other Side": Ethnostatus Distinctions in Western Subarctic Native Communities, pp. 279-95, in F.L. Barron and James B. Waldram (Editors): *1885 and After: Native Society in Transition.* Regina: Canadian Plains Research Centre.

Woodcock, George
  1975   *Gabriel Dumont: the Métis Chief and his Lost World.* Edmonton: Hurtig.

CONCLUSION

Samuel W. Corrigan

The chapters preceding these few words present a past, a present and a future. They show the clear beliefs of the Métis of Manitoba in a system of law and legal administration based upon the expressed wish of the members of the community. They then outline the demise of Métis government, and show the horrible consequences of racism, loss of economic and social opportunity, and massive devaluation by the rnajority. Finally they point the way to a future of some promise, provided the governments of Canada and Manitoba can recognize the important opportunity now appearing before them. Whether or not they will do so is an open question.

In times of financial stress, it is customary for government to reject any new initiatives, no matter how cost efficient they might be, on the grounds that both they and the taxpayers simply cannot afford the inevitable expense of something new. How they can manage to afford the impressive expense of demonstrably unworkable penal systems is, of course, open to question. Just one example of unnecessary waste in the system will suffice, in this case an example which dramatically affects Métis children and families.

In the 1970s the Manitoba government determined that a new jail should be built in Brandon to serve the western Manitoba region. As it was intended to serve minimum, medium and maximum security prisoners, the architects designed it as a maximum security facility. They also incorporated a separate youth facility within the same basic structure. This was a separate and secure wing of the building which could not be reached from the rest of the institution without going through numerous locked doors and security checkpoints. Following its completion, somebody decided that this constituted having both youth and adults in the same facility, something which is clearly improper. But the chances of youths needing to be held for short periods was high. Could youths be held there for at least short periods? Yes, they could indeed. For how long? For four days, but no more.

Consequently, youths from the immediate region who are in that jail, and thus near their families and their lawyers, are transported to Winnipeg on Thursdays of each week. As those whose cases have not been heard will still have to appear in court in Brandon, however, they are trundled back to that same jail on Monday, there to wait until the following Thursday for the next van to Winnipeg. Youths who are arrested and held in the region on Thursdays after the van has left, of course, are required to remain in the jail until the following week, requiring of course the full staff for that period, even if only for one child. The cost of maintaining a staff for that section of the jail is high. The cost—and danger—of transporting the youths far from their families and lawyers, twice a week, especially on icy winter roads is great. The cost of custom designing, building and equipping an eight bed separate facility for children in Brandon could be no more than $250,000. But I suggest that will not be done until a van goes off the road and children die. Such is the mentality of the present penny-wise, pound-foolish system.

The quality of a justice system is measured not by either the low proportion of errors which it entails, or the level of satisfaction of that majority which are never its victims, but rather by the nature and extent of its effects upon people and their lives. What was the quality of the justice and land system for Urbain Ross? Urbain was the child of a "half-breed head of household" and was thus entitled to receive land under Section 31 of *The Manitoba Act*. Young Urbain was allotted parts of Sections 10 and 15 in Township 10, near Dakotah, Manitoba, some 240 acres in all. The allotment was made in 1880, when Urbain was 15 years old. Six years later, in 1886 when he turned 21 and thus arrived at his majority, he learned that he no longer had any land. It seems the Province of Manitoba decreed that persons 18 years of age and older were subject to land taxes. Urbain, not being able to gain title to his allotment while still a minor - that is until he turned 21 - did not pay taxes. Accordingly the land was seized and sold for taxes shortly before his 21st birthday. It was, of course, perfectly legal. It might not have been fair, but it was legal.

What of the woman near Dauphin whose children were taken for placment for a short time, who was assured she would be told where and how they were? Ten years later she still waits, waiting for word of her sons, waiting, knowing she will never be told, but waiting every day nonetheless. What is the quality of a family service responsible for that wait?

What is the quality of life for Métis youths on the streets in Winnipeg, sunk in a morass of drugs and prostitution? Is it the fault of children that 16 and 17 year olds are substantially ignored by the child welfare agencies acting under provincial law? Is it just that a Métis child and family service can exist, but not be funded to do the job?

218

The Métis say they can do the job. They say they can design and develop appropriate systems, of justice and family service especially, and history leads one to believe they can do just that. Self-determination will lead to justice, and conversely justice may not be possible without self-determination. Surely, after the success of the Métis up to 1870, and the notable lack of success of non-Aboriginal systems since then, the Métis should receive that opportunity. It is, after all, the same opportunity granted in some measure to other Canadians. It cannot help Urbain Ross, but it might well help his great-great grandchildren.

BIBLIOGRAPHY

Aboriginal Women's Justice Committee

    1988   *Aboriginal women in conflict with the law: The Ikwewak Project.*
            Winnipeg: Aboriginal Women's Justice Committee.

Adams, Howard
    1975   *Prison of Grass, Canada from the Native Point of View.* Toronto:
            General Publishing.

Adelberg E., and C. Currie
    1987   *Canadian Women in Conflict with the Law, Too Few to Count.*
            Vancouver: Press Gang Publishers.

Attorney General's Department of Manitoba.
    1989   *Submission to the Aboriginal Justice Inquiry.* Winnipeg,
            Manitoba, Attorney General's Department.
    1987   *Rural Courts Preparing for the Future: Northern Justice
            Thompson Court Service.* Winnipeg: Manitoba, Attorney
            General's Department

Barkwell, L.J.
    1990   Judicial Inquiries - Implications. Paper presented at the Prairie
            Justice Research consultation, *Strategies to Increase
            De-carceration of Aboriginal Offenders.* Prince Albert,
            Saskatchewan, March 30, 1990.
    1989   *Observation on Discrimination and Dehumanization in the
            Criminal Justice System.* Presentation to the Aboriginal Justice
            Inquiry, Dec. 15, 1988. Winnipeg: Four Season Reporting Ser-
            vices Ltd., 1989.
    1989   Report on Justice Committee Workshops. *Proceedings of the
            Manitoba Métis Federation 21st Annual Assembly.* Winnipeg:
            Manitoba Métis Federation Inc.
    1981   Differential treatment of juveniles on probation: An evaluative
            study. In W. A. Morrison (Ed.) *Juvenile Delinquency - An Action
            Systems Theory Reader.* Lexington, Mass.: Ginn & Co., 1981,
            pp 230 - 242
    1980   Differential probation treatment of delinquency. In R. Ross and
            P. Gendreau (Eds.), *Effective Correctional Treatment* (pp. 279-
            297). Toronto: Butterworths.

Barkwell, L. J., and D. N. Chartrand
  1989   *Devalued People: The Cycle Leading into Demoralization and Victimization*. Presentation to the Aboriginal Justice Inquiry, Nov. 1989. Winnipeg: Manitoba Métis Federation Inc.

Barkwell, L. J., D. N. Gray, R. H. Richard, D. N. Chartrand and L. N. Longclaws
  1989.   *Research and Analysis of the Impact of the Justice System on the Metis*. Winnipeg: Manitoba Métis Federation, Inc.

Barkwell, L. J., D. N. Gray, D. N. Chartrand, L. N. Longclaws and R. H. Richard
  1989   Devalued People: The status of the Métis in the justice system. *Canadian Journal of Native Studies,* Vol 9, (1) pp 121 - 150.

Barkwell, L. J., L. N. Longclaws and D. N. Chartrand,
  1989   The status of Métis children in the child welfare system. *Canadian Journal of Native Studies,* Vol. 9, (1) pp 33 - 53.

Barron, L. F. and J. B. Waldram (Eds.)
  1986   *1885 and After: Native Society in Transition*. Regina: Canadian Plains Research Centre, University of Regina.

Beal, Bob and Ron MacLeod
  1984   *Prairie Fire: The 1885 North-West Rebellion.* Edmonton: Hurtig Publishers

Bienvenue, Rita and A. H. Litif
  1974   Arrests, Disposition, Recidivism: A Comparison of Indians & Whites. *Canadian Journal of Criminology and Corrections,* 2 (16), 105 - 116.

Bourgeault, R.
  1988   Race and Class under Mercantilism: Indigenous People in 19th Century Canada. In B.S. Bolaria and P.S. Li (Editors): *Racial Oppression in Canada*, 2nd edition. Toronto: Garamond Press.
  1983   The Indian, the Métis and the Fur Trade. *Studies in Political Economy*, 12:45-80.

Brogden, M. E.
  1990   Origins of the South African Police: Institutional versus Structural Approaches'. *Acta Juridica XV*:1- 19.
  1988   *Criminalizing the One-and-a-Half-Men: Law and political struggle in the subjugation of the Metis*. Liverpool: Unpublished

1987   An Act to Colonize the Internal Lands of the Island: Empire and origins of the professional police. *International Journal of the Sociology of Law*, May, (15):179-208

1984   From Henry III to Liverpool 8. *International Journal of the Sociology of Law* (12) 1 37-58.

Brogden, M. E., T. Jefferson, and S. Walklate
1988   *Introducing Policework*. London: Unwin Hyman.

Brown, Lorne and Caroline Brown
1973   *An Unauthorized History of the RCMP.* Toronto: James Lorimer & Co..

Canada, Saskatchewan, and the Federation of Saskatchewan Indian Nations
1985   *Joint Canada-Saskatchewan-FSIN Studies of Certain Aspects of the Justice System as they Relate to Indians in Saskatchewan.* Volumes I-V. Ottawa: Department of Justice.

Canadian Bar Association.
1988   *Aboriginal Rights in Canada: An Agenda for Action.* Ottawa: Canadian Bar Association.

Canadian Corrections Association
1967   *Indians and the Law*. Ottawa: Queen's Printer.

Canadian Centre For Justice Statistics
1989   *Young Offender Custodial Key Indicator Report.* Ottawa: Statistics Canada.

1988   *1987 Crime Statistics*. Ottawa: Statistic Canada.

Caputo, T., and D. Bracken
1988   Custodial dispositions and the Young Offenders Act. In J. Hudson, B. Burrows, and J. Hornick (Eds.), *Justice and the Young Offender in Canada* (pp. 123 - 143). Toronto: Wall and Thompson.

Chambliss, W.
1964   A Sociological Analysis of the Law of Vagrancy. *Social Problems* 12:66-77.

Chartier, Clem
1988   *In the Best Interest of the Métis Child.* Saskatoon: University of Saskachewan Native Law Centre.

Conroy, John
   1988   *Introduction, Overview and Summary of Recommendations of the Special Committee on Imprisonment and Release.* Ottawa: Canadian Bar Association.

Congressional Document Series
   1851   #613, *Treaty Journal 1851.* Washington D.C.

Cooper, Barry
   1988   *Alexander Kennedy Isbister: A Respectable Critic of the Honorable Company.* Ottawa: Carleton University Press.

Crawford, John C.
   1983   Speaking Michif in Four Métis Communities. *Canadian Journal of Native Studies*, (3)1:47-55.

Daubney, D.
   1988   *Taking Responsibility, Report of the Standing Committee on Justice and Solicitor General, Review of sentencing, conditional release and related aspects of correction.* Ottawa: House of Commons.

Demers, Donald J.
   1978   *Discretion, Disparity, and the Parole Process.* Ph.D. Dissertation, University of Alberta: Unpublished.

Dershowitz, Alan M.
   1982   *The Best Defense.* New York. Vintage Books, Random House.

Desmeules, Larry
   1988   The Métis family and Métis futures. Paper presented at the *Second National Métis Child Care Conference.* Winnipeg: Métis Association of Alberta.

Dobbin, Murray
   1981   *The One-And-A-Half Men: The Story of Jim Brady and Malcolm Morris, Métis Patriots of the Twentieth Century.* Vancouver: New Star Books.

Dusenberry, Verne
   1985   Waiting for a day that never comes: The dispossessed Métis of Montana. In J. Peterson and J. Brown (Eds.) *The New Peoples: Being and Becoming Métis in North America.* Winnipeg: U of M Press

Ekstedt, John, and C. Griffiths (Editors)
   1988   *Corrections in Canada.* Toronto: Butterworths.

Ens, Gerhard
 1988 Dispossession or Adaptation? Migration and Persistence of the Red River Métis, 1835-1890, pp. 120-144. *Canadian Historical Association Historical Papers*, Windsor.
 1983 Métis Lands in Manitoba 1870-1887. *Manitoba History* 5:2-11.

Erasmus, Peter
 1976 *Buffalo Days and Nights.* Calgary: Glenbow-Alberta Institute

Fine, Sean
 1989 Near 1 in 4 Family Murders Among Native, Study Says. *The Globe and Mail,* October 4. Toronto.

First National Métis Child Welfare Conference.
 1987 Exercising authority and control over Métis child welfare matters. *Proceedings Report.* Calgary.

Flanagan, Thomas
 1991 The Market for Métis Lands in Manitoba: an Exploratory Study. *Prairie Forum* 3:79-90

Foster, John F.
 1973 *The Country-Born in the Red River Settlement: 1820-50.* Edmonton University of Alberta Press

Frideres, J.S.
 1974 *Canada's Indians: Contemporary Conflicts.* Toronto: Prentice Hall.

Friesen, Gerald
 1984 *The Canadian Prairies: A History.* Toronto: Toronto University Press.

Gendreau, P., B. A. Grant and M. Leipeiger
 1979 Self-esteem, incarceration and recidivism. *Criminal Justice and Behavior*, 6, 3-17.

Gibson, D. and L. Gibson
 1972 *Substantial Justice: Law and Lawyers in Manitoba.* Winnipeg: Penguin.

Giraud, M.
 1986 *The Métis in the Canadian West* 2 volumes, translated by G. Woodcock, Edmonton: University of Alberta Press.

Glueck, A. C.
 1973 *Manitoba and the Hudson's Bay Company,* Winnipeg: University of Winnipeg Press.

1965   *Minnesota and the Manifest Destiny of the Canadian North-West*, Toronto: University of Toronto Press.

Gosselin, Luc
1982   *Prisons in Canada.* Montreal: Black Rose Books.

Griffiths, C. and Simon Verdun-Jones
1989   *Canadian Criminal Justice.* Toronto: Butterworths

Greenland, C.
1987   The Last Public Execution in Canada. *Criminal Law Quarterly* (29) 4:415-420.

Greenwood, L. M.
1984   The Chartrand Murder Trial. *Criminal Justice History* 125:59.

Gunn, D. and C.R. Tuttle
1880   *History of Manitoba.* Ottawa: Rogers and Co.

Gyles, Harold ff.
1987   The Manitoba Court Communicator Program. A Report to the Attorney General Department of Research and Planning. Winnipeg.

Harding, James
1990   Evolution of Research. Paper presented at *Strategies to Reduce the Over-Incarceration of Canada's Aboriginal Peoples: A Research Consultation.* Prince Albert: Prairie Justice Research.
1989   Native People must receive fairer treatment from the law. Regina: *The Leader Post,* March 22, 1989.

Havemann, Paul
1983   The Indigenization of Social Control in Canada. Paper presented at the *XIth International Congress of Anthropological and Ethnological Sciences.* Vancouver, August, 19-23, 1983.

Havemann, Paul et al.
1985   *Law and Order for Canada's Indigenous People.* Regina: Prairie Justice Research.

Hector, Ron, and Mary Young
1988   *Proceedings of the Aboriginal Justice Inquiry.* Winnipeg.

Hogg, Peter
1977   *Constitutional Law of Canada.* Toronto: The Carswell Company Limited.

Hourie, Audreen

1989   *Survey of Federal/Provincial Corrections involvement at selected Metis Communities.* Winnipeg: Manitoba Métis Federation Inc.

1989   *Letter to the Aboriginal Justice Inquiry, re Métis Adoptions.* Winnipeg: unpublished

Howard, James

1977   *The Plains-Ojibwa or Bungi* (Reprint). Lincoln, Nebraska: J. & L. Reprint Co.

Howard, Joseph K..

1974   *Strange Empire - Louis Riel and the Métis People,* (Reprint of 1952 edition) Toronto: James Lewis and Samuel, Publishers.

Hylton, John

1981   The Native Offender in Saskatchewan, some implications for crime prevention planning. In *Selected Papers of the Canadian Congress for the Prevention of Crime.* Winnipeg: Canadian Association for the Prevention of Crime.

Jackson, M.

1988   *Locking up Natives in Canada. Report of the Canadian Bar Association on Imprisonment and Release.* Toronto: Canadian Bar Association.

Jobson, Keith.

1977   Dismantling the System. *Canadian Journal of Criminology and Corrections,* Vol. 19, No. 3, pp. 254 - 264.

Justice Reform Committee.

1988   *Access to Justice, Justice Requirements of Natives.* Vancouver: Government of British Columbia.

Kappler, Charles

1903   *Indian Affairs: Laws and Treaties,* Vol. II. Senate Documents, 57th Congress, Ist Session, Document 452, Washington.

Kimelman, Edwin.

1985   *No Quiet Place.* Final Report to the Minister of Community Services. Winnipeg: Manitoba Community Services.

1984   *File Review Report, Review Committee on Indian and Métis Adoptions and Placements.* Winnipeg: Manitoba Community Services.

1983   *Group Home Review, Report of the Review Committee on Indian and Métis Adoptions and Placements.* Winnipeg: Manitoba Community Services.

Knafla, L.A.
    1986   From Oral to Written Memory: The Common Law Tradition in Western Canada. In L. Knafla (Editor) *Law and Justice in a New Land: Essays in Western Canadian Legal History.* Toronto: Carswell.
    1986   *Law & Justice in a New Land.* Toronto: Carswell Co. Ltd.
    1981   *Crime and Criminal Justice in Europe and Canada.* Waterloo: Wilfred Laurier University Press.

Lajeunesse, T.
    1987   *The Manitoba Court Communicator Program - A Review.* Winnipeg: Research and Planning, Manitoba Attorney General.

La Prairie, Carol
    1988   The Young Offenders Act and Aboriginal youth. In J. Hudson, J. Hornick, and B. Burrows (Eds.), *Justice and the Young Offender in Canada.* (pp. 159 - 169) Toronto: Wall and Thompson.
    1987   Native women and crime: A theoretical model. *Canadian Journal of Native Studies* Vol. 8 (1), pp. 121-137.

Latimer, C.A.
    1986   *Winnipeg Youth Courts and the Young Offenders Act.* Winnipeg: Attorney General, Research Planning and Evaluation.

Lautt, Melanie.
    1979   Natives and justice. In D. Hepworth (Ed.) *Explorations in Prairie Justice Research.* (pp. 55-114) Regina: Canadian Plains Research Centre.

Lavalee, Guy, D.
    1990   The Michif French Language: A Symbol of Métis Group Identity at St. Laurent Manitoba. Paper presented at the *Annual Meeting of the Canadian Anthropology Society.* Calgary: May 1990.
    1988   *The Métis People of St. Laurent Manitoba: An Introductory Ethnography.* Vancouver: M.A. Thesis, University of British Columbia.

Lee, G.
    1981   Some Structural Aspects of Police Deviance. In C. Shearing (Editor) *Organizational Police Deviance.* Toronto: Butterworths.

Longclaws, L., G. Barnes, L. Grieve and R. Dumof
1980   Alcohol and drug use among the Brokenhead Ojibwa. *Journal of Studies on Alcohol,* 41 (1), 21 - 36.

Longclaws, Lyle
1989   *An Implementation Strategy Proposal that Ensures an Orderly Development Plan for Establishing Incorporated Métis Child and Family Service Agencies in All MMF Regions.* Winnipeg: Manitoba Metis Federation Inc.
1988   *Contemporary Trends Within Aboriginal Society, for Awareness Purposes.* Winnipeg: Native Clan Organization Inc.
1981   Native adolescents, strangers in our schools. In *Selected Papers of the Canadian Congress for the Prevention of Crime.* Winnipeg: Canadian Association for the Prevention of Crime.

Lussier, Antoine S.
1983   The Métis Since 1870. Special Issue: *Canadian Journal of Native Studies,* Vol. 3 (1)

Lussier, Antoine, and Bruce Sealey
1980   *The Other Natives: Les Métis Vol 3.* Winnipeg: Manitoba Métis Federation Press.

MacGregor, J. G.
1978   *Senator Hardisty's Prairies: 1849-1889.* Saskatoon: Western Producer Prairie Books

MacLeod, Margaret
1963   *Cuthbert Grant of Grantown: Warden of the Plains of Red River.* Toronto: McClelland and Stewart.

Mandlebaum, David
1979   *The Plains Cree.* Regina: Canadian Plains Research Centre.

Manitoba Association of Friendship Centres Inc.
1987   *Court Communicator Program Workshop Report.* Portage La Prairie.

Manitoba Community Services.
1988   *1987-88 Annual Report*

Manitoba Community Services, Child and Family Support 1984
1984   *Directive #18 respecting procedures of the placement of Native children.* Winnipeg: Government of Manitoba.

Manitoba Métis Federation Inc.
1989   *Submission to the task force on literacy.* Winnipeg: Manitoba
        Métis Federation Inc.

Manitoba Métis Federation Justice Committee
1989   *Research and Analysis of the Impact of the Justice System on
        the Métis: Submission to the Aboriginal Justice Inquiry*
        Winnipeg: Manitoba Métis Federation Inc.

Manitoba Métis Rights Assembly
1983   *Manitoba Métis Rights Position Paper: Métis Anoutch.*
        Winnipeg: Manitoba Metis Federation Inc.

Manitoba Society of Criminology
1973   *Report of the Conference of Northern Justice.* Winnipeg:
        Manitoba Society of Criminology.

Martin, Fred V.
1991   Federal and Provincial Responsibility in the Métis Settlements
        of Alberta. In David C. Hawkes (Ed.) *Aboriginal Peoples and
        Government Responsibility.* Ottawa: Carleton University Press.

McCaskill, D.
1985   *Patterns of Criminality and Correction among Native Offenders
        in Manitoba: A Longitudinal Analysis.* Saskatoon: Prairie
        Region, Correctional Service of Canada
1970   *A Study of the Needs and Resources Related to Offenders of
        Native Origin in Manitoba.* Ottawa: Solicitor General of Canada

McDougall, John
1903   *The Days of the Red River Rebellion.* Toronto: W. Briggs.

McKenzie, Wayne
1985   Metis Self-Government in Saskatchewan. In L. Barron & J.
        Waldram (Eds.) *1885 and After: Native Society in Transition.*
        Regina: Canadian Plains Research Centre. University of
        Regina.

McKinley, Patrick
1989   Natives Blamed for Woes. *Winnipeg Free Press.* October 14,
        1989.

McLean, Don
1988   *1885—Métis Rebellion or Government Conspiracy?* Winnipeg:
        Pemmican Publications Inc.

McLeod, R. C.
1976 *The NWMP and Law Enforcement.* Toronto: Butterworths.

Meade, Buddy, M. Penner and Mervin Moar
1987 Manitoba Métis Child and Family Services. In *Proceedings of the First National Métis Child Welfare Conference.* Calgary.

Métis and Non-Status Indian Crime and Justice Commission
1977 *1977 Commission Report.* Ottawa.

Métis Association of Alberta and J. Sawchuk, P. Sawchuk and T. Ferguson
1981 *Métis Land Rights in Alberta: A Political History.* Edmonton: Métis Association of Alberta.

Métis National Council
1989 *Canada and the Métis: A Proposal for Remedies and Reparations.* Saskatoon: Métis National Council

Moar, Mervin
1989 *Some Highlights on Metis Child and Family Service Issues.-* Winnipeg: Manitoba Metis Federation.

Morse, Bradford W.
1980 Indian and Inuit Family Law and the Canadian Legal System. *American Indian Law Review,* Vol. 8, 199-258.

Morton, W. L.
1965 *Manitoba: Birth of a Province.* Winnipeg: Manitoba Record Society.
1957 *Manitoba: A History.* Toronto: University of Toronto Press

National Film Board
1986 *Richard Cardinal: Cry from a Diary of a Metis Child.* Montreal: National Film Board of Canada.

Native Counselling Services of Alberta
1989 *Working Together: Criminal Justice Initiatives for Native People in Alberta.* Edmonton: Native Counselling Services of Alberta and the Alberta Solicitor General.

Native Probation Caucus
1989 *Submission to the Aboriginal Justice Inquiry.* Winnipeg: Four Seasons Reporting.

O'Brien, John
1979 *An Overview of the Balanced Service System.* Atlanta: Responsive Systems Associates.

Ombudsman, Manitoba
    1989   *Nineteenth Annual Report of the Ombudsman.* Winnipeg: Queen's Printer for the Province of Manitoba

Ontario Federation of Indian Friendship Centres
    1985   *Young Offenders Act Manual: A Native Perspective.* Toronto: Ontario Federation of Indian Friendship Centres.

Ontario Ministry of the Attorney General, Department of Justice Canada, The Ontario Federation of Indian Friendship Centres
    1989   *Report of the Steering Committee on the Evaluation of the Ontario Native Courtworker Program.* Administered by the Ontario Federation of Indian Friendship Centres. Toronto: SPR Associates Inc.

Payment, Diane
    1990   *The Free People—Otipemisiwak.* Ottawa: Minister of Supply and Services.
    1985   Batoche after 1885: A Society in Transition in F. L. Barron and J. B. Waldram (Editors) *1885 and After: Native Society in Transition* Regina: University of Regina.

Pelletier, Emile
    1977   *A Social History of the Manitoba Metis.* Winnipeg: Manitoba Métis Federation Press.

Peterson, J. and J. Brown, Eds.
    1987   *The New Peoples: Being and Becoming Metis in North America.* Winnipeg: University of Manitoba Press.

Ramsey, Alexander and A. C. Morrill
    1863   *Journal of the Proceedings Connected with the Negotiation of a Treaty with the Red Lake and Pembina Bands of Chippewas, October 2, 1863.* Washington: Treaty File, Records of the Bureau of Indian Affairs, National Archives.

Redbird, Duke
    1980   *We are Métis: A Métis View of the Development of a Native Canadian People.* Toronto: Ontario Metis and Non-Status Indian Association.

Robertson, Eleanor
    1988   *Native Women In Conflict with the Law.* Winnipeg: Unpublished.

Ross, A.
    1972   *The Red River Settlement.* (Reprint of the 1856 Smith Elder & Co. edition). Edmonton: Hurtig.

Ryant, Joseph
1988   *Métis Child and Family Services*. Winnipeg: Manitoba Métis
        Federation Inc.

Ryant, J. and C. Heinrich
1988   Youth Court Committees in Manitoba. In J. Hudson, J. Hornick,
        and B. Burrows (Eds.) *Justice and the Young Offender in
        Canada*. (pp 93 - 104) Toronto: Wall and Thompson.

St-Onge, Nicole
1985   The Dissolution of a Métis Community: Pointe a Grouette,
        1860-1885, *Studies in Political Economy* 18:149-172

Saskatchewan Association of Friendship Centres
1983   *Native Courtworker Services of Saskatchewan Program
        Evaluation*. Regina: Saskatchewan Assoication of Friendship
        Centres.

Sawchuk, Joe
1978   *The Métis of Manitoba: Reformulation of an Ethnic Identity*.
        Toronto: Peter Martin Associates Ltd.

Sealey, D. Bruce and Antoine S. Lussier
1975   *The Métis: Canada's Forgotten People*. Winnipeg: Manitoba
        Métis Federation Press.

Sinclair, Murray
1977   *An Evaluation of Manitoba's Court Communicator Program*.
        Winnipeg.

Skinner, S., O. Driedger, and B. Grainger
1981   Corrections: An Historical Perspective of the Saskatchewan
        Experience. *Canadian Plains Reports #4*. Regina: Canadian
        Plains Research Centre.

Sloan, R.
1987   *Legal Aid in Manitoba: An Evaluation Report*. Winnipeg: Social
        Planning Council of Winnipeg.

Social Planning Council of Winnipeg
1989   *Winnipeg Census Data, Insights and Trends 1981 - 1986:
        Natives*. Winnipeg: Social Planning Council of Winnipeg.

Solicitor General of Canada
1990   *Native and Non-Native Admissions to Federal, Provincial and
        Territorial Correctional Institutions*. Ottawa: Solicitor General of
        Canada

1989   *Task Force on Aboriginal Peoples in Federal Corrections: Final Report*. Ottawa: Solicitor General of Canada.

1988   Correctional Issues Affecting Native Peoples. *Correctional Law Review, Working Paper #7*. Ottawa: Solicitor General of Canada.

1985   *Native and Non-Native Admissions to Federal, Provincial and Territorial Correctional Institutions*. Ottawa: Solicitor General of Canada

1975   *Native People and Justice*. Ottawa: Solicitor General of Canada.

Sprague, D. N.
1988   *Canada and the Métis*. Waterloo: Wilfred Laurier U.P.

1980a   The Manitoba Land Question, 1870-1882. *Journal of Canadian Studies* 15:74-84.

1980b   Government Lawlessness in the Administration of Manitoba Land Claims 1870-1887, *Manitoba Law Journal*. 10:415-441.

Sprague, D. N. and Frye, R. P
1983   *The Genealogy of the First Métis Nation: the Development and Dispersal of the Red River Settlement*. Winnipeg: Pemmican Publications Inc.

Stanley, George F. G.
1963   *Louis Riel,* Toronto: University of Toronto Press.

1936   *The Birth of Western Canada: A History of the Riel Rebellions* London: Longmans Green and Company. Reprinted 1960, Toronto: University of Toronto Press.

Statistics Canada
1989   *Canadian Social Trends: Violence in the Family.* Ottawa: Statistics Canada.

Steel, T.
1974   *The Life and Death of St. Kilda*. Glasgow: Fontana

Steele, S.
1972   *Forty Years in Canada*. Toronto: Ryerson

Stubbs, Roy
1967   *Four Recorders of Rupert's Land.* Winnipeg: Peguis Publishers.

Subcommittee on the Penitentiary System in Canada
1977   *Report to Parliament.* Ottawa: Minister of Supply and Services.

Taylor, John
    1983   An Historical Introduction to Métis Claims in Canada. *Canadian Journal of Native Studies,* (3)1:151-181.

Tough, Frank
    1987   *Native People and the Regional Economy of Northern Manitoba: 1870-1930s.* Ph.D. Thesis, Toronto: York University, unpublished
    1984   The establishment of a commercial fishing industry and the demise of Native fisheries in Northern Manitoba. *Canadian Journal of Native Studies,* (4)2:304 - 321

Tremaudan, A. H.
    1982   *Hold High Your Heads* Winnipeg: Pemmican Publications.

Turk, A.
    1982   *Political Criminality.* Beverley Hills: Sage.

Turtle Mountain Indian Reservation
    1985   *St. Annes's Centennial: Turtle Mountain Treaty and Claims.* Belcourt: Turtle Mountain Indian Reservation.

University of Manitoba Research Ltd.
    1988   *Manitoba Métis Federation: Survey of Members.* Winnipeg: University of Manitoba Research Ltd.

Voegelin, Erminie Wheeler and Harold Hickerson
    1974   *Chippewa Indians*, Volumes 1 and 2. New York: Garland Publishing Inc.

Waldram, James
    1988   *As Long As Rivers Run: Hydroelectric Development and Native Communities in Western Canada.* Winnipeg: University of Manitoba Press.
    1986   The "Other Side": Ethnostatus Distinctions in Western Subarctic Native Communities, pp 279-295, in F. L. Barron and James B. Waldram (Eds.): *1885 and After: Native Society in Transition.* Regina: Candian Plains Research Centre.

Wells, E.L.
    1989   Self-enhancement through delinquency: A conditional test of self-derogation theory. *Journal of Research in Crime and Delinquency.* 26 (3) (pp. 226 - 252)

Wiebe, M.
    1984   *Native Culture and Canadian Law.* Kingston: Queens Theological College.

Winnipeg Police Department.
    1988   *1988 Statistical Report.*

Wolfensberger, Wolf
    1972   *The Principle of Normalization in Human Services.* Toronto:
            Leonard Crainford and NIMR.

Woodcock, G.
    1976   *Gabriel Dumont: The Métis Chief and his Lost World.*
            Edmonton: Hurtig Publishers.

York, Geoffrey
    1989   *The Dispossessed: Life and Death in Native Canada.* Toronto:
            Lester & Orpen Ltd.

Zimbardo, Phillip, and Maslach, Christina
    1973   Dehumanization in institutional settings. Paper presented at the
            American Psychological Association Convention. Montreal.